No. 2985
$24.95

101
Solderless
Breadboarding
Projects

Delton T. Horn

TAB BOOKS Inc.

Blue Ridge Summit, PA

FIRST EDITION
FIRST PRINTING

Copyright © 1988 by TAB BOOKS Inc.
Printed in the United States of America

Library of Congress Cataloging in Publication Data

Horn, Delton T.
101 solderless breadboarding projects / by Delton T. Horn.
p. cm.
Includes index.
ISBN 0-8306-0385-9   ISBN 0-8306-2985-8 (pbk.)
1. Electronics—Amateurs' manuals.   I. Title.   II. Title: One hundred one solderless breadboarding projects.   III. Title: One hundred and one solderless breadboarding projects.
TK9965.H638   1988
621.381—dc19   87-33588
                                                    CIP

Questions regarding the content of this book
should be addressed to:

Reader Inquiry Branch
TAB BOOKS Inc.
Blue Ridge Summit, PA 17294-0214

Contents

Introduction   **v**

List of Projects   **vi**

1 The Breadboarding System   **1**

What Is Breadboarding?—Complete Breadboarding Systems—Precautions

2 The 555 Timer   **6**

The Basic Timer Modes—Features of the 555 Timer IC—Basic Monostable
Circuits—Switch Debouncer—Timer Operated Relay—Astable Circuits—Triangle
Wave Generator—Sound Pocket Generator—The 556 Dual Timer—The 558 Quad
Timer—Long Range Timers—Sequential Timer—Ramp Timer—Ramp Astable—
Complex Wave Generation—Some Unusual Applications—The 7555 CMOS Timer

3 The XR2240 Programmable Timer   **45**

The Time Periods—The Monostable Circuit—Sequential Timer—The Astable
Circuit—Complex Tone Generators

4 The 741 and Other Op Amps   **60**

The Ideal Op Amp—The 741 Op Amp—Inverting Amplifier Circuits—Non-Inverting
Amplifier Circuits—Difference Amplifiers—Comparators—Summing Amplifiers—
Other Mathematical Functions—Filters—Signal Sources—Chapter Summary

5 The LM339 Quad Comparator   **126**

The Chip—Hysteresis—Loading—Limit Comparator—Monostable Multivibrator—
Astable Multivibrator—Light Detector—Bargraph—Capacitance Meter—Summary

6 The LM380 and Other Audio Amplifiers   **138**

The LM380 Audio Amplifier IC—The Basic Amplifier Circuit—Phono Amplifier—
Bridged Amplifier—The LM386 Audio Amplifier IC—The HA-2400 Programmable
Amplifier

7 Sound Effects Generators   **156**

The SN76477 Complex Sound Generator IC—SN76477 Circuits—The SN94281
Complex Sound Generator

8 Digital Gates   **176**

The Basic Gates—Combining Gates—Signal Generators—LED Flasher—Logic
Probe—Switch Debouncer—Touch Switch—Binary Adder—Linear Amplifier

9 Flip-Flops   **206**

Flip-Flop Dividers—Counters—Sequencer—Shift Register—Summary

Index   **215**

Introduction

MANY BOOKS OF ELECTRONIC PROJECTS HAVE BEEN PUBLISHED, BUT I THINK SOMETHING is missing. Most published projects are completed designs. The hobbyist simply duplicates what the author built.

You can learn more by experimenting with circuits on a breadboard. In addition, by breadboarding a circuit before constructing it permanently, you can easily customize a project to suit your individual needs.

This book presents over 100 circuits and variations suitable for breadboarding. Extensive suggestions for experimentation and modification are provided.

With a little bit of practice and creativity on your part, this could be the most useful project book you have ever bought.

List of Projects

PROJECT	TITLE	FIGURE	PAGE
1	Monostable Multivibrator Demonstrator	2-6	12
2	Voltage-Controlled Monostable Multivibrator	2-7	14
3	Inverted Input Monostable Multivibrator	2-9	16
4	Switch Debouncer	2-10	16
5	Timer Controlled Relay	2-11	17
6	Astable Multivibrator Demonstrator (Low Frequencies)	2-16	22
7	Astable Multivibrator Demonstrator (Audio Frequencies)	2-17	24
8	Triangle Wave Generator	2-18	25
9	Sound Pocket Generator	2-21	27
10	Tone Burst Generator	2-23	28
11	Cascaded Timer	2-27	31
12	Long Duration Timer	2-29	32
13	Sequential Timer	2-30	34
14	Linear Ramp Monostable	2-31	35
15	Linear Ramp Astable	2-32	37
16	Complex Sound Generator	2-33 / 2-34	38

17	Second Complex Sound Generator	2-35	40
18	Missing Pulse Detector	2-37	41
19	Frequency Divider Circuit	2-38	42
20	Light-Off Alarm	2-41	43
21	Light-On Alarm	2-42	44
22	XR2240 Monostable Multivibrator	3-4	51
23	Sequential Timer	3-5	52
24	Low-Frequency Astable	3-7	54
25	Multiple LED Flasher	3-8	55
26	Audio Frequency Astable Multivibrator	3-9	56
27	Complex Tone Generator	3-10	57
28	Alternate Complex Tone Generator	3-12	59
29	Inverting Amplifier	4-11	60
30	Negative Input Inverting Amplifier	4-13	72
31	Variable Gain Inverting Amplifier	4-15	73
32	Non-Inverting Amplifier	4-19	75
33	Difference Amplifier	4-21	81
34	Comparator	4-22	82
35	Improved Comparator	4-23	84
36	Inverting Summing Amplifier	4-25	85
37	Logarithmic Amplifier	4-27	91
38	Antilogarithmic Amplifier	4-30	94
39	Multiplier	4-32	97
40	Division Circuit	4-34	100
41	Exponential Circuit	4-36	102
42	Sine Amplifier	4-38	104
43	Absolute Value Circuit	4-39	105
44	Low-Pass Filter	4-42	107
45	High-Pass Filter	4-44	111
46	Band-Pass Filter	4-48	113
47	Band-Reject Filter	4-51	117
48	Sine Wave Generator	4-53	118
49	Square Wave Generator	4-54	120
50	Variable Frequency Square Wave Generator	4-55	122
51	Variable Width Pulse Generator	4-56	122
52	Triangle Wave Generator	4-58	124
53	Sawtooth Wave Generator	4-59	124
54	Comparator Demonstration Circuit	5-3	128
55	Digital Gate Driver	5-5	130
56	Limit Comparator	5-6	132
57	Monostable Multivibrator	5-7	133
58	Astable Multivibrator	5-8	134
59	Light Detector	5-9	135
60	Bargraph	5-10	136
61	Capacitance Meter	5-11	137
62	Basic LM380 Amplifier	6-4	142

63	Audio Amplifier	6-6	144
64	Ceramic Cartridge Phono Amplifier	6-7	145
65	RIAA Phono Amplifier	6-8	145
66	Bridged Amplifier	6-9	147
67	LM386 Amplifier—Gain of 20	6-11	149
68	LM386 Amplifier—Gain of 200	6-12	150
69	Programmable Inverting Amplifier	6-15	153
70	Programmable Sine Wave Oscillator	6-16	155
71	Programmable Multifunction Circuit	6-17	155
72	Space "Phaser" Sound Effect	7-5	168
73	Steam Engine Sound Effect	7-6	170
74	Explosion / Gunshot Sound Effect	7-7	171
75	Speeding Car and Crash Sound Effect	7-8	172
76	SN94281 Steam Engine Train Sound Effect	7-12	175
77	AND Gate Demonstrator	8-4	179
78	NAND Gate Demonstrator	8-8	181
79	OR Gate Demonstrator	8-12	183
80	NOR Gate Demonstrator	8-15	184
81	X-OR Gate Demonstrator	8-17	185
82	Complex Gate Circuit #1	8-19	187
83	Complex Gate Circuit #2	8-23	193
84	Clock Generator	8-25	194
85	Gated Clock Generator	8-26	195
86	X-OR Clock Generator	8-27	195
87	Phase Shift Oscillator	8-28	196
88	Dual Waveform Function Generator	8-29	197
89	LED Blinker	8-30	198
90	Simple Logic Probe	8-31	199
91	Improved Logic Probe	8-32	199
92	Switch Debouncer	8-33	201
93	Simple Touch Switches	8-34	202
94	Timed Touch Switch	8-35	203
95	Binary Adder	8-36	204
96	Digital Linear Amplifier	8-37	205
97	Divide-By-Two Circuit	9-4	208
98	Divide-By-Three Circuit	9-5	209
99	Divide-By-Five Circuit	9-6	210
100	Eight Step Counter	9-7	211
101	Sequencer	9-8	212
Bonus	Shift Register	9-9	213

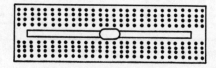

1

The Breadboarding System

THE CIRCUITS PRESENTED IN THIS BOOK ARE NOT INTENDED AS FINISHED PROJECTS. THEY are simply starting places for your own experimentation. It is strongly recommended that you breadboard each circuit before you hard-wire a permanent version.

WHAT IS BREADBOARDING?

A breadboarding system is simply a method of temporarily hooking up electronics circuits for purposes of testing and experimenting.

The best way to learn is by doing, so you should put together as many of the circuits described in this book as possible. Of course, you could hard-wire and solder each test circuit, as if it was intended for permanent use. But this would be awkward at best. In order to experiment with different component values, you would have to do repeated soldering and desoldering.

Also, building each circuit in this book permanently would be unnecessarily expensive. You could conceivably cut costs by desoldering each circuit when you are through with it and reusing the components as much as possible. Desoldering tends to be very tedious, time consuming, and quite inconvenient. Besides, the repeated heating of their leads can damage some components. Semiconductors, including ICs, tend to be very heat sensitive. It is all too easy to destroy a delicate semiconductor crystal with a soldering iron. Semiconductors, especially ICs, tend to be the most expensive components in the majority of circuits.

Fortunately, there is a much easier way to set up temporary circuits—breadboarding.

There are many possible approaches to breadboarding. All involve making electrical connections between various components without soldering.

1

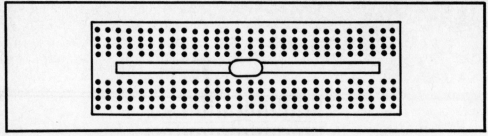

Fig. 1-1. Breadboarding is made easy with a solderless socket.

In the early days of electronics, an actual breadboard (a piece of wood, such as might be used for cutting bread) was used as a base for the circuit. Spring-loaded clips of some sort were mounted on the board, and component leads were held by the clips. This was inelegant, and usually rather ugly, but it did the job.

I doubt if anybody is still using this type of breadboarding, but the name has stuck.

Today there are more convenient and elegant means of breadboarding. In its simplest form, a modern breadboard is a solderless socket. Various component leads and wires can easily and quickly be plugged into or pulled out of the socket holes. A typical solderless socket is shown in Fig. 1-1.

The various holes in this type of socket are electrically interconnected within the body of the socket. Various interconnection patterns may be used. The most frequently used, and probably most versatile interconnection pattern is shown in Fig. 1-2.

These sockets can make experimentation and circuit design much, much easier than any other method of breadboarding. The socket holes are placed to accommodate the pins of integrated circuits. All of the projects in this book are IC based.

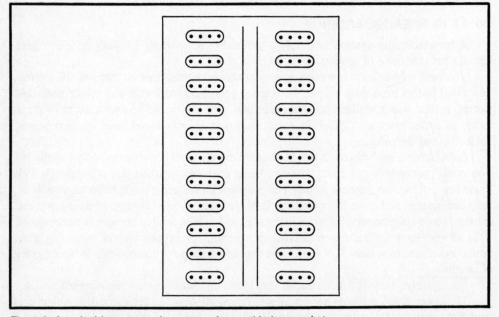

Fig. 1-2. A typical interconnection pattern for a solderless socket.

Solderless breadboarding sockets are available in a variety of sizes. Many can be purchased for less than ten dollars apiece.

COMPLETE BREADBOARDING SYSTEMS

A complete breadboarding system makes experimentation even easier and more convenient. A breadboarding system includes a solderless socket and various commonly used sub-circuits in a single package. A typical system of this type is shown in Fig. 1-3.

A variable power supply is almost always included in a breadboarding system. The power supply converts ac house current into the appropriate dc voltage(s) to operate the constructed circuit. In some cases, the power supply may also be used as a source of reference voltage for testing.

The most useful power supplies are continuously variable from zero up to 15 or 20 volts dc. Ideally, the power supply should be of the dual-polarity type. That is, both positive and negative voltages (with reference to ground) are available. For maximum versatility, the positive and negative supply voltages should be independently variable.

In some cases you may want to use ordinary batteries instead of, or possibly in addition to the power supply.

Many breadboarding systems also provide a connection point for 60 Hz ac house current, although usually at a voltage lower than the 110 volts supply. The house current is passed through a step-down transformer and is then made available for use within the circuit.

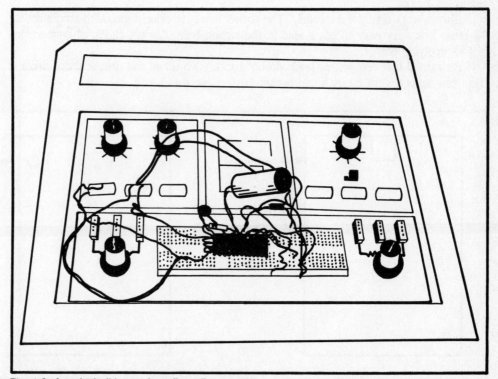

Fig. 1-3. A typical all-in-one breadboarding system.

A breadboarding system should also include some sort of variable signal source. This is usually just a variable frequency oscillator. It is desirable to have a choice of waveshapes for maximum versatility. In some cases, the signal amplitude is also adjustable.

Some breadboarding systems include output devices such as LEDs, seven-segment readouts, and/or speakers.

Finally, most breadboarding systems also have one or more potentiometers and switches handily available for use in experimental circuits. Such components are difficult to connect to a solderless socket, so it is convenient to have them built into the system housing.

You could build a customized breadboarding system yourself, using any suitable circuits, standard power supply, oscillator, and whatever else you might need frequently. Several commercial manufacturers market breadboarding systems. Heathkit, for example, offers several models for different types of circuitry. A Heathkit breadboard is shown in Fig. 1-3.

Having commonly used circuits, such as power supplies and signal sources, is extremely convenient. You could breadboard all the supporting circuitry each time along with the circuit you want to experiment with, but that would obviously be a big nuisance.

PRECAUTIONS

The whole point of breadboarding is to experiment with the circuits. Try to build as many of the circuits described in this book as you can. Experiment with each circuit. Try different component values. Advice on such experimentation will be given with each project. You will also be told which components are critical and should not change to avoid unnecessary risk.

Always work slowly and carefully. The socket holes are closely spaced to accommodate IC pins. It is very easy to put a lead in the wrong hole. Always check all connections before applying power.

Be careful that component leads do not touch each other and create short circuits. This can happen very easily when breadboarding, so watch out.

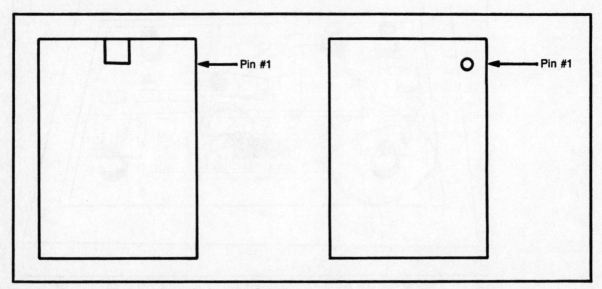

Fig. 1-4. ICs are marked to indicate the location of pin #1.

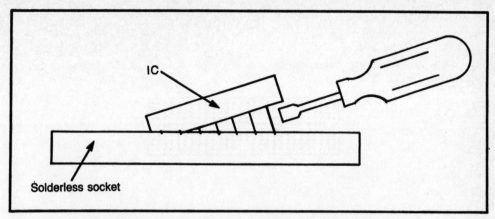

Fig. 1-5. A small screwdriver can be used to remove an IC from the socket.

Use shielded hook-up wire for all jumpers. Solid wire works better than the stranded type with solderless sockets. It will help to use hook-up wire with different colored shielding. This makes tracing connections a lot easier.

All of the projects in this book utilize integrated circuits, which should be handled with special care. Make sure all the pins are straight and properly aligned before you try inserting an IC in a socket. Make sure that none of the pins get bent up under the body of the IC. Be especially careful that the IC is oriented properly. Connecting the power supply to the wrong pins could prove disastrous. ICs are marked to indicate the location of pin #1. Two of the most common markings used for this purpose are illustrated in Fig. 1-4. These drawings are looking at the top (or back) of the IC. The pins point away from the bottom (or front).

ICs usually have short leads and fit very snugly into a solderless socket. You should exercise care in removing an IC to prevent bending or breaking one or more pins. IC removal tools are available or you can use a small (jewelers) screwdriver to pry the IC out of the socket. Be careful! Fit the tip of the screwdriver under one end of the body of the IC. Wiggle the screwdriver gently until the body of the IC moves up slightly. Now put the tip of the screwdriver under the opposite end of the IC and repeat the process. Repeat this, moving from one end to the other, as many times as needed until the IC pops free from the socket. Work slowly and very gently. Do not try to force the IC.

Of course, if you are working with several projects using the same IC, there is no need (or point) in removing the IC between circuits. Just leave the IC in place, and remove only the off-chip components. This will save wear and tear on the IC pins.

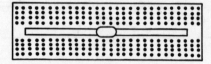

2

The 555 Timer

PROBABLY THE TWO MOST POPULAR TYPES OF ICS ARE TIMERS AND OP AMPS. OP AMPS are discussed in Chapter 4. This chapter will examine the unquestioned "king" of the timer chips, the 555.

Many electronics applications require some kind of timing signal to keep various stages in synchronization, or to trigger events periodically or at a specific time. Not surprisingly, a circuit that handles such timing functions is called a timer.

Timer ICs, such as the 555, have countless applications and are quite easy to use.

There are two basic types of timer circuits. Both are *multivibrator* (square wave) circuits. They are the monostable multivibrator and the astable multivibrator. The 555 can be operated in either mode. Because the output signal is a square wave, it can be used in digital as well as analog applications. The 555 is an analog device, but it is compatible with most digital logic families.

THE BASIC TIMER MODES

As stated above, the 555 can be operated in either of the two basic timer modes. Specific circuits will be presented later in this chapter. For now, here is a brief review of the basic principles.

The Monostable Mode

A monostable multivibrator has one stable state, which may be either HIGH or LOW, depending on the specific design used. The output will normally remain in the stable state until a triggering signal is received at the timer input. Upon being triggered, the

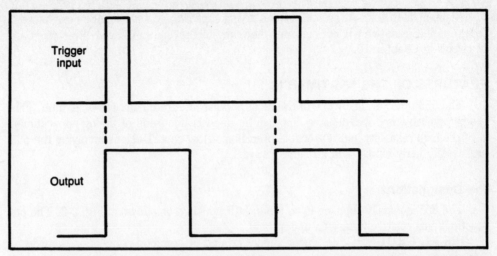

Fig. 2-1. A monostable multivibrator has a single stable state to which it reverts after its time period.

output switches to the opposite (unstable) state for a fixed period of time. The length of the input trigger pulse has no effect on the length of the output pulse.

At the end of the timing cycle, the output reverts to its normal, stable state. The action of a monostable multivibrator is illustrated in Fig. 2-1.

Because there is one output pulse for each input (trigger) pulse, this type of circuit is sometimes called a *one-shot*. A monostable multivibrator may also be called a *pulse stretcher* since the output pulse is usually significantly longer than the input pulse.

The Astable Mode

The other common type of timer circuit is the astable multivibrator. This circuit has no stable output states. The output continuously switches back and forth between the two possible states (HIGH and LOW) at a regular rate determined by component values within the circuit. The action of an astable multivibrator is illustrated in Fig. 2-2.

An astable multivibrator is really nothing more than a square-wave generator, or oscillator. When used for timing purposes, this type of circuit is often referred to as a *clock*.

The Bistable Multivibrator

In the interest of completeness, I should also mention the *bistable multivibrator,* which has two stable output states. Either output state may be held indefinitely. When a trigger pulse is received at the input, the output reverses state.

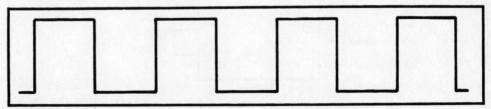

Fig. 2-2. An astable multivibrator oscillates between two unstable states.

Bistable multivibrators are not used in timing applications, and cannot be constructed from timer ICs, so we will not consider them any further here. We will cover this type of circuit in Chapter 10.

FEATURES OF THE 555 TIMER IC

The 555 timer is surely one of the most popular integrated circuits of all time. This readily available and inexpensive chip can be used in hundreds of timing applications. It offers high reliability and reasonable precision at low cost. Designs involving the 555 are usually fairly simple and straightforward.

Pin Designations

The 555 is usually supplied in an 8-pin, DIP housing, as shown in Fig. 2-3. The pin functions are relatively easy to understand.

Pin #1, GROUND: The power supply ground or common connection is made to this pin.

Pin #2, TRIGGER: The input trigger pulse is applied to this pin to initiate a timing cycle.

Pin #3, OUTPUT: The output pulse is taken from this pin.

Pin #4, RESET: This pin is used to cancel the current timing cycle.

Pin #5, CONTROL VOLTAGE: This pin permits an external voltage signal to control the timing cycle. In most applications this pin is not used.

Pin #6, THRESHOLD: The voltage on this pin determines the internal switching point.

Pin #7, DISCHARGE: This pin is used to discharge the external timing capacitor, and sense the end of the timing cycle.

Pin #8, Vcc: This is the connection point for the positive supply voltage.

A simplified diagram of the 555's internal circuitry is shown in Fig. 2-4.

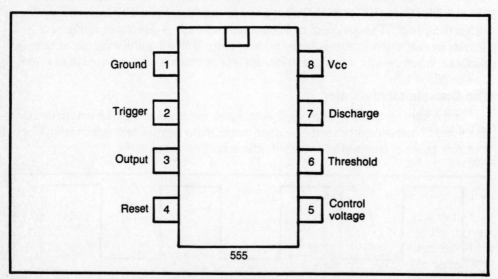

Fig. 2-3. The 555 timer is one of the most popular ICs.

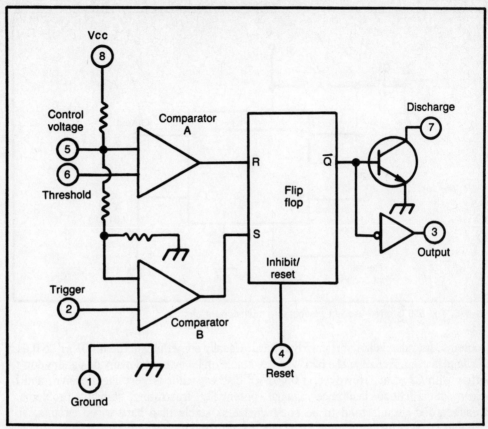

Fig. 2-4. The basic internal structure of the 555 timer IC.

Power Supply Specifications

The 555 is quite flexible in its power supply requirements. The timing cycle is relatively immune to fluctuations in the supply voltage, so close regulation is not essential, as it is for many other ICs.

The 555 can be operated at any potential from +4.5 volts to +18 volts. For most applications, +9 volts to +12 volts will give the best performance.

If the 555 is to be used with digital ICs, it should use the same supply voltage as the digital devices. For example, TTL gates must be operated on +5 volts. The 555 will work fine on this voltage too, and will deliver pseudo-digital signals at the correct levels for TTL circuitry.

BASIC MONOSTABLE CIRCUITS

Our experimentation will start with the 555 timer IC in the monostable mode. The basic circuit is shown in Fig. 2-5.

Notice how few external components are required—just two capacitors and a resistor. As a matter of fact, one of the capacitors can often be omitted. Resistor R1 and capacitor C1 determine the timing cycle of the circuit. Capacitor C2 is used to prevent instability

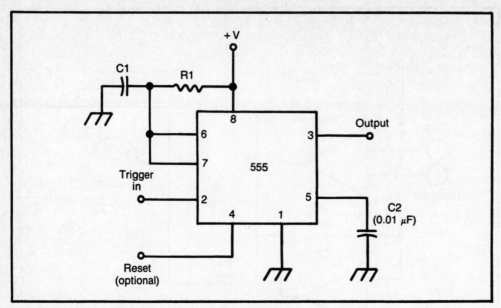

Fig. 2-5. The 555 is often used in monostable multivibrator circuits.

problems. Its value is not particularly critical. Usually something in the 0.001 μF to 0.01 μF range is used. Actually, the 555 is pretty stable on its own, and many designers don't bother with C2 at all. However, a 0.001 μF disc capacitor is very inexpensive, and I believe it is cheap insurance against potentially frustrating stability problems. Breadboarded circuits tend to be somewhat less stable than hard-wired circuits, so including C2 is probably a good idea, but it's up to you.

The normal stable state for the output of this basic monostable circuit is LOW (near ground potential). When a negative-going trigger pulse is received, the output snaps to a HIGH state for a time period determined by the values of R1 and C1. The formula is simple enough;

$$T = 1.1R_1C_1$$

For example, if R1 is a 22 k resistor, and C1 is a 0.33 μF capacitor, the time period will be;

$$\begin{aligned} T &= 1.1 \times 22,000 \times 0.00000033 \\ &\cong 0.008 \text{ second} \\ &= 8 \text{ ms} \end{aligned}$$

By selecting the proper component values, a very wide range of timing periods can be set up. Remember that the tolerance ratings of the components used will have an effect on the accuracy of the timing period. Resistors with no more than 5 percent tolerance should be used in timer applications. In critical applications, 1 percent resistors should be used. Capacitors usually have wider tolerances than resistors and should be carefully selected for use in timer circuits. As a rule, you should not use capacitors with high dielectric absorption for anything but the most non-critical applications. Capacitor types to be avoided for any degree of precision include paper capacitors, mica capacitors, and ceramic capacitors. These types of capacitors will function in a timing circuit, but the timing period will not be very accurate. Generally, the highest accuracy in timing can be achieved with plastic film capacitors, such as polystyrenes and polycarbonates.

For larger capacitor values (1 μF to about 10 μF), tantalum capacitors may be used. For capacitances greater than about 10 μF, the experimenter is usually forced to rely on electrolytic capacitors. Unfortunately, electrolytics have the widest tolerances of all. They are also prone to high leakage (especially for large values) and mediocre stability.

To compensate for the inevitable inaccuracies of the capacitance value, the resistance may be made variable to permit fine tuning to the desired timing period. For a high-precision application, a ten-turn trimpot should be used, but for experimenting (and other less critical applications) an ordinary potentiometer may be used.

The value of R1 may be anywhere from 100 ohms to 13 megohms, but for the most reliable and stable operation, it is best to keep the resistance in the range of 10 kilohms to 1 megohm.

The value of C1 is limited mainly by leakage. Higher value capacitors tend to have more leakage than lower value units. At some point, the leakage becomes unacceptable, but it is impractical to give a definite maximum level because different applications may be more or less tolerant of errors due to leakage. At the other extreme, C1 should have a minimum value of at least 100 pF to avoid problems due to stray capacitances in the circuit.

The 555 can produce output pulses as short as 10 milliseconds. Theoretically, there is no upper limit, but in practical circuits the restraints on the resistor and capacitor values limit the maximum length of the output pulse.

A Practical Monostable Demonstration Circuit

Figure 2-6 shows a practical circuit for demonstrating the operation of a monostable multivibrator. The only differences from the basic circuit are a switch to enter input pulses manually and an LED to indicate the output state. A partial parts list for this project is given in Table 2-1. Notice that the values for resistor R1 and capacitor C1 are not included in the parts list. These components determine the timebase of the circuit, and various values will be used in these experiments.

Switch S1 is a momentary-contact push-button with normally-open (NO) contacts. The basic 555 monostable multivibrator circuit is triggered by a negative-going input pulse. Closing the switch briefly grounds pin #2 (the trigger input). When the switch is opened, resistor R2 holds the input at a HIGH level. When the switch is closed, the input goes from HIGH to LOW.

Since a switch is hard to mount on a solderless breadboarding socket, and momentary switches often are not included in breadboarding systems, you might want to simulate the switch by touching the bare ends of two jumper wires together when you want to close the switch. This is inelegant, and a little awkward, but it will work for experimental purposes.

At the output, there is an LED and a resistor going to ground. The LED is oriented so that it will light (be forward-biased) when the timer output goes HIGH. Resistor R3 simply limits the current flow through the LED to avoid possible damage.

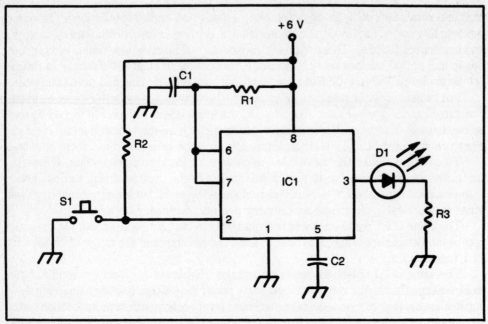

Fig. 2-6. A practical monostable multivibrator demonstration circuit. PROJECT #1

The output of the timer is normally LOW, so the LED will normally remain dark. During the timing cycle, the output goes HIGH, illuminating the LED.

Capacitor C2 is for improved stability of the circuit as discussed earlier.

The values of R2, R3, and C2 are not particularly critical. Use anything close to the specified values that you happen to have handy. There is not much point in experimenting with these values, because they do not have much noticeable effect on the operation of the circuit.

Breadboard the circuit, using a 33 kilohm resistor for R1 and a 0.1 microfarad capacitor for C1. Double-check all connections carefully before applying power. (This should be done every time you breadboard any circuit—better safe than sorry.)

Once you are sure that everything is hooked-up correctly, apply power to the circuit. A 6-volt supply is specified in the schematic, but this isn't terribly critical. When power is applied, nothing should happen. The LED may flash briefly due to false triggering,

Table 2-1. Parts List for the Monostable Multivibrator Circuit in Fig. 2-6.

IC1	555 timer IC
D1	LED (Light-Emitting Diode). Any type may be used, but a large LED will be more visible and easier to use.
R1	see text
R2	10 kΩ resistor
R3	470 ohm resistor
C1	see text
C2	0.01 μF capacitor
S1	N.O. push-button switch (SPST)

but that is nothing to worry about. If the LED lights up and stays lit, something is wrong. Remove power from the circuit and re-check your work; something is shorted. While it is remotely possible, it is very unlikely that the problem is within the IC. The trouble-spot is most likely in the external circuitry. Make sure that no component leads are accidentally touching each other. Check the switch to make sure that its contacts are open.

Assuming there is no problem with the circuit when you apply power, you are ready to test its operation. While watching the LED, close switch S1 briefly. The LED should flash and go off again very quickly. Watch carefully, because the timebase of this circuit is very short. Nominally, the output pulse time should be;

$$
\begin{aligned}
T &= 1.1 R_1 C_1 \\
&= 1.1 \times 33{,}000 \times 0.0000001 \\
&= 0.00363 \text{ second} \\
&= 3.63 \text{ ms}
\end{aligned}
$$

Of course, the component tolerances may change the timing period in either direction.

If you don't see the LED flash, don't panic yet. The component values may be on the low side, and the flash may be too brief for the eye to catch.

Replace capacitor C2 with a 25 μF capacitor and R1 with a 100 kΩ resistor. (Always remove power from any circuit before changing any of the components. There are *no* exceptions to this rule.)

Repeat the experiment with these new component values. You will probably have to use an electrolytic capacitor for C2, but that is all right for this application. The only thing that will be hurt is the accuracy of the time-base equation.

You should have no trouble seeing the LED light up this time. With these component values, the nominal length of the output pulse should be;

$$
\begin{aligned}
T &= 1.1 \times 100{,}000 \times 0.000025 \\
&= 2.75 \text{ seconds}
\end{aligned}
$$

Experiment with other values for R1 and C1. Be sure to remove power from the circuit before making any changes.

With long time-bases, you can check the timing accuracy with a time-base. Here are some examples;

$$
\begin{aligned}
R_1 &= 470 \text{ k}\Omega \\
C_1 &= 50 \text{ }\mu\text{F} \\
T &= 1.1 \times 470{,}000 \times 0.00005 \\
&= 25.85 \text{ seconds}
\end{aligned}
$$

$$
\begin{aligned}
R_1 &= 1 \text{ M}\Omega \\
C_1 &= 100 \text{ }\mu\text{F} \\
T &= 1.1 \times 1{,}000{,}000 \times 0.0001 \\
&= 110 \text{ seconds} \\
&= 1 \text{ minute, } 50 \text{ seconds}
\end{aligned}
$$

$$R_1 = 1 \text{ M}\Omega$$
$$C_1 = 500 \ \mu\text{F}$$
$$T = 1.1 \times 1,000,000 \times 0.0005$$
$$= 550 \text{ seconds}$$
$$= 9 \text{ minutes, } 10 \text{ seconds}$$

The last one will probably give you enough time for a quick cup of coffee.

You will almost surely measure times greater or less than the calculated values. This is due to component tolerances.

Increasing capacitance, generally reduces the stability of a capacitor. Capacitances in parallel add. Try generating some long time periods with two or more paralleled capacitors in place of a single C1. Does this help or hurt the overall accuracy?

Voltage-Controlled Monostable Circuit

Remove capacitor C2 from the circuit, and feed a dc voltage into pin 5. A convenient way to do this is to use a resistive voltage divider network to tap off part of the supply voltage, as shown in Fig. 2-7. This arrangement is good because there is no way for the applied control voltage to exceed the supply voltage, which could cause problems.

The specific resistor values are not particularly critical. For best results, the fixed resistors (Ra and Rb) should be equal in value and somewhat smaller than the value of

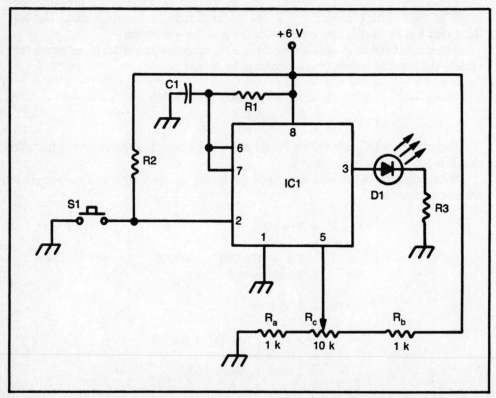

Fig. 2-7. Using pin #5 creates a voltage-controlled monostable multivibrator. PROJECT #2

the potentiometer (Rc). I used 1 kΩ resistors for Ra and Rb, and a 10 k potentiometer for Rc.

Repeat some of the experiments described in the last section with different voltages applied to pin #5. How does the control voltage input affect the timing cycle?

Inverted Input Monostable

Ordinarily, the 555 is triggered by a negative-going input pulse. In some applications you may need to trigger a timer with a positive-going input pulse. The simple network shown in Fig. 2-8 will do the trick. Figure 2-9 shows the complete circuit for an inverted-input, monostable multivibrator.

SWITCH DEBOUNCER

Before moving on to the astable mode, consider a few examples of practical applications for 555 monostable multivibrators.

One application is switch debouncing. A mechanical switch does not make or break contact cleanly. It bounces back and forth several times before settling down to its new position. This is inevitable. Mechanical parts vibrate.

Usually switch bouncing does not make much difference. In certain critical applications, such as digital counters, multiple switch closures could confuse the circuit, resulting in erratic or incorrect operation. For example, a digital counter may count each bounce as a new switch closure, destroying any semblence of an accurate count.

The solution is a switch debouncer circuit, like the one shown in Fig. 2-10. This is simply a monostable multivibrator with a timing cycle long enough to give the mechanical switch contacts time to settle into position firmly. Once the timing cycle has been initiated, additional input pulses (switch bounces) will be ignored until the 555 has timed out.

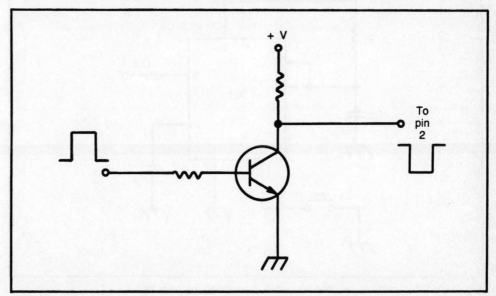

Fig. 2-8. In some applications it may be necessary to invert the trigger signal before applying it to a 555 timer.

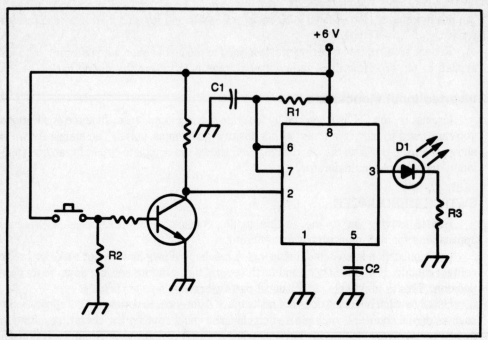

Fig. 2-9. An inverted input monostable multivibrator circuit. PROJECT #3

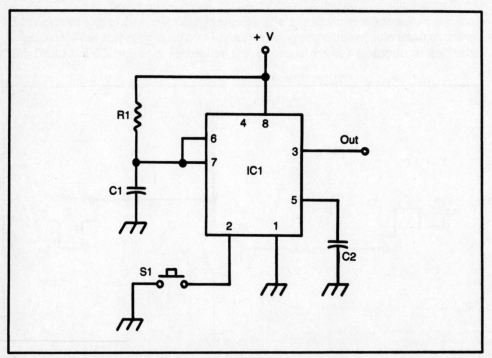

Fig. 2-10. This circuit can be used for switch debouncing. PROJECT #4

IC1	555 timer IC
C1	0.5 μF capacitor
C2	0.01 μF capacitor
R1	470 k resistor
S1	N.O. SPST push switch

Table 2-2. Parts List for the Switch Debouncer in Fig. 2-10.

Using the component values listed in Table 2-2, the timing cycle will be approximately 0.1 second, which should be long enough to cover the bounciest switch without slowing down operation.

TIMER OPERATED RELAY

Most monostable multivibrators are used to turn something on or off after a specific time delay. Small dc loads, such as the LEDs used in the demonstrator circuits, can be powered directly from the 555's output. This IC cannot put out much power, hence for larger loads, there must be some sort of intermediate device, such as a relay.

Figure 2-11 shows a circuit for a timer-operated relay. The parts list for this project is given in Table 2-3. The diodes protect the IC from back-emf across the relay coil. Resistor R1 and capacitor C1 are selected for the desired time period.

A negative-going input pulse could be used to trigger this circuit in place of switch S1. In this case, resistor R2 would also be eliminated.

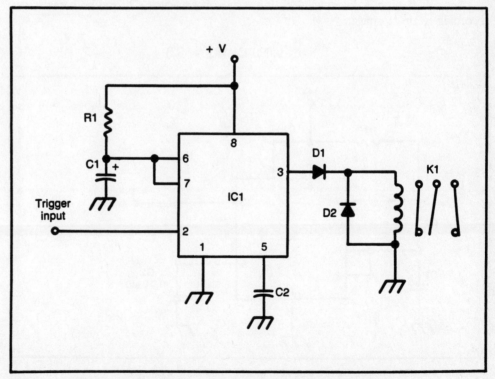

Fig. 2-11. A relay can be controlled by a monostable timer circuit. PROJECT #5

Table 2-3. Parts List for the Timer-Operated Relay Circuit in Fig. 2-11.

IC1	555 timer IC
C1	*
C2	0.01 μF capacitor
R1	*
D1, D2	1N4148, 1N914, or similar diode
K1	relay—6 V, 500 Ω, 12 mA coil—contacts to suit application

* select for desired time period

ASTABLE CIRCUITS

The 555 timer can also be operated in the astable mode. An astable multivibrator has no stable output states. The output continuously switches back and forth between the LOW and HIGH states. The rate of this switching is determined by the timing cycle of the circuit.

The basic 555 astable multivibrator circuit is shown in Fig. 2-12. Notice how similar this circuit is to the monostable multivibrator circuits presented earlier.

There are actually *two* time periods to calculate in this circuit. These are the time the output holds the HIGH state and the time it is in the LOW state. The complete cycle time is the sum of the HIGH and LOW times. The transition time between states is so short it has no noticable effect on the total cycle time.

The HIGH time is determined by the values of capacitor C1, and both resistors, according to this formula;

$$T_h = 0.693 \, C1 \, (R1 + R2)$$

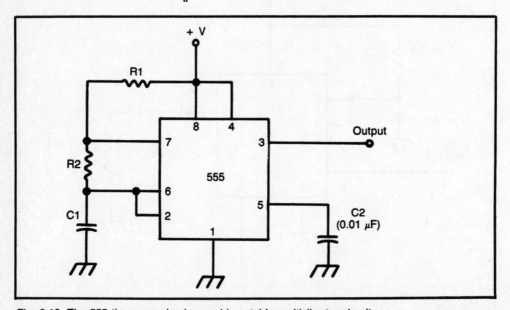

Fig. 2-12. The 555 timer can also be used in astable multivibrator circuits.

For example, if we assume the following component values;

$$C_1 = 0.22 \ \mu F \ (0.00000022 \ farad)$$
$$R_1 = 39 \ k\Omega \ (39,000 \ ohms)$$
$$R_2 = 68 \ k\Omega \ (68,000 \ ohms)$$

then the HIGH time will be approximately equal to;

$$T_h = 0.693 \times 0.00000022 \times (39,000 + 68,000)$$
$$= 0.693 \times 0.00000022 \times 107,000$$
$$= 0.0163132 \ second$$

For the LOW time, resistor R1 is ignored. Only R2 and C1 determine the LOW time. The formula for finding this part of the cycle is;

$$T_l = 0.693 \ C_1 \ R_2$$

Continuing with our sample component values, we find that the LOW time is approximately equal to;

$$T_l = 0.693 \times 0.00000022 \times 68,000$$
$$= 0.0103672$$

Notice that since the LOW equation uses only one resistor, and the HIGH equation uses both, the LOW time will always be at least slightly less than the HIGH time.

The total cycle time is simply the sum of the HIGH time and the LOW time. In this example:

$$T_t = T_h + T_l$$
$$= 0.0163132 + 0.0103672$$
$$= 0.0266804 \ second$$

Since the astable multivibrator is essentially an oscillator, or signal generator, it is usually more convenient to talk about the waveform in terms of frequency instead of cycle time. The frequency is simply the reciprocal of the cycle time. That is;

$$F = 1/T_t$$

In the example;

$$F = 1/0.0266804$$
$$= 37.480697 \ Hz$$

By algebraically rearranging the formula, it is possible to find the frequency directly from the component values, without bothering with the HIGH, LOW, and cycle times at all;

$$F = 1/T_t$$
$$= 1/(T_h + T_l)$$
$$= 1/((0.693\ C_1\ (R_1 + R_2)) + (0.693\ C_1\ R_2))$$
$$= 1/(0.693\ C_1\ (R_1 + 2R_2))$$

The ratio of the HIGH cycle time to the total cycle time determines the waveshape. The 555 timer in the astable mode puts out rectangle waves. But there are an infinite variety of possible rectangle waves. In each case, the difference is the *duty cycle*, or the ratio of HIGH time to total cycle time.

In a perfect square wave, the output is HIGH for at exactly half of each cycle. A square wave is illustrated in Fig. 2-13. The duty cycle is 1:2, or 50%.

Most waveforms are made up of a fundamental (base frequency) and a number of harmonics, or additional frequency components that are exact integer multiples of the fundamental.

A square wave includes only the odd harmonics. Any harmonic that is a multiple of two is missing. For example, a 500 Hz square wave would have the following frequency components;

500 Hz	Fundamental
1,500 Hz	Third harmonic
2,500 Hz	Fifth harmonic
3,500 Hz	Seventh harmonic
4,500 Hz	Ninth harmonic

and so forth. The harmonics grow weaker as they get higher (further from the fundamental).

A non-square rectangle wave is shown in Fig. 2-14. In this waveform, the HIGH

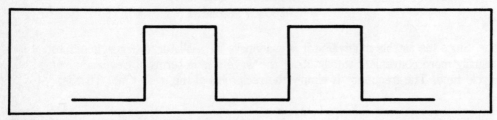

Fig. 2-13. A square wave has a duty cycle of 1:2.

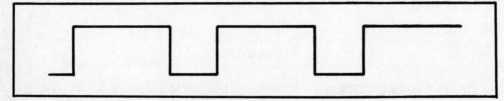

Fig. 2-14. This rectangle wave has a duty cycle of 1:3.

time is one third of the total cycle time, so the duty cycle is 1:3 or 33.33%. This time, every third harmonic is missing;

500 Hz	Fundamental
1,000 Hz	Second harmonic
2,000 Hz	Fourth harmonic
2,500 Hz	Fifth harmonic
3,500 Hz	Seventh harmonic
4,000 Hz	Eighth harmonic
5,000 Hz	Tenth harmonic

and so on.

Another rectangle wave is shown in Fig. 2-15. This one has a duty cycle of 1:5, or 20%. Every fifth harmonic is absent from this waveform;

500 Hz	Fundamental
1,000 Hz	Second harmonic
1,500 Hz	Third harmonic
2,000 Hz	Fourth harmonic
3,000 Hz	Sixth harmonic
3,500 Hz	Seventh harmonic
4,000 Hz	Eighth harmonic
4,500 Hz	Ninth harmonic
5,500 Hz	Eleventh harmonic

and so on.

You should have spotted a pattern by now. For a rectangle wave with a duty cycle of 1:X, where X is an integer, all harmonics that are integer multiples of X will be absent. Calculating the harmonic content when X is not an integer is rather difficult. Fortunately, it is rarely necessary. Generally you can come close enough for most purposes simply by rounding X off to the nearest integer value.

Low-Frequency Astable Multivibrator

Figure 2-16 shows a practical astable multivibrator demonstration circuit. The parts list is given in Table 2-4, except for the frequency determining components (C1, R1, and R2).

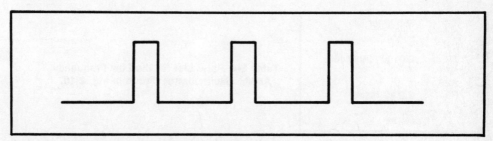

Fig. 2-15. This rectangle wave has a duty cycle of 1:5.

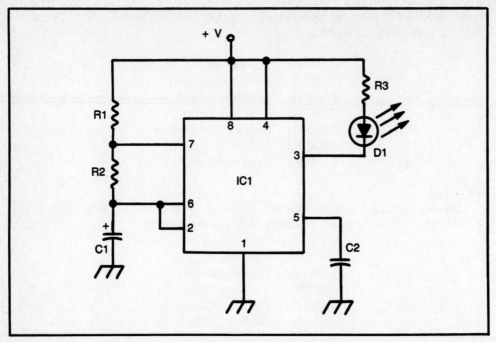

Fig. 2-16. This circuit demonstrates the operation of an astable multivibrator at low frequencies. PROJ-ECT #6

Breadboard the circuit using the following component values;

$$C_1 = 0.22 \ \mu F$$
$$R_1 = 470 \ k\Omega$$
$$R_2 = 470 \ k\Omega$$

When you apply power to this circuit, the LED should blink on and off to indicate the pulses being generated at the output. Using these component values, the output frequency should be approximately equal to;

$$F = 1/ \ (0.693 \ C_1 \ (R_1 + 2R_2))$$
$$= 1/(0.693 \times 0.00000022 \times (470,000 + (2 \times 470,000)))$$
$$= 1/(0.693 \times 0.00000022 \times (470,000 + 940,000))$$

IC1	555 timer IC
D1	LED
C1	*
C2	0.01 μF capacitor
R1	*
R2	*
R3	2.2 kΩ resistor
	* see text

Table 2-4. Parts List for the Low Frequency
Astable Multivibrator Circuit in Fig. 2-16.

$$= 1/(0.693 \times 0.00000022 \times 1,410,000)$$
$$= 1/0.2149686$$
$$= 4.65 \text{ Hz}$$

The LED should blink about four and a half times per second. This is a little fast to measure by eye, so let's substitute a larger capacitor in place of C1. We will use a 50 μF electrolytic capacitor. Remember to remove power before making any changes in the circuit.

The positive lead of the capacitor should be connected to pin 6.

Now the nominal output frequency of the circuit should be in the neighborhood of;

$$F = 1/(0.693 \times 0.00005 \times 1,410,000)$$
$$= 1/48.8565$$
$$= 0.02 \text{ Hz}.$$

Each cycle should take over 48 seconds. Time the LED blinks with a stop watch. Actually, you may measure a time period several seconds longer or shorter than the calculated value. This is due to the component tolerances. Electrolytic capacitors in particular have very wide tolerances.

Check how long the LED is on compared to its off time. When R1 is equal to R2 we do *not* get a 1:2 duty cycle. It is not possible to achieve a true square wave with the basic 555 astable circuit. You can come very close by making the value of R1 very small when compared to R2. Try replacing R1 with a 1 kΩ resistor. Repeat the experiment. The ON and OFF times should be very close to equal. You may not even be able to measure the difference with just your eye and stop watch.

Note that changing the duty cycle changed the frequency significantly. Experiment with other combinations of component values on your own. Here's one more set of component values to try with this circuit;

$$C_1 = 0.01 \ \mu\text{F}$$
$$R_1 = 2.2 \text{ k}\Omega$$
$$R_2 = 4.7 \text{ k}\Omega$$

What happens when you apply power to the circuit this time? The LED should appear to be lit continuously. Actually, it is blinking on and off at a rate that is too high for the eye to distinguish. The nominal frequency is equal to;

$$F = 1/(0.693 \times 0.00000001 \times (2200 + (2 \times 4700)))$$
$$= 1/(0.693 \times 0.00000001 \times (2200 + 9400))$$
$$= 1/(0.693 \times 0.00000001 \times 11,600)$$
$$= 1/0.0000803$$
$$= 12,453 \text{ Hz}$$

For frequencies above a few hertz, the simple LED just won't do as an output indicator device.

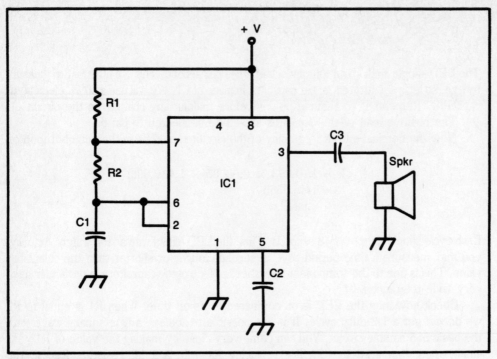

Fig. 2-17. An astable multivibrator circuit for audio frequencies. PROJECT #7

Audio-Frequency Astable Multivibrator Demonstrator

Figure 2-17 shows how the circuit can be adapted for audio output. Capacitor C3 protects the speaker from any dc component in the output signal. Such a dc component could be harmful to a speaker.

The parts list for this project is given in Table 2-5, except for the frequency determining components. Why not start out with the values used in the last experiment?

$$C_1 = 0.01 \ \mu F$$
$$R_1 = 2.2 \ k\Omega$$
$$R_2 = 4.7 \ k\Omega$$

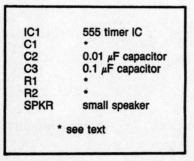

IC1	555 timer IC
C1	*
C2	0.01 μF capacitor
C3	0.1 μF capacitor
R1	*
R2	*
SPKR	small speaker
	* see text

Table 2-5. Parts List for the Audio
Frequency Astable Multivibrator Circuit in Fig. 2-17.

When you apply power, you should hear a high pitched tone from the speaker.

Experiment with other component values on your own. Notice how each change alters the tone. Pay particular attention to the difference in sound with variations in the duty cycle.

TRIANGLE WAVE GENERATOR

The 555 is designed only for rectangle waves, but it can be "fooled" into producing other waveforms in some circumstances. The circuit shown in Fig. 2-18 is a triangle wave generator. Actually, it generates a pseudo-triangle wave. Sometimes.

At moderately high frequencies (several kilohertz), the output closely resembles a triangle wave, as shown in Fig. 2-19. At lower frequencies, the output pulses become increasingly separated, as shown in Fig. 2-20. This waveform may be useful in some circumstances, but it is certainly not a triangle wave.

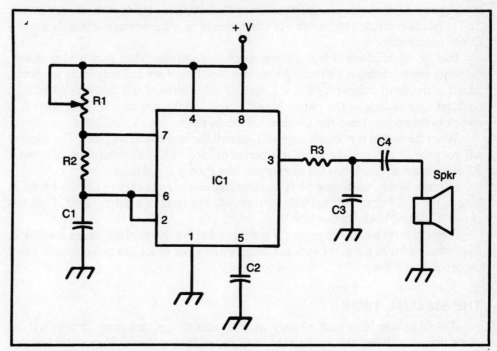

Fig. 2-18. This circuit generates pseudo-triangle waves. PROJECT #8

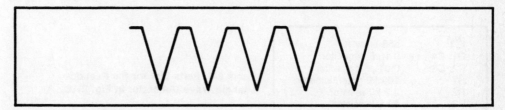

Fig. 2-19. An approximation of a triangle wave at high frequencies.

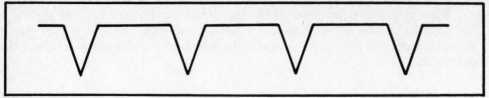

Fig. 2-20. The output signal from the circuit in Fig. 2-18 at low frequencies.

A parts list for this project is given in Table 2-6. Notice that potentiometer R1 controls both the output frequency and the waveshape. Try experimenting with other values for R2 and C1 too.

SOUND POCKET GENERATOR

Figure 2-21 shows an unusual variation on the basic 555 astable multivibrator circuit. The output is controlled by switch S1, which should be a momentary-action (Normally-Open) push-button.

Initially, when power is first applied, there is no output. When switch S1 is closed, the timer starts putting out a rectangle wave whose frequency and duty cycle are determined in the usual manner by C1, R1, and R2. The speaker will continue sounding a constant tone as long as the switch is held closed. So far, we have nothing special. A switch between pin 3 and the speaker will do as much.

When the switch is released (opened), something interesting happens. The speaker will continue to produce the tone for a period defined by the time constant of resistor R3 and capacitor C3. When C3 discharges, the tone will cease.

In other words, each time S1 is momentarily closed, a pocket of sound at least as long as the R^3/C^3 time constant will be produced. For want of a better name, I call this circuit a "sound pocket generator."

A typical parts list for this project is given in Table 2-7. None of the values are critical. Experiment with all the parts values. Changing the value of R4 has no noticeable effect on circuit operation.

THE 556 DUAL TIMER

The 555 timer IC is such a handy and versatile device that many circuits will use more than one. When this is the case, it is generally convenient to use the 556 dual timer IC. This 14-pin chip contains two complete and independent (except for the supply voltage) 555-type timers in a single package. The pinout diagram for the 556 dual-timer

IC1	555 timer IC
C1, C4	0.1 μF capacitor
C2, C3	0.01 μF capacitor
R1	100 kΩ potentiometer
R2	2.2 kΩ resistor
R3	12 kΩ resistor
SPKR	small speaker

Table 2-6. Parts List for the Pseudo-Triangle Wave Generator in Fig. 2-18.

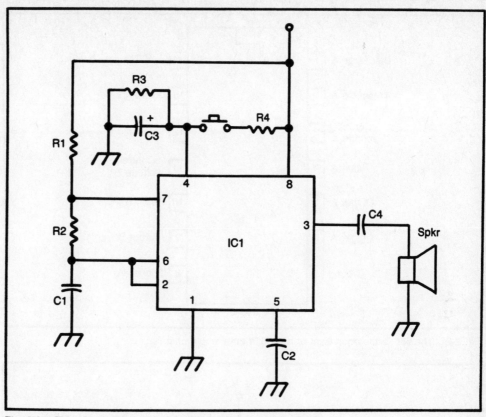

Fig. 2-21. This circuit puts out a "pocket" of sound. PROJECT #9

Table 2-7. Parts List for the Sound Pocket Generator Circuit in Fig. 2-21.

IC1	555 timer IC
C1, C4	0.1 μF capacitor
C2	0.01 μF capacitor
C3	50 μF electrolytic capacitor
R1	2.2 kΩ resistor
R2	22 kΩ resistor
R3	120 kΩ resistor
R4	3.9 kΩ resistor
S1	N.O. SPST push switch
SPKR	small speaker

IC is shown in Fig. 2-22. Half a 556 can be used in any application calling for a 555. Of course you must watch out for the differences in the pin numbers.

Figure 2-23 shows a fairly typical application for the 556 dual timer. This is a tone burst generator. In a sense, it is rather like an automated version of the circuit in Fig. 2-21. In this circuit the output will contain bursts of a regular tone, separated by periods of silence. The basic waveform is illustrated in Fig. 2-24.

Naturally, this circuit could also be built using two separate 555s, as shown in Fig. 2-25. This circuit is functionally 100 percent identical to the one in Fig. 2-23, but it is a little easier to see what is going on here. We have two astable multivibrators, one

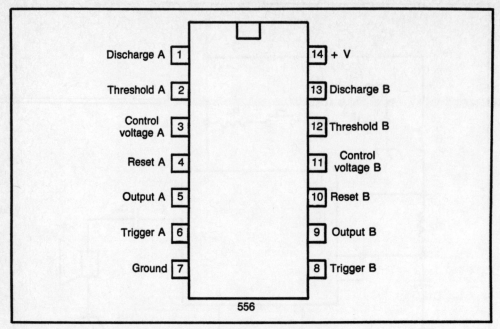

Fig. 2-22. The 556 is the equivalent of two 555s on a single chip.

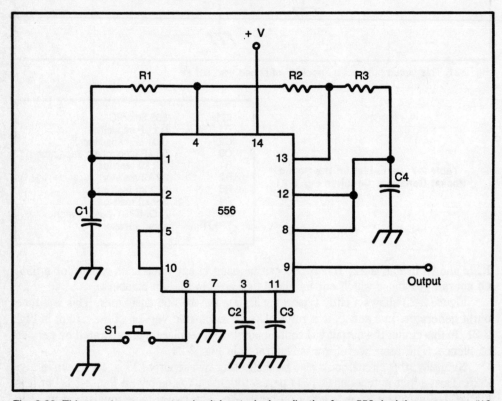

Fig. 2-23. This tone burst generator circuit is a typical application for a 556 dual timer. PROJECT #10

Table 2-8.		
Parts List for the Waveform	2	555 timer ICs
Tone Burst Generator	or	
Circuit in Figs. 2-23 and 2-25.	1	556 dual timer IC
	R1	330 kΩ resistor
	R2	12 kΩ resistor
	R3	4.7 kΩ resistor
	C1, C4	0.1 μF capacitor
	C2, C3	0.01 μF capacitor
	S1	Normally Open SPEST push switch

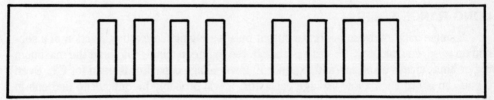

Fig. 2-24. The tone burst generator circuit shown in Fig. 2-23 produces this type of signal.

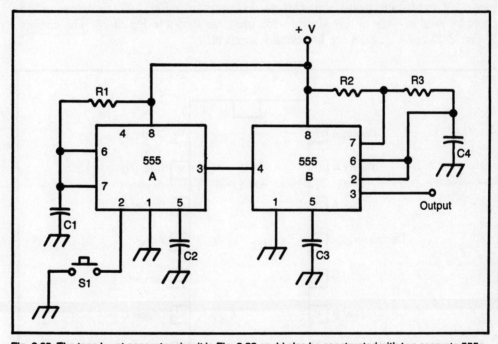

Fig. 2-25. The tone burst generator circuit in Fig. 2-23 could also be constructed with two separate 555s.

of which is controlling the other. Timer B generates the tone. Timer A generates a slower (lower frequency) rectangle wave which turns the output of timer B on and off at regular intervals.

Another frequent application for a 556 dual timer (or a pair of separate 555 timers) is to increase the time period of a monostable multivibrator. Projects for accomplishing this will be discussed shortly.

THE 558 QUAD TIMER

A quad-timer IC is also available, for high density circuits. This is the 558, shown in Fig. 2-26. This device contains four 555-type timer stages that can be used in most, but not all, standard 555 applications. The timers in the 558 are limited for some applications because not all functions are brought out to the IC pins as they are with the 555 and the 556. The 558 timer stages are primarily designed for monostable operation, but one stage can be operated in the astable mode.

The timer stages in a 556 dual timer are *exact* replacements for 555 timers. The timer stages in a 558 quad-timer are merely close approximations of true 555 timers.

LONG RANGE TIMERS

A single 555 timer can generate output pulses ranging from a tiny fraction of a second up to several minutes. As a rule of thumb, ten to fifteen minutes is about the maximum upper limit, unless a special (and expensive) low-leakage capacitor is used for C1. Even if you can afford such a low-leakage capacitor, it will probably be difficult to find one in the desired value.

It is often more practical to achieve longer time periods by cascading two (or even more) 555 monostable multivibrator stages, as illustrated in Fig. 2-27. Of course, a 556 could be used in place of the separate 555 units, as shown in Fig. 2-28. The circuits in Fig. 2-27 and Fig. 2-28 are functionally identical.

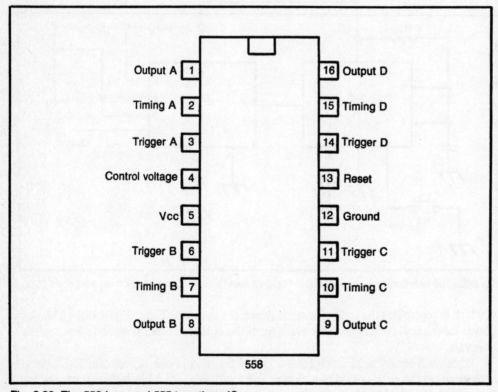

Fig. 2-26. The 558 is a quad 555-type timer IC.

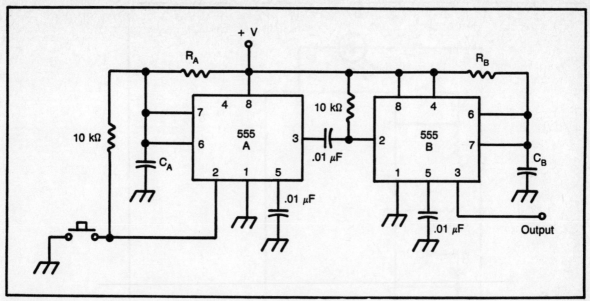

Fig. 2-27. A pair of 555s can be cascaded to create a longer time period. PROJECT #11

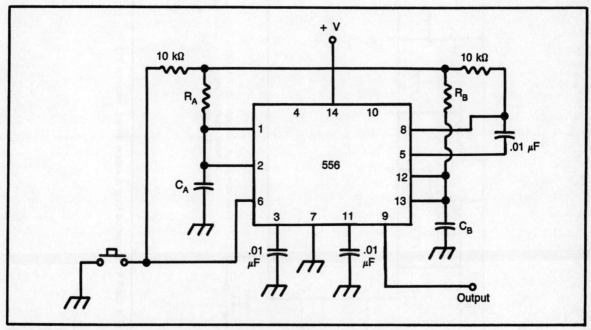

Fig. 2-28. The circuit in Fig. 2-27 can be simplified by using a 556 dual timer IC.

The 558 is particularly well-suited for cascading timer stages for long duration time periods. A typical four-stage circuit is shown in Fig. 2-29. No parts list is given for this project, because component values should be selected for the specific application.

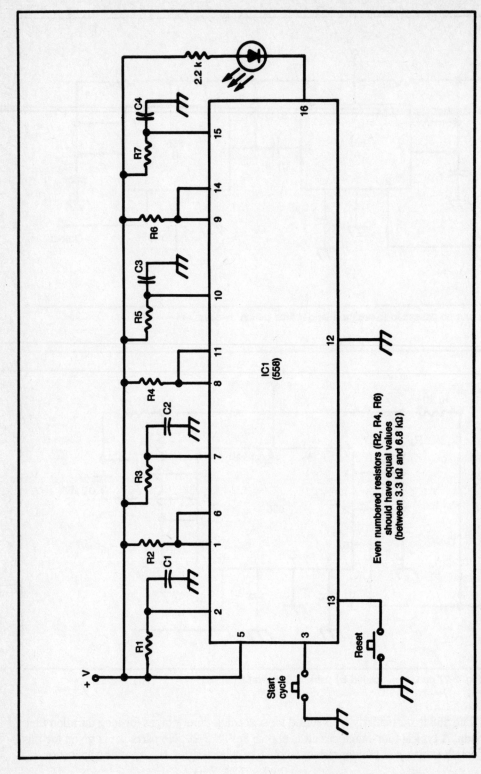

Fig. 2-29. The 558 is ideal for cascaded long duration timers. PROJECT #12

Since there are four timer stages, there are four time constants to set up;

Stage 1:	R_1	C1
Stage 2:	R_3	C2
Stage 3:	R_5	C3
Stage 4:	R7	C4

The four time constants add to create the total output delay.

The LED and its associated resistor provide a visual indication of the output. You can use this circuit to drive other circuits or devices. The final output is taken off at pin 16.

The even numbered resistors (R2, R4, and R6) should have equal values. The exact resistance is not critical. Anything between 3.3 kΩ and 68 kΩ should do.

Each of these cascaded long-duration timers works in pretty much the same way. Refer back to Fig. 2-27. For the time being, ignore timer B and its associated components. Timer A functions as a monostable multivibrator. Normally its output is LOW. When it is triggered by a negative-going pulse, the output goes HIGH for a fixed period. After the timer times out, the output switches from HIGH back to LOW.

The output of timer A is connected to the trigger input of timer B. When A times out, B senses a negative-going pulse, triggering its own timing cycle. The timer stages take turns, first A, and then B.

It's simple, and best of all, it works.

SEQUENTIAL TIMER

Since a long duration timer is made up of individual timer stages that operate one after the other, you might wonder why the intermediate outputs cannot be tapped for sequential operation. The answer is, they can be. Figure 2-30 shows a typical sequential timer circuit. You should notice that it is pretty much the same as the long duration timer circuit of Fig. 2-29 with the additional outputs tapped.

With a circuit like this, multiple events can be triggered in sequence, with any desired delay between any two adjacent events.

RAMP TIMER

Ordinarily, the output of a 555 timer circuit is a pulse. The time it takes to switch from full LOW to full HIGH (or vice versa) is so short, we can almost say the switching is instantaneous.

All of this is just fine for the vast majority of timing applications. But in some cases a simple time-activated switch may not be desirable. A voltage that increases linearly from LOW to HIGH in a given time period may be preferable.

There are two simple tricks needed to accomplish this. First, do not use the nominal output of the timer. Tap a ramp output across the timing capacitor. The timing cycle is the time it takes this capacitor to charge, so the voltage across this component will gradually increase throughout the timing cycle.

Unfortunately, a capacitor normally charges in an exponential, rather than a linear fashion. This might not make much difference in some applications. When you need a true linear ramp, you have to use the second trick.

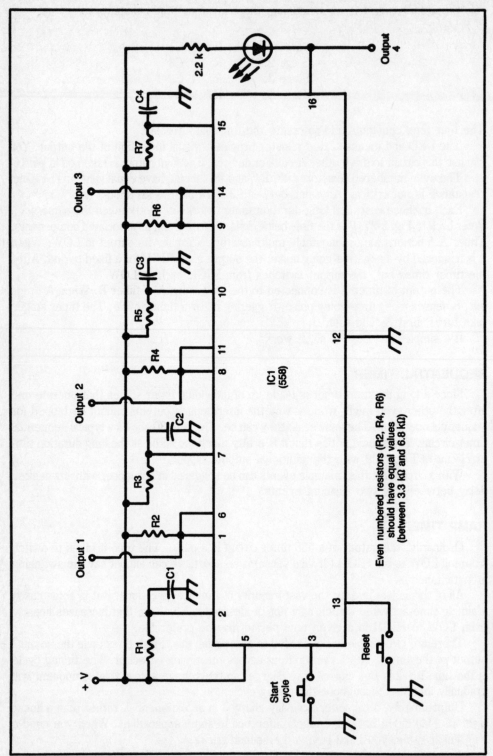

Fig. 2-30. The 558 is also used in this sequential timer circuit. PROJECT #13

Even numbered resistors (R2, R4, R6)
should have equal values
(between 3.3 kΩ and 6.8 kΩ)

A capacitor can be charged linearly through a constant-current source. In the circuit of Fig. 2-31, the timing resistor has been replaced with a transistor which functions as a constant-current source. Notice that the normal pulse output is still available, even if the ramp output is also used.

The resistor (R1) in the emitter circuit of the transistor is the new timing resistor, although the equation for the time period is somewhat more complex here.

$$T = V_c C_1 / I_t$$

where T is the time period in seconds, C1 is the value of the timing capacitor (in farads), V_c is the voltage applied to pin #5, and I_t is the current supplied by transistor Q1. The transistor current output is determined by the value of R1 and the supply voltage. Assuming a +15 volt supply, the I_t current will be approximately;

$$I_t = 4.2/R_1$$

This equation is not precise, but it will be close enough for most applications. Algebraically rearranging these two equations gives an approximate formula for the timing period;

$$T = 0.24 V_c C_1 R_1$$

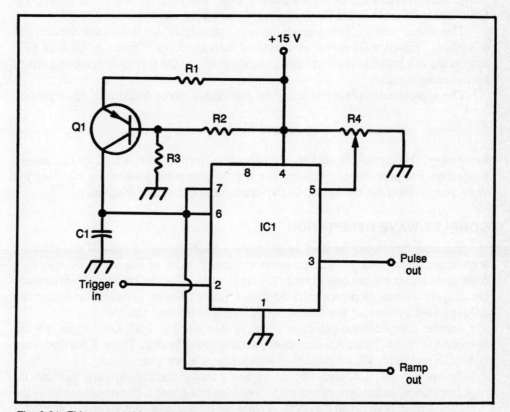

Fig. 2-31. This monostable multivibrator circuit produces a linear ramp output. PROJECT #14

IC1	555 timer
Q1	pnp transistor (2N3906, or similar)
C1	0.005 μF capacitor
R1	100 kΩ resistor
R2	4.7 kΩ resistor
R3	10 kΩ resistor
R4	10 kΩ potentiometer

Table 2-9. Parts List of the Ramp Timer Circuit in Fig. 2-31.

It is important to remember that this equation assumes a supply voltage of +15 volts, which is the recommended supply voltage for this circuit. It will work with lower supply voltages, but at a loss in accuracy and overall stability.

A typical parts list for this project is given in Table 2-9. Experiment with different values for R1 and C1 to achieve different time periods.

To see how this circuit works, connect a flashlight bulb to the ramp output. When the circuit is triggered, the bulb should light dimly, and gradually increase to full brightness, then cut off at the end of the timer cycle.

RAMP ASTABLE

Can you use the same tricks to generate ramp (or sawtooth) waves in the astable mode? Sure. A typical circuit is shown in Fig. 2-32. The parts list is given in Table 2-10. Once again, R1 and C1 are the frequency determining components.

This circuit works in pretty much the same manner as the monostable version just described. Transistor Q1 serves as a constant current source. Transistor Q2 is an FET functioning as a buffer to prevent loading the timer due to the output device being driven by the ramp signal.

The approximate output frequency for this circuit can be found with this equation;

$$F = 0.91/(R_1 C_1)$$

Remember, this formula is only an approximation, further complicated by component tolerances. For precision applications, use a multi-turn potentiometer for R1. This will allow you to fine tune the circuit to the exact, desired, output frequency.

COMPLEX WAVE GENERATION

555 type timers can be used to generate a wide variety of unusual and complex waveforms. Refer back to the tone-burst generator circuit of Fig. 2-23. By operating **both** timer sections in the audible range (50 Hz up to 15 kHz), the two signals will interact, creating enharmonic (non-harmonic) sidebands. Many different complex waveforms can be generated by altering the relative frequencies of the two timers.

Another complex-tone-generator circuit is shown in Fig. 2-33. Once again, we use two timer sections. Timer A is an ordinary astable multivibrator. Timer B is a frequency divider. This circuit will be presented separately in a few pages.

Except for C2, C4, and C5, all of the passive components are suitable for experimentation. In fact, you may want to construct this circuit with variable components. A deluxe version is shown in Fig. 2-34. A parts list for this project is given in Table 2-11.

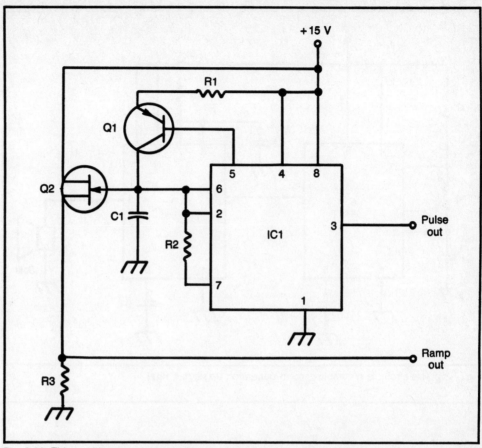

Fig. 2-32. This modification of the astable circuit generates a ramp (sawtooth) waveform. PROJECT #15

Switch S1 is a rotary type, permitting you to select any of the capacitors. It acts as a range switch. R1 and R2 control the frequency and waveshape of the original signal, which may be tapped off at point A. R3 controls the timing of the frequency divider section and has a drastic effect on the resulting sound. Finally, R4 is simply a volume control. If you enjoy weird sounds, this one should keep you busy for hours.

Another way to achieve some very novel waveshapes is to combine the outputs of two or more astables through one or more digital gates. A sample circuit is shown in

Table 2-10. Parts List for the Ramp Astable Circuit in Fig. 2-32.

IC1	555 timer
Q1	pnp transistor (2N3906, or similar)
Q2	FET (2N4681, or similar)
C1	0.01 μF capacitor
R1	680 kΩ resistor
R2	4.7 kΩ resistor
R3	10 kΩ resistor

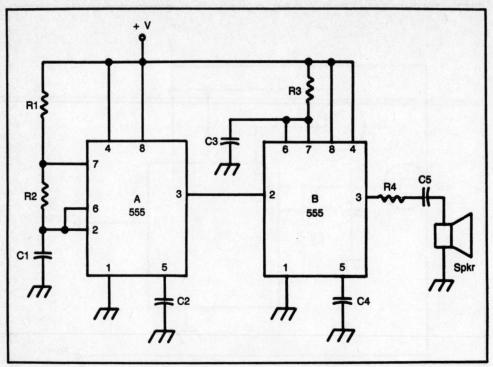

Fig. 2-33. This circuit is a complex sound generator. PROJECT # 16(a)

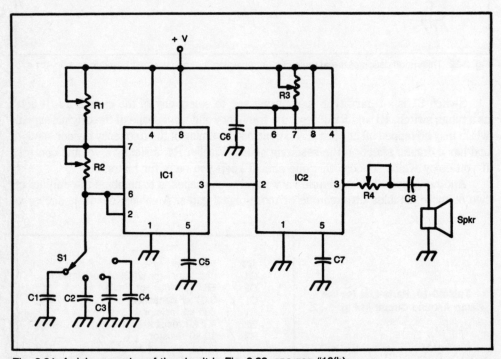

Fig. 2-34. A deluxe version of the circuit in Fig. 2-33. PROJECT #16(b)

IC1, IC2	555 timer
C1	0.01 μF capacitor*
C2	0.05 μF capacitor*
C3	0.1 μF capacitor*
C4	0.5 μF capacitor*
C5, C7	0.01 μF capacitor
C6	0.02 μF capacitor
C8	0.1 μF capacitor
R1, R2	250 kΩ potentiometer
R3	500 kΩ potentiometer
R4	5 kΩ potentiometer
S1	SP4T rotary switch

* experiment with other values

Fig. 2-35. No parts list is given for this project. Just select the component values surrounding each 555 as if you were designing a simple astable multivibrator.

Any type of digital gate may be used to combine the timer outputs. An AND gate is shown here. The output will be HIGH if and only if both inputs to the gate are HIGH. If either timer output is a LOW, the output at that instant will be LOW. Typical signals in this circuit are illustrated in Fig. 2-36. There are countless possibilities to be obtained by altering the relative frequencies (and phase) of the astables and by using other digital gates (such as OR, X-OR, NOR, or NAND, or even some combinations. For more information on digital gates refer to Chapter 9).

SOME UNUSUAL APPLICATIONS

Most applications for the 555 timer IC are essentially variations on the basic monostable or astable circuits, but some of the variations are not as obvious as others. Here are the more novel applications for the 555.

Missing Pulse Detector

The circuit shown in Fig. 2-37 will produce a negative-going pulse when it detects a gap in a stream of pulses at the input. Missing pulse detectors like this are used in continuity testers and security alarms, among other applications.

Basically, this circuit is a monostable multivibrator that is continually retriggered by new pulses at the input before it has a chance to time out. Transistor Q1 adds this retriggering ability to the timer.

Ordinarily, a new pulse is received at the input before the timer has finished its time period. A new timing cycle is started by each input pulse. This can continue indefinitely as long as there is a steady stream of input pulses. The output remains a constant HIGH.

Suppose one of the incoming pulses is missing for some reason. The 555 will have a chance to time out, and the output will go LOW until the input pulse stream starts up again. External circuitry can easily detect this condition.

Resistor R1 and capacitor C1, as usual, should be selected to give the desired time period for your specific application. The time period should be just slightly longer than the normal spacing between the input pulses.

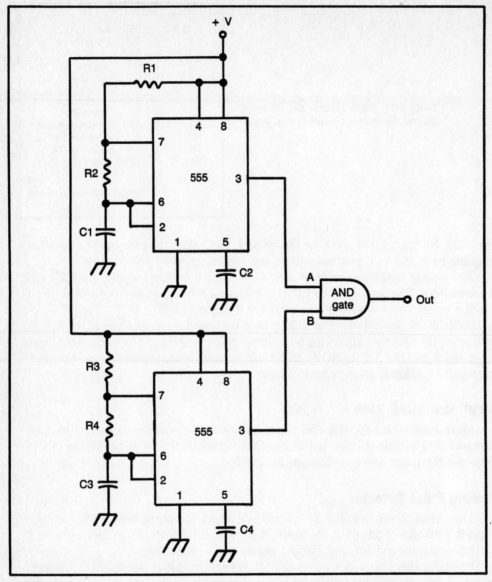

Fig. 2-35. Digital gates can combine the outputs of multiple astables to produce various unusual waveshapes. PROJECT #17

Capacitor C2 is the stability capacitor. As always, this capacitor should have a value between about 0.001 μF and 0.01 μF. Transistor Q1 may be almost any low-power pnp transistor. The exact type is not particularly critical. Since there are so few components in this circuit, no parts list is given here.

Frequency Divider

Suppose you have a signal that is at too high a frequency for some particular application. This often happens in large systems, where a high frequency is required

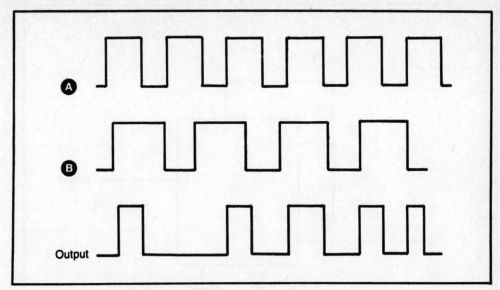

Fig. 2-36. A typical set of signals for the circuit in Fig. 2-35.

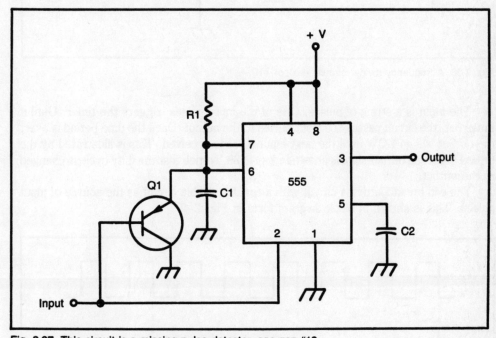

Fig. 2-37. This circuit is a missing pulse detector. PROJECT #18

by some stages, while other stages have a slower response. The solution is to use a frequency divider.

Figure 2-38 shows how the 555 can be used as a straightforward frequency divider. You should recognize this circuit as a simple variant of the basic monostable multivibrator circuit.

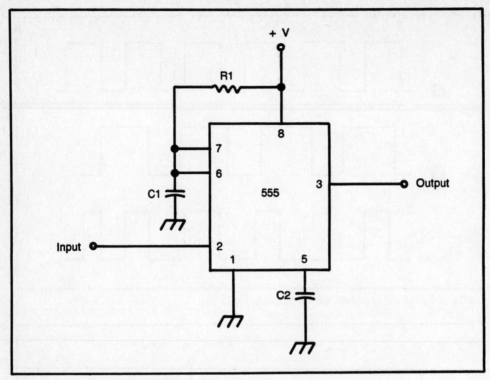

Fig. 2-38. A frequency divider circuit. PROJECT #19

The input is a string of pulses. One of the input pulses triggers the timer. Until it times out, the circuit passes the input pulses to the output. Once the time period is over, the output will go LOW until the next input pulse is received. This is illustrated by the typical input and output signals shown in Fig. 2-39. Notice that the duty cycle is changed at the output.

You can breadboard this circuit with a regular astable circuit as the source of input pulses. This is shown in block diagram form in Fig. 2-40.

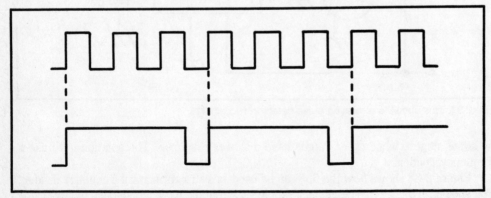

Fig. 2-39. Typical input and output signals for the circuit in Fig. 2-38.

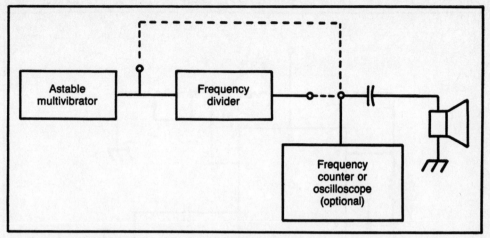

Fig. 2-40. Block diagram of the circuit in Fig. 2-38 in use.

Light-Triggered Timers

A simple CdS photocell can make the 555 respond to the presence or absence of light. The circuit shown in Fig. 2-41 will produce a tone when the photocell is dark. As long as the photocell is exposed to light, the speaker will be silent.

Potentiometer R3 is used to adjust the sensitivity of the circuit. A fixed resistor may be substituted, if you prefer. By reversing the positions of R3 and the photocell, you can get the opposite response.

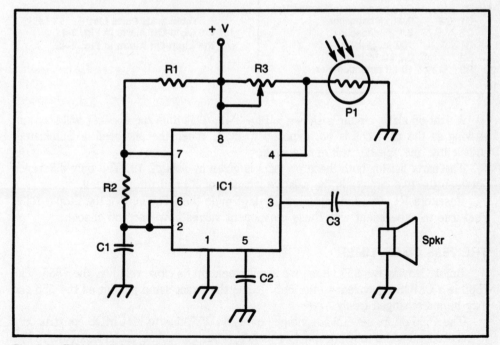

Fig. 2-41. This is a light-off alarm. PROJECT #20

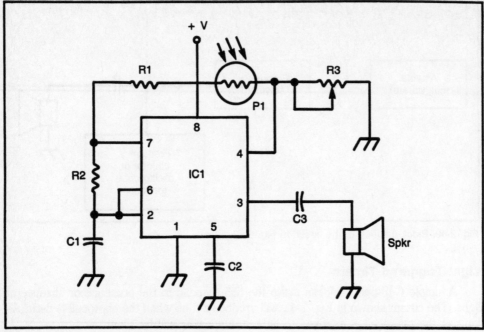

Fig. 2-42. This is a light-on alarm. PROJECT #21

IC1	555 timer
P1	CdS photocell (photoresistor)
C1, C2	0.01 μF capacitor
C3	0.1 μF capacitor
R1	100 kΩ resistor
R2	2.2 kΩ resistor
R3	10 kΩ potentiometer

Table 2-12. Parts List
for the Light-Off Alarm in Fig. 2-41
and the Light-On Alarm in Fig. 2-42.

A light-on alarm circuit is shown in Fig. 2-42. This time the speaker will be silent as long as the photocell is *not* exposed to light. When the photocell is illuminated, sufficiently, the speaker will emit a tone.

The parts list for both these projects is given in Table 2-12. The only difference between the two circuits is the relative location of R3 and the photocell.

Resistors R1, R2, and capacitor C1 determine the frequency of the output tone. Feel free to experiment with these component values however you choose.

THE 7555 CMOS TIMER

Before leaving the 555 timer, we should mention its close relative, the 7555. The 7555 is a CMOS equivalent to the 555. It has the exact same pin-out as the 555 and may be interchanged freely.

The 7555 offers several advantages over the 555, due to its CMOS construction. It will accept a wider range of supply voltages, while consuming much less power. The 7555 can also produce longer timing cycles than the 555.

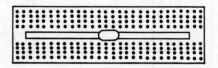

3

The XR2240
Programmable Timer

CHAPTER 2 EXPLORES SOME OF THE MANY APPLICATIONS FOR THE 555 TIMER. NOW YOU can turn your attention to a device that might be considered the 555's big brother. The XR2240 programmable timer is shown in Fig. 3-1.

Because the XR2240 has more pins than the 555, it might appear more difficult to use. Many people might be intimidated by the programmable aspect. Actually, in many ways, the XR2240 is even easier to use than the 555.

Fully half the pins are multiple outputs the user can pick or choose from in any combination. Selecting the desired output (or outputs) is all that is involved in "programming" this device.

A simplified block diagram of the XR2240's internal circuitry is shown in Fig. 3-2. Essentially it consists of a basic timer (not dissimilar to the 555) followed by an eight-bit binary counter which provides the multiple outputs. This will be explained shortly.

THE TIME PERIODS

You should recall from Chapter 2 that the basic time period for the 555 is given by:

$$T = 1.1 \, RC$$

For the XR2240 the constant (1.1) is eliminated and the basic timer period is:

$$T = RC$$

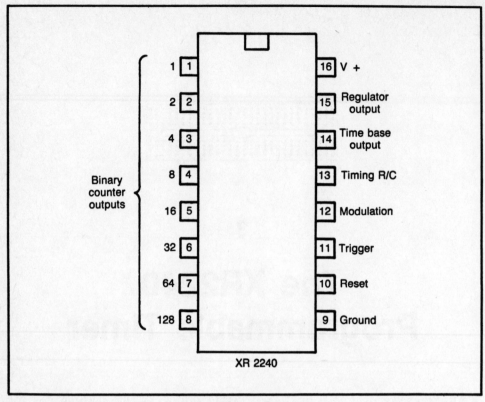

Fig. 3-1. Pinout diagram of the XR2240 programmable timer IC.

Using a single combination of a resistor and a capacitor, the XR2240 programmable timer can provide 255 different time periods. Each of these is an integer multiple of the basic time period set by the resistor and capacitor.

The multiple outputs increase the basic time period by binary intervals.

Pin #	Time Period
1	1T
2	2T
3	4T
4	8T
5	16T
6	32T
7	64T
8	128T

Each successive output simply doubles the time period of its immediate predecessor.

The operation of the XR2240 programmable timer is easiest to understand through an example. Assume that R is a 1 megohm (1,000,000 ohms) resistor and C is a 0.1

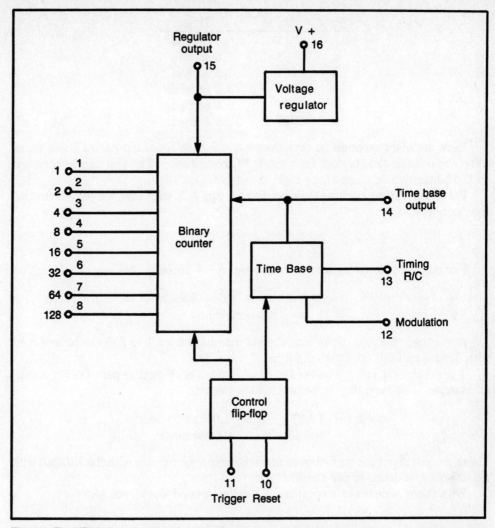

Fig. 3-2. The XR2240 programmable timer IC contains an eight-bit binary counter along with the basic timer circuitry.

μF (0.0000001 farad) capacitor. In this case, the basic time period would be;

$$T = RC$$
$$= 1,000,000 \times 0.0000001$$
$$= 0.1 \text{ second.}$$

At each of the counter output pins we would find the following time periods;

Pin #	Value	Time
1	1T	0.1 second
2	2T	0.2 second

Pin #	Value	Time
3	4T	0.4 second
4	8T	0.8 second
5	16T	1.6 second
6	32T	3.2 seconds
7	64T	6.4 seconds
8	128T	12.8 seconds

Here are eight separate outputs from a single time base, but earlier I said there were 255 possible time periods for a single RC combination. The rest can be achieved by combining two or more of the eight direct outputs.

For instance, if we combine the outputs from pins 2, 5, and 7, we will get an effective time period of;

$$T_x = 2T + 16T + 64T$$

For our example (using a basic time base of 0.1 second), this works out to;

$$T_x = 0.2 + 1.6 + 6.4$$
$$= 8.2 \text{ seconds}$$

Any integer multiple of the fundamental time base from 1 to 255 can be achieved with some combination of the output pins.

The counter outputs can be used to create some very long time periods. Try another example. This time the component values will be;

$$R = 1 \text{ M}\Omega = 1,000,000 \text{ ohms}$$
$$C = 500 \text{ }\mu\text{F} = 0.0005 \text{ farad}$$

These are just about the maximum component values we can use with the XR2240 with reasonable confidence of fair stability.

With these component values, the basic time period works out to;

$$T = 1,000,000 \times 0.0005$$
$$= 500 \text{ seconds}$$
$$= 83 \text{ minutes, 20 seconds}$$
$$= 1 \text{ hour, 23 minutes, 20 seconds}$$

For convenience of discussion, simply round this off to 1.5 hours. Component tolerances could account for that much error.

This is already a rather long period for a timer. It is really longer than can be reasonably and reliably achieved with the 555.

By using the binary counter outputs of the XR2240 we can get even longer time periods. Considerably longer;

Pin #	Value	Time
1	1T	1.5 hour
2	2T	3 hours
3	4T	6 hours

4	8T	12 hours
5	16T	24 hours
6	32T	48 hours
7	64T	96 hours
8	128T	192 hours

By combining all eight of the binary counter outputs (for a total multiplier of 255), the maximum effective time period becomes;

$$
\begin{aligned}
T &= 255T \\
&= 255 \times 1.5 \text{ hour} \\
&= 382.5 \text{ hours} \\
&= 15 \text{ days, } 22.5 \text{ hours}
\end{aligned}
$$

How often are you likely to need a time period longer than that? Clearly the XR2240 programmable timer is truly a wide range device by any standards.

THE MONOSTABLE CIRCUIT

The basic XR2240 programmable timer monostable circuit is illustrated in Fig. 3-3. The output will have a time period of;

$$
T = nRC
$$

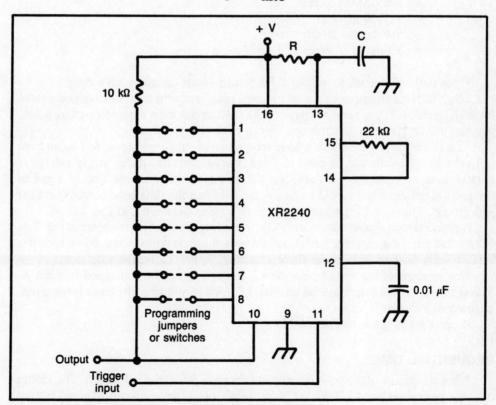

Fig. 3-3. The basic XR2240 monostable multivibrator circuit.

where n is the programmed value (from 1 to 255) set up by connecting the appropriate pins (1 through 8), R is the value of the timing resistor in ohms, and C is the value of the timing capacitor in farads.

The acceptable range of the resistor is 1 kΩ to 10 MΩ, and the capacitor may have any value from 0.01 μF to 1000 μF. However, there will be a significant decrease in circuit stability if values greater than about 1 MΩ or 500 μF are used.

Within these limits, the time period can be as short as;

$$n = 1$$
$$R = 1 \text{ k}\Omega \qquad\qquad = 1000 \text{ ohms}$$
$$C = 0.01 \text{ μF} \qquad\quad = .00000001 \text{ farad}$$
$$T = 1 \times 1000 \times 0.00000001$$
$$= 0.00001 \text{ second}$$

At the other end of the scale, the time period may be as long as;

$$n = 255$$
$$R = 10 \text{ M}\Omega \qquad\qquad = 10,000,000 \text{ ohms}$$
$$C = 1000 \text{ μF} \qquad\quad = 0.001 \text{ farad}$$
$$T = 255 \times 10,000,000 \times 0.001$$
$$= 2,550,000 \text{ seconds}$$
$$= 42,500 \text{ minutes}$$
$$= 708 \text{ hours, 20 minutes}$$
$$= 29 \text{ days, 12 hours, 20 minutes}$$

From 0.01 millisecond to almost a full month—quite an impressive range!

The XR2240 is triggered by a positive-going pulse, rather than a negative-going pulse (as with the 555). If you need to trigger a XR2240 circuit from a negative-going pulse, you can use an inverter, like the one shown back in Fig. 2-8.

This IC can be powered with a fairly wide range of supply voltages. Any value from +5 volts to +15 volts can be used to drive XR2240 circuits. If the supply voltage is greater than, or equal to, +7 volts, and the timing capacitor is less than or equal to 0.1 μF, a shunt capacitor should be connected between the time base output (pin #14) and ground. This shunt capacitor should have a value between 250 and 300 pF.

A practical monostable demonstration circuit using the XR2240 is shown in Fig. 3-4. Notice that the shunt capacitor mentioned above is shown in dotted lines. When in doubt, it is probably best to include the shunt capacitor, just to be on the safe side.

One or more of the output pins (pins 1 through 8) can be connected to point X. The selected pins will determine the time the LED will stay lit after the timer is triggered, as discussed above.

A parts list is given in Table 3-1.

SEQUENTIAL TIMER

A simple variant on the basic monostable circuit is illustrated in Fig. 3-5. This circuit uses the same parts listed in Table 3-1, with the addition of seven more LEDs and current limiting resistors.

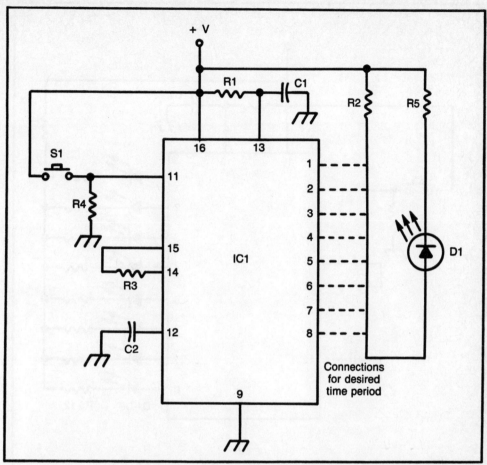

Fig. 3-4. Here is a practical XR2240 monostable multivibrator demonstration circuit. PROJECT #22 ᐧ

Each output pin controls its own LED. All eight LEDs will light up when the timer is triggered, then they will be extinguished sequentially, number one first, and number eight last.

The outputs can drive other devices besides LEDs. Buffers may be needed if the load requires a significant amount of current. This circuit allows multiple devices to be turned on simultaneously and turned off at staggered intervals.

Table 3-1. Parts List for the Monostable Multivibrator Circuit of Fig. 3-4.

IC1	XR2240 programmable timer
D1	LED
R1	(see text)
R2	10 kΩ resistor
R3	22 kΩ resistor
R4	1 MΩ resistor
R5	470 Ω resistor
C1	(see text)
C2	0.01 μF capacitor
S1	Normally Open SPST push switch

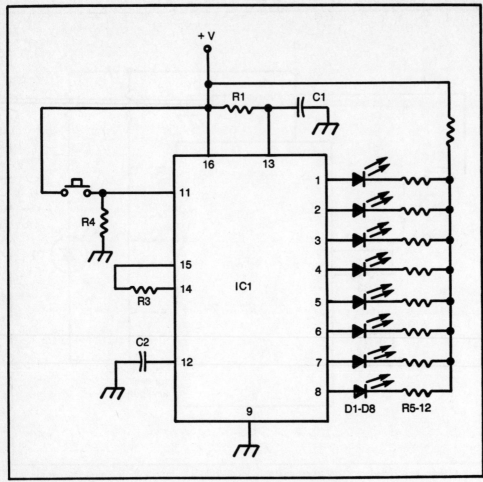

Fig. 3-5. The XR2240 can be used as a sequential timer. PROJECT #23

If your application calls for staggered turn-on times, you can still use this circuit. You could invert the output pulses, or you could use the XR2420 to drive a 555 based timer operated relay, as shown in Fig. 2-11. You should recall that the 555 is triggered by a negative-going pulse; therefore, the relay won't be energized until the end of the appropriate time period. The 555's time period will determine how long the relay remains energized.

THE ASTABLE CIRCUIT

The XR2240 programmable timer IC can also be operated in the astable mode. The XR2240 astable multivibrator is quite similar to the monostable multivibrator circuit shown in Fig. 3-3. The astable version is shown in Fig. 3-6. The primary difference between this astable circuit and the monostable version is that the reset input (pin #10) is *not* connected to the output here. The circuit may be force-reset with an external signal, if desired, otherwise, this pin is simply ignored.

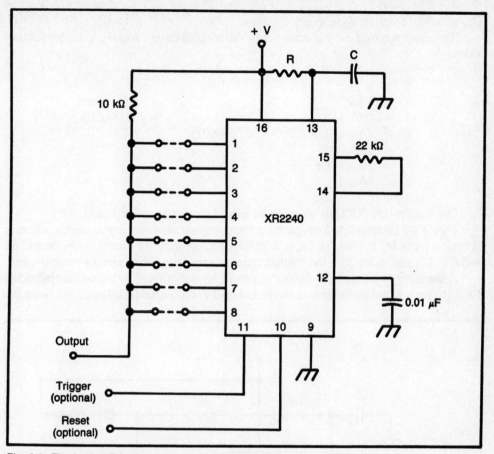

Fig. 3-6. The basic XR2240 astable multivibrator circuit.

The output frequency of an XR2240 astable multivibrator can be found with this simple formula;

$$F = 1/(2nRC)$$

where n is the programmed output value (1 to 255) set up by the selection of pins 1 through 8. R is the timing resistance (1 kΩ to 10 MΩ), and C is the timing capacitance (0.01 μF to 1000 μF).

If you are familiar with algebra, you should realize that the minimum frequency is achieved when all three values are at their maximums;

N = 255
R = 10 MΩ = 10,000,000 ohms
C = 1000 μF   = 0.001 farad
F = 1/(2 × 255 × 10,000,000 × 0.001)
   = 1/5,100,000
   = 0.0000002 Hz

Or, about 1 complete cycle every 59 days.

The maximum frequency is achieved by reducing all three variables to their minimum values;

$$N = 1$$
$$R = 1\ k\Omega \qquad\qquad = 1000\ \text{ohms}$$
$$C = 0.01\ \mu F \qquad\qquad = 0.0000001$$
$$F = 1/(2 \times 1 \times 1000 \times 0.0000001)$$
$$= 1/0.00002$$
$$= 50,000\ Hz$$
$$= 50\ kHz$$

Once again, the XR2240 gives us an incredible range to work with.

Figure 3-7 shows a low-frequency astable demonstration circuit you can breadboard. A typical parts list is given in Table 3-2. Experiment with the timing components, R1 and C1. Connect point X to the various outputs singularly, or in various combinations.

A fascinating multiple LED flasher can easily be constructed by connecting individual LEDs to each of the output pins, as shown in Fig. 3-8. Additional LEDs could be connected

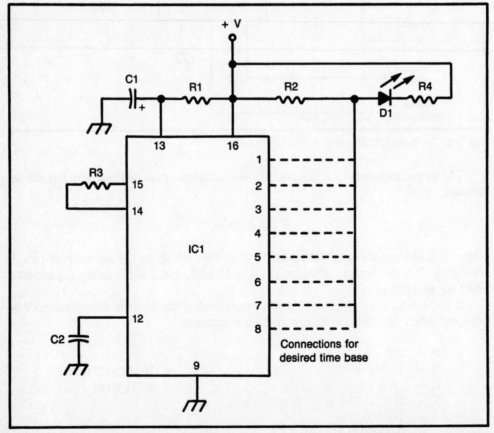

Fig. 3-7. This circuit demonstrates the XR2240's astable operation at low frequencies. PROJECT #24

Table 3-2. Parts List for the Low-
Frequency Astable Multivibrator Circuit of Fig. 3-7.

IC1	XR2240 programmable timer
D1	LED
R1	(see text)
R2	10 kΩ resistor
R3	22 kΩ resistor
R4	470 Ω resistor
C1	(see text)
C2	0.01 μF capacitor

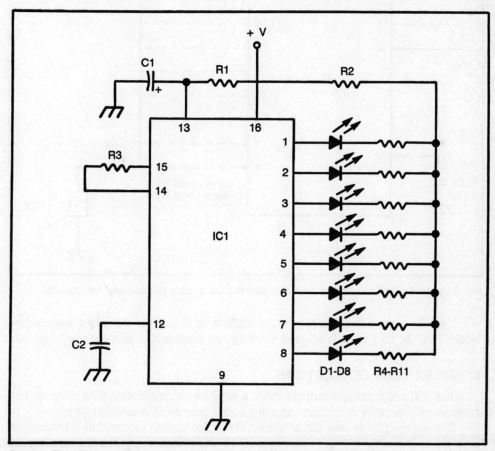

Fig. 3-8. The XR2240 can be used at the heart of a fascinating multiple LED flasher circuit. PROJECT #25

in parallel with the ones shown here. You might want to build a permanent version of this project. If so, it's best to mount the LEDs on a separate panel in an eye-catching pattern, rather than just in a row.

Figure 3-9 shows another XR2240 astable demonstration circuit. This one is designed for you to experiment with frequencies in the audible range. A typical parts list is given in Table 3-3. Once again, experiment with different timing components, R1 and C1, and single and multiple outputs.

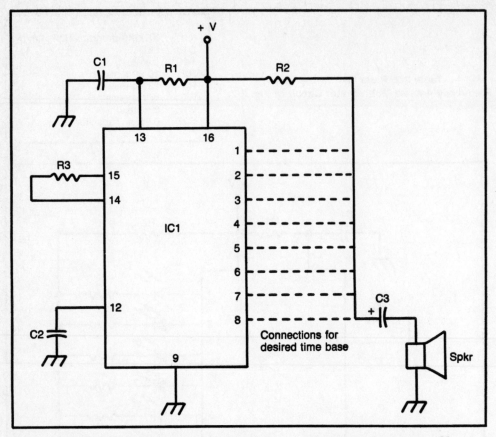

Fig. 3-9. The XR2240 demonstrates astable operation at audible frequencies. PROJECT #26

If you have an oscilloscope handy, you might want to monitor the output waveshapes. Notice how the duty cycle is affected when two or more output pins are used together.

COMPLEX TONE GENERATORS

The XR2240's multiple outputs make it ideal for experimenting with complex tone generators. The trick is to combine the various outputs in non-standard ways.

One approach is to use digital gates. There are countless possible combinations. Just one is illustrated in Fig. 3-10. Figure 3-11 shows how the gates alter the signals. A typical parts list for this project is given in Table 3-4, but by all means use your

IC1	XR2240 programmable timer
R1	(see text)
R2	10 kΩ resistor
R3	22 kΩ resistor
C1	(see text)
C2	0.01 μF capacitor
C3	10 μF electrolytic capacitor
SPKR	small 8 Ω speaker

Table 3-3. Parts List for the Audio-Frequency Astable Multivibrator Circuit of Fig. 3-9.

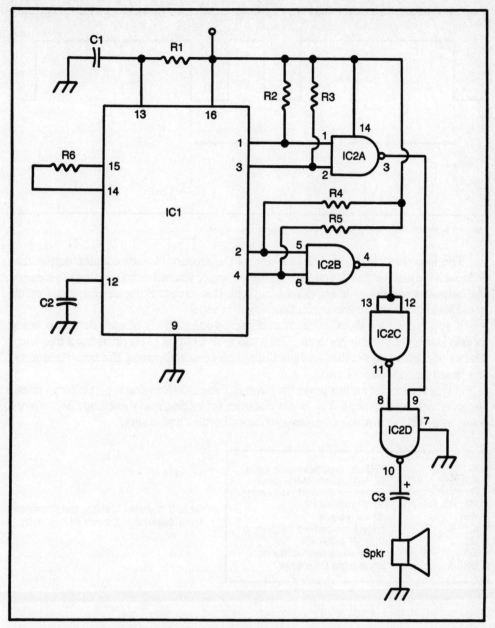

Fig. 3-10. Combining digital gates with a XR2240 produces a complex tone generator. PROJECT #27

imagination and experiment. There are countless variations you can build on this simple, basic idea.

Another approach to complex tone generation with the XR2240 is shown in Fig. 3-12. Here, each output passes through a variable resistance, or potentiometer. For breadboarding purposes, you might want to substitute fixed resistors. Experiment with various values.

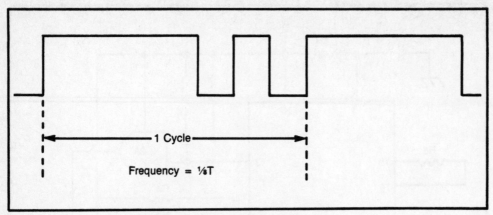

Fig. 3-11. Some typical signals for the circuit of Fig. 3-10.

The individual output resistances control the amount of each counter output that will reach the final output. If you have an oscilloscope, you will definitely want to monitor the output waveform while experimenting with this circuit. Some combinations result in outputs that don't resemble rectangle waves at all.

If you know a lot about music or acoustics, you can think of each output as being an individually controllable harmonic. Each successive output pin is providing a frequency exactly one octave higher than its immediate predecessor. Octaves, like binary counters, are based on multiples of two.

A typical parts list for this project is given in Table 3-5. No value is particularly critical, so, as always, experiment. You might discover something really exciting. At the very least, you will learn which combinations work better than others.

IC1	XR2240 programmable timer
IC2	CD4011 quad NAND gate
R1	(select for desired frequency)
R2, R3, R4, R5	10 kΩ resistor
R6	22 kΩ resistor
C1	(select for desired frequency)
C2	0.01 μF capacitor
C3	10 μF electrolytic capacitor
SPKR	small eight Ω speaker

Table 3-4. Parts List for the Complex Tone Generator Circuit of Fig. 3-10.

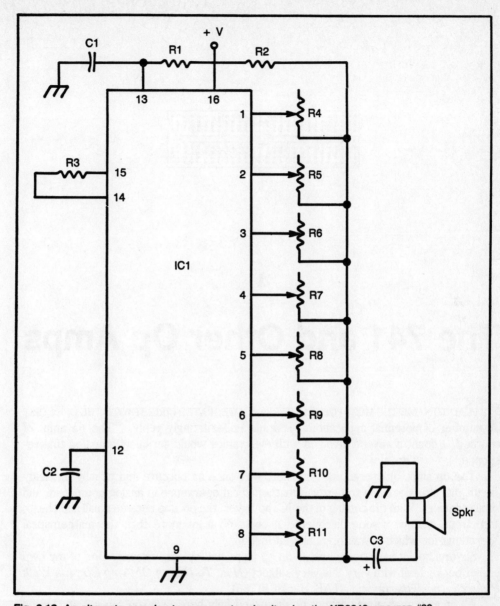

Fig. 3-12. An alternate complex tone generator circuit using the XR2240. PROJECT #28

Table 3-5. Parts List for the Complex Tone Generator Circuit of Fig. 3-12.

IC1	XR2240 programmable timer
R1	(select for desired frequency)
R2	10 kΩ resistor
R3	22 kΩ resistor
R4 - R11	100 kΩ potentiometers
C1	(select for desired frequency)
C2	0.01 μF capacitor
C3	10 μF electrolytic capacitor
SPKR	small eight Ω speaker

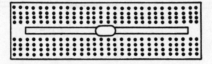

4

The 741 and Other Op Amps

IF I HAD TO NAME THE MOST POPULAR TYPE OF INTEGRATED CIRCUIT WITH THE GREATEST number of potential applications, I would unhesitatingly reply, "The op amp, of course." I doubt if anyone involved with electronics would seriously question that response.

The op amp, or operational amplifier, was once an obscure and usually unwieldy circuit that was designed to perform mathematical operations in analog computers and similar devices. With the coming of the IC, however, the op amp became small and cheap, and circuit designers soon discovered it could do a lot more than the mathematical operations for which it was originally intended.

Several books have been written on op amps and op amp circuits. One of my own earlier books dealt with very this very subject (*How To Design Op Amp Circuits With Projects And Experiments*—TAB Books #1765).

All op amp applications cannot be discussed fully here, but you can get started on some breadboarding experiments.

THE IDEAL OP AMP

Before delving into the practical circuits, you should have at least some idea of what an op amp is, and how it works. The op amp is easiest to understand by imagining an impossible, ideal device. No practical op amp ever achieves the ideal performance described here, although a few high performance devices come remarkably close.

The op amp normally has two inputs—one inverting, and the other non-inverting—and a single output. In theory, all op amps require a dual-polarity power supply (above and below ground potential). Some newer designs have ways around this requirement, but such devices will be ignored for the time being. The dual-polarity supply voltage is necessary to allow the output to swing in both the positive and the negative directions, as determined by the signal(s) at the input(s). In most circuits, the two power supply voltages will be equal except for the polarity.

The schematic symbol for the op amp is shown in Fig. 4-1. Notice that there is no direct connection to ground (supply common), although all input and output signals are referenced to ground potential.

If only the non-inverting input is used, the output signal will always have the same polarity as the input. If only the inverting input is used, the output signal will always have the opposite polarity of the input.

The op amp is designed to use both inputs simultaneously. In many applications one of the inputs is tied to ground for an effective input value of zero. The output is controlled by the difference between the signals fed to the two inputs. The larger of the two signals will determine the polarity of the output signal.

Assuming both input signals are positive, there are three basic combinations possible. Call the inverting input A, and the non-inverting input B;

Condition	Output Polarity
A < B	+
A = B	0
A > B	−

If the larger input signal is negative, the output polarities will be reversed.

The most basic op amp circuit is the differential amplifier. The theoretical circuit is shown in Fig. 4-2. Notice that the power supply connections are omitted for simplicity. This is often done in schematic diagrams. The supply connections are always assumed.

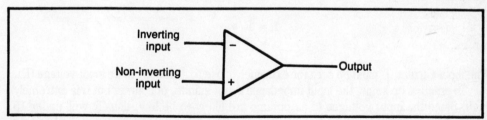

Fig. 4-1. The schematic symbol for an op amp.

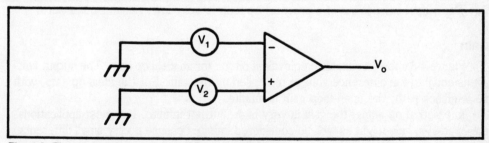

Fig. 4-2. The op amp is basically a difference amplifier.

Call the output voltage V_0, the inverting input V_1, and the non-inverting input V_2. For any combination of input values, the output voltage can always be calculated with this simple formula;

$$V_0 = (V_2 - V_1)G$$

G represents the amount of gain, which will be discussed shortly.

Many op amp applications are essentially variations, often quite disguised, of the basic differential amplifier. Ideally, a perfect op amp will exhibit a number of characteristics, as described below.

Common-Mode Rejection Ratio

If the exact same signal is fed to both inputs simultaneously, they are said to be in the common-mode. Ideally, the output should be exactly zero under these circumstances. How well the op amp can cancel out identical input signals is described by a specification called the common-mode rejection ratio, or CMRR.

An ideal op amp has an infinite CMRR figure. For practical op amps, the CMRR is very high—the higher the better.

Input and Output Impedances

The input impedance of an ideal op amp is infinite, while the output impedance is zero.

The theoretically infinite input impedance has a special significance. According to Ohm's law;

$$I = E/R$$

Since R is infinity;

$$I = E/\infty$$
$$= 0$$

The input current (I) must be zero (or extremely close to it) for any finite input voltage (E).

In practical op amps, the input impedance is not infinite, of course, but it is extremely high. Since the input voltages to an op amp are likely to be low, usually well under 15 volts, the current flow will be essentially zero. The inputs are placed at virtual ground as far as current flow is concerned.

The output impedance of a practical op amp is very low, but not quite zero.

Gain

Figure 4-3 shows a simplified equivalent circuit for an ideal op amp. The output voltage is equal to the difference voltage multiplied by the gain. For the ideal op amp, with no feedback path, the open-loop gain is infinite.

In practical op amps, the gain is very high, but not infinite. For most applications, the open-loop gain might as well be considered infinite because a very small differential voltage at the inputs will drive the output into saturation.

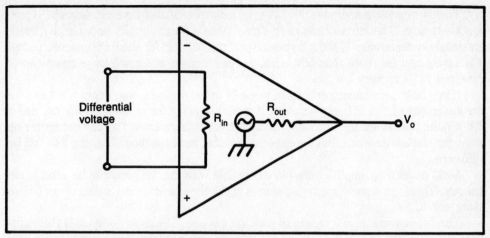

Fig. 4-3. The equivalent circuit for an ideal op amp.

Generally, most op amp circuits include a feedback path from the output back to the inverting input to reduce the gain. Somewhat different equations are used to find the gain for different circuit configurations. The appropriate gain equations will be given when the circuits are discussed.

Bandwidth

An ideal op amp has an infinite bandwidth. That is, the gain is exactly the same at all frequencies.

Offset

If the input is zero, the output should also be zero. Any deviation from zero at the output is called offset. An ideal op amp features zero offset. For a practical op amp, the offset should be as small as possible.

Many op amp devices include extra pins for external circuitry to adjust the offset. An ideal op amp also exhibits zero drift.

THE 741 OP AMP

Most of the projects in this chapter were designed with the 741 in mind. This is probably the single most popular IC on the market today.

A lot of technicians today disregard the 741. More recent op amp devices offer better specifications, but unless you are dealing with a high precision application, the 741 can be adequate. The 741 is also readily available and cheap. It is convenient for experimentation because if you accidentally ruin it, replacement is not expensive.

You could use a higher grade op amp in these projects if you wish, but there is not much to be gained.

The biggest disadvantage of the 741 compared to some other more recent devices is that the 741 does require a dual-polarity power supply. Since a good breadboarding system should have a dual polarity power source anyway (if nothing else, for positive and negative test voltages), this is not much of a limitation.

The current low esteem for the 741 is an indication of how far electronics has come in a short time. The introduction of this chip made a lot of circuits possible that were previously inconceivable. When it first came out, the 741 sold for about $50 apiece. Today, it is rarely sold for more than 50¢ each. Surplus houses often sell large quantities of untested 741's at very low prices.

If you build permanent versions of some of these projects, you might want to take the limitations of the 741 into account. It is rather noisy for audio applications, and it is not quite precise enough for many measurement applications. You can get better op amps for just a little more, but for experimentation and breadboarding, the 741 will be sufficient.

Most modern op amp IC's are pin compatible with the 741, and can be substituted directly. There are some exceptions; always check the manufacturer's data sheet before using any IC.

The 741 is available in a variety of packaging styles. The most common is the eight-pin DIP, as shown in Fig. 4-4. In the projects, the pin numbers will correspond to this version.

Some 741s come in 14-pin DIP housings as shown in Fig. 4-5. An 8-pin round can is also used. This style is illustrated in Fig. 4-6.

The major specifications for the 741 are listed in Table 4-1.

The 741, like most modern op amp IC's, features internal frequency compensation. Some early op amp IC's required external components for frequency compensation to avoid severe instability problems in some applications.

Closely related to the 741 are the 747 and the 324.

The 747 contains two independent 741-type op amps in a single 14-pin DIP package, as shown in Fig. 4-7.

Either half of a 747 may be used as a direct substitute for a single 741. Watch the pin numbers.

The negative supply voltage (pin #4) is common to both internal op amp circuits, but independent positive supply voltages may be applied (pin #13 for op amp A, and pin #9 for op amp B). In most practical circuits, these two pins will simply be tied together, using a single positive voltage source.

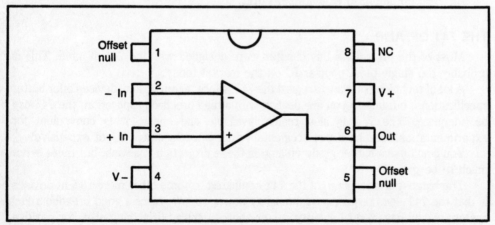

Fig. 4-4. The 741 op amp is most frequently housed in an eight-pin DIP package.

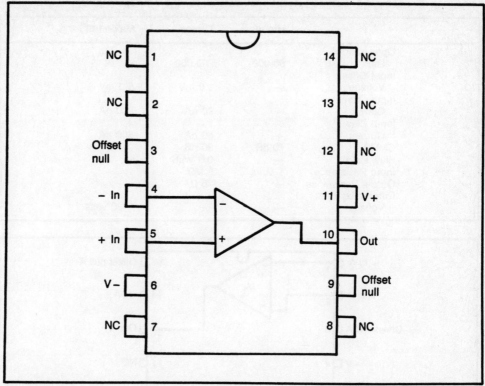

Fig. 4-5. The 741 is also available as a fourteen-pin DIP.

Figure 4-8 shows the 324 quad op amp IC. It contains four independent op amp sections, each similar to the 741, although with some slightly improved electrical characteristics.

Besides the convenience of having four op amps in a single compact package, the 324 offers the advantage of using only a single polarity supply voltage.

Fig. 4-6. Sometimes the 741 comes in an eight-pin round can housing.

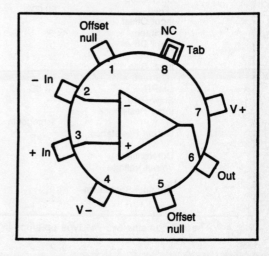

Table 4-1. Some Typical Specifications for the 741 Op Amp IC.

	Minimum	Typical	Maximum
Open-Loop Gain	50,000	200,000	—
Input Offset Voltage	—	1.0 mV	5.0 mV
Input Offset Current	—	20 nA	200 nA
Input Bias Current	—	80 nA	500 nA
CMRR	70 dB	90 dB	—
Slew Rate	—	0.5 V/μS	—
Input Resistance	1 MΩ	6 MΩ	—
Output Resistance	—	75 Ω	—
Differential Input Voltage	—	—	±30 volts

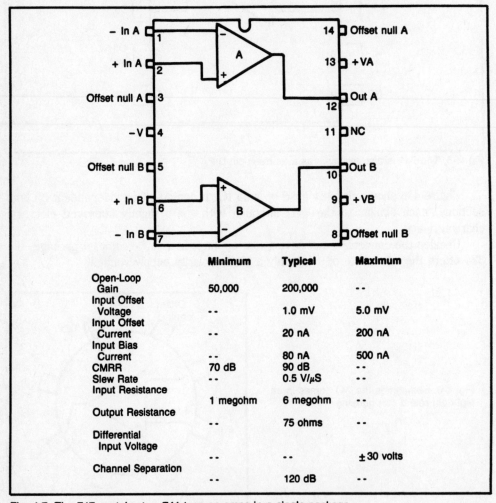

	Minimum	Typical	Maximum
Open-Loop Gain	50,000	200,000	--
Input Offset Voltage	--	1.0 mV	5.0 mV
Input Offset Current	--	20 nA	200 nA
Input Bias Current	--	80 nA	500 nA
CMRR	70 dB	90 dB	--
Slew Rate	--	0.5 V/μS	--
Input Resistance	1 megohm	6 megohm	--
Output Resistance	--	75 ohms	--
Differential Input Voltage	--	--	±30 volts
Channel Separation	--	120 dB	--

Fig. 4-7. The 747 contains two 741 type op amps in a single package.

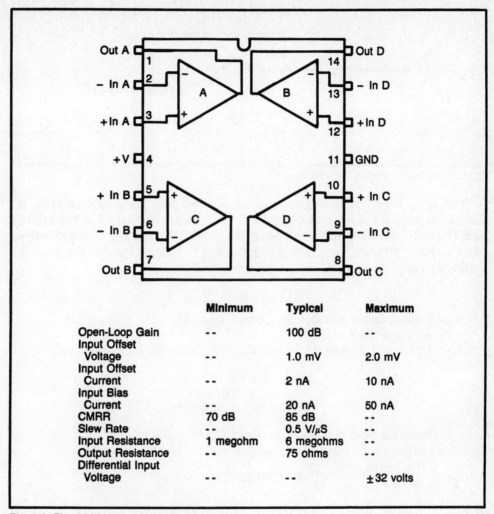

	Minimum	Typical	Maximum
Open-Loop Gain	--	100 dB	--
Input Offset Voltage	--	1.0 mV	2.0 mV
Input Offset Current	--	2 nA	10 nA
Input Bias Current	--	20 nA	50 nA
CMRR	70 dB	85 dB	--
Slew Rate	--	0.5 V/μS	--
Input Resistance	1 megohm	6 megohms	--
Output Resistance	--	75 ohms	--
Differential Input Voltage	--	--	$\pm$32 volts

Fig. 4-8. The 324 is a quad op amp IC.

INVERTING AMPLIFIER CIRCUITS

There are three basic op amp circuits, the differential amplifier which uses both inputs, the inverting amplifier which uses only the inverting input, and the non-inverting amplifier which uses only the non-inverting input. In the single input circuits, the unused input is grounded. As far as the op amp is concerned, it has an applied signal voltage of 0.

The inverting amplifier is probably the most widely used configuration. The basic circuit is illustrated in Fig. 4-9.

(Note that the power supply connections are not shown here. This is often done to simplify schematic diagrams. Remember, all op amps must have power applied to the correct pins, whether this is shown explicitly or not.)

Since the inverting input is used in this circuit, the polarity of the output signal will always be the opposite of the input signal. That is, a positive input will result in a negative output, and vice versa.

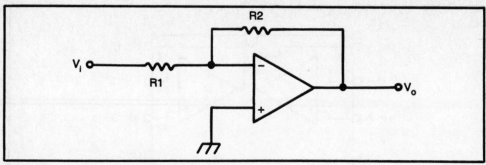

Fig. 4-9. The basic inverting amplifier circuit.

This circuit is extremely simple, requiring only two resistors in addition to the IC itself. R1 is the input resistor (R_i), and R2 is the feedback resistor (R_f). The ratio of these two resistances determines the gain of the circuit. The gain may be negative (less than 1 — R2 < R1), unity (equal to 1 — R2 = R1) or positive (greater than 1 — R2 > R1). The gain can be determined with this formula;

$$G = -R2/R1$$

The negative sign simply indicates the polarity inversion.

Here are a few quick examples.

First, let R1 = 1 kΩ and R2 = 100 kΩ. The gain in this case would be;

$$
\begin{aligned}
G &= -R2/R1 \\
&= -100,000/1000 \\
&= -100
\end{aligned}
$$

If, for example, the input is 1 mV, the output will be −100 mV, or −0.1 volt.

If both resistors are made equal, say 100 kΩ, the result is unity gain;

$$
\begin{aligned}
G &= -100,000/100,000 \\
&= -1
\end{aligned}
$$

The output voltage will be equal to the input voltage, except the polarity is reversed.

There is a special case here. If both resistors are eliminated, as shown in Fig. 4-10, the functional resistances are now zero, so;

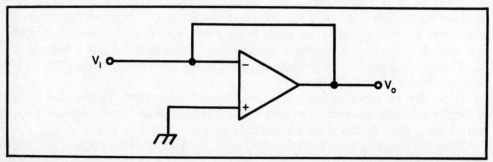

Fig. 4-10. Omitting the feedback and input resistors results in a gain of 1 (unity) for an inverting voltage follower.

$$G = -0/0$$
$$= -1$$

This special case circuit is known as an inverting voltage follower. It is used to change a signal's polarity or as a buffer to avoid loading down successive stages in a large circuit or both.

There is one more possible combination. R1 may be made larger than R2. In this case, there is negative gain, or attenuation. For example, if R1 = 100 kΩ, and R2 = 10 kΩ;

$$G = -10,000/100,000$$
$$= -1/10$$
$$= -0.1$$

If a 10 mV signal is fed to the input, for example, the output will be −1 mV.

Very large, or very small gains are usually not practical, because of the large resistance ratios that would be required. As a rule of thumb, resistor values should be kept more or less between 1 kΩ and 1 MΩ.

Figure 4-11 shows a practical inverting amplifier circuit for you to breadboard. A typical parts list is given in Table 4-2. Notice that no values are given for R3 (R_i) and R4 (R_f). These are the gain determining components, and you should experiment with various values.

R1 and R2 are a simple voltage divider used to present a variable voltage to the input of the circuit for experimental purposes.

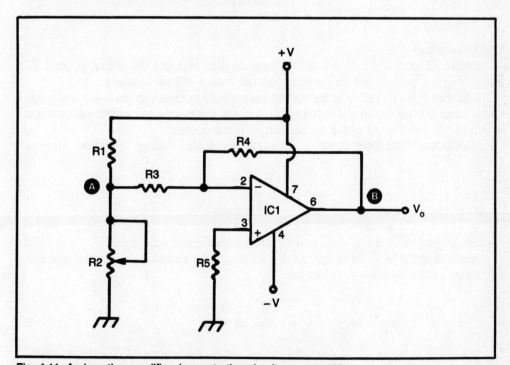

Fig. 4-11. An inverting amplifier demonstration circuit. PROJECT #29

Table 4-2. Parts List for the Inverting Amplifier Demonstration Circuit in Fig. 4-11.

Use any standard voltmeter to measure the signal at the input (A), and at the output (B). If you have two voltmeters, it would be convenient to use both of them so you can monitor the input and output voltages simultaneously. If you only have one voltmeter available, you can just move the leads back and forth between points A and B as needed throughout the course of your experimentation. Remember that the output of an inverting amplifier is always the opposite of the input, so watch the polarity of your test leads.

The gain for this circuit is simply;

$$G = -R4/R3$$

Experiment with various values for these two resistors. As an example, let's say R3 is 10 kΩ, and R4 equals 47 kΩ. In this case the gain is nominally;

$$G = -47,000/10,000$$
$$= -4.7$$

or approximately five.

Adjust R2 for an input of +1 volt at point A, then measure the output at point B. Remember the polarity will be inverted, so the output will be negative.

You should get a reading at the output somewhere between about −4.4 and −5.0 volts. Ideally, it should be −4.7 volts, but resistor tolerances and minor inaccuracies within the IC itself could cause a slight error in the output.

Now increase the input signal to +2 volts. The output voltage should be close to;

$$V_o = V_i \times G$$
$$= 2 \times -4.7$$
$$= -9.4 \text{ volts}$$

A reading between −9 and −9.75 volts can be considered acceptable.

Now adjust R2 for an input voltage of 4.5 volts. What should the output voltage be? According to the equation it should be;

$$V_o = 4.5 \times -4.7$$
$$= -21.15 \text{ volts}$$

When you measure the output voltage, you will probably get a reading that is a little under −15 volts. What went wrong? Nothing, you have simply saturated the op amp.

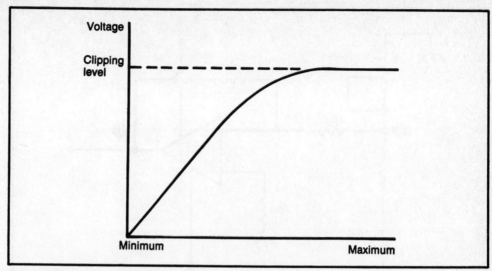

Fig. 4-12. A typical input/output graph for Fig. 4-11.

It cannot deliver more voltage at the output than its supply voltage. This limitation should be accounted for in any design involving op amps.

The input voltage must never exceed the supply voltage, or the op amp could be damaged.

Try other settings of R2. Calculate and measure the output voltage for various other input voltages. (See Fig. 4-12.)

When you are finished experimenting with this version of the circuit, substitute other values for R3 and R4. Calculate the gain, and repeat your experiments. Be sure to try combinations in which R3 is greater than, equal to, and less than R4.

The circuit of Fig. 4-11 uses only positive input voltages. Rewire the circuit as shown in Fig. 4-13. In this version of the circuit, the input voltage will be negative, and the output voltage will be positive.

Repeat the experiments described for Fig. 4-11.

If you have a signal generator or oscillator and an oscilloscope, you might want to check the operation of the inverting amplifier on ac signals. You will need a dual trace oscilloscope to display the input and output signals simultaneously. The output should be 180° out of phase with the input, as illustrated in Fig. 4-14.

Figure 4-15 shows yet another variation on the basic inverting amplifier circuit. This time the feedback resistor (R4) is a variable potentiometer, allowing you to vary the gain of the amplifier without physically rewiring the circuit.

Set R2 for a specific input voltage, then change the gain via R4 while monitoring what happens to the output signal. If you set the gain too high, the output will become saturated.

By this point you should have a good understanding of the operation of the inverting amplifier circuit.

NON-INVERTING AMPLIFIER CIRCUITS

You might be wondering why the inverting amplifier was treated first. Logically,

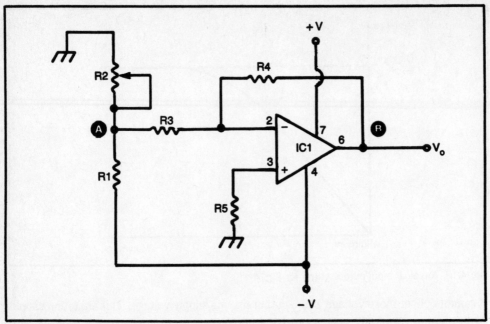

Fig. 4-13. This variation on the inverting amplifier demonstration project uses negative input voltages.
PROJECT #30

shouldn't the non-inverting amplifier be at least slightly simpler to understand? If nothing else, there is no need to worry about polarity inversion.

Actually the non-inverting amplifier is somewhat more complex than the inverting amplifier. It is also more limited.

In most applications involving amplification with op amps, the inverting amplifier is more commonly used. The non-inverting amplifier is generally used only when the polarity inversion is specifically undesirable for some strong reason. Even then, a two-stage

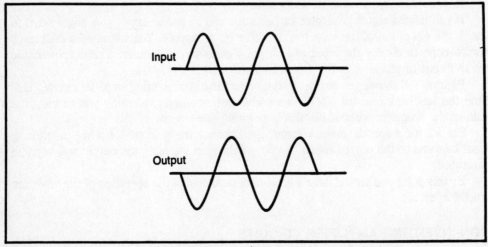

Fig. 4-14. The output of an inverting amplifier is 180° out of phase with the input.

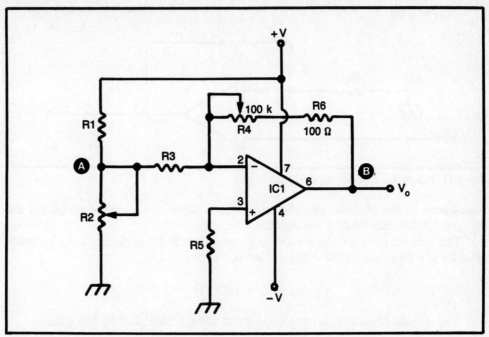

Fig. 4-15. This inverting amplifier circuit features variable gain. PROJECT #31

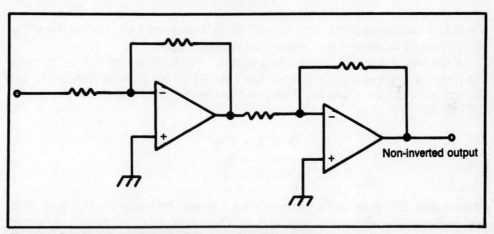

Fig. 4-16. Two inverting stages result in a non-inverted output.

inverting amplifier is sometimes used, as shown in Fig. 4-16. Usually the second stage will simply be an inverting voltage follower with a gain of −1. The first stage does the actual amplification and inverts the signal 180°. The second stage just re-inverts the signal another 180°. The output of the second stage is essentially in phase with the original input signal.

The basic non-inverting amplifier circuit is illustrated in Fig. 4-17. Notice that even though the input signal is fed to the non-inverting input of the op amp, the feedback path and the gain determining resistors are connected to the inverting input. The feedback

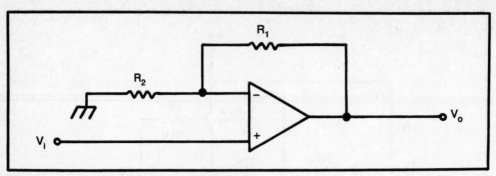

Fig. 4-17. The basic non-inverting amplifier circuit.

signal must be out of phase with the original input signal so the open-loop gain of the op amp can be reduced to a manageable level.

The gain equation for the non-inverting amplifier circuit is slightly more complex than for the inverting amplifier circuit, but not very much so;

$$G = 1 + (R2/R1)$$

The output, of course, is simply the input voltage multiplied by the gain;

$$V_o = V_iG$$

There is no negative sign this time because there is no polarity (phase) inversion. The output signal is in phase (same polarity) as the input signal.

If you look at the gain equation for a minute, you should realize that the gain of a non-inverting amplifier *must* be greater than unity (1) for any possible values of R1 and R2, with one important exception. If both resistors are zero (eliminated from the circuit), the gain is;

$$
\begin{aligned}
G &= 1 + (0/0) \\
&= 1 + 0 \\
&= 1
\end{aligned}
$$

or unity gain. This is the non-inverting voltage follower. It is shown in Fig. 4-18. A direct feedback path, with no resistors, is used. The gain is unity, and there is no polarity

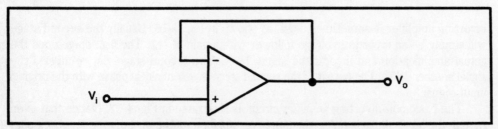

Fig. 4-18. The resistorless non-inverting voltage follower is the only non-inverting amplifier circuit with unity gain.

inversion or phase shift. The output of a non-inverting voltage follower is the same as the input. This circuit is used strictly for buffering between stages.

The resistorless circuit of Fig. 4-18 is the only way to achieve unity gain in the non-inverting mode. In an inverting amplifier, you can get unity gain by making the two resistors equal in value. But that doesn't work for a non-inverting amplifier. As an example, let's give both resistors a value of 10 kΩ;

$$G = 1 + (10,000/100,000)$$
$$= 1 + 1$$
$$= 2$$

In a non-inverting amplifier, equal-valued resistors will always result in a gain of two.

It is possible to achieve a gain just slightly greater than unity by making R1 very large with respect to R2. For instance;

$$R1 = 10 \ M\Omega$$
$$R2 = 1 \ k\Omega$$
$$G = 1 + (1000/10,000,000)$$
$$= 1 + 0.0001$$
$$= 1.0001$$

No combination of resistances will give a gain of less than unity (attenuation) for a non-inverting amplifier circuit.

A practical demonstration of a non-inverting amplifier circuit is shown in Fig. 4-19. The parts list is given in Table 4-3.

Resistor R1 and potentiometer R2 form a voltage divider to provide a variable (positive) dc input voltage.

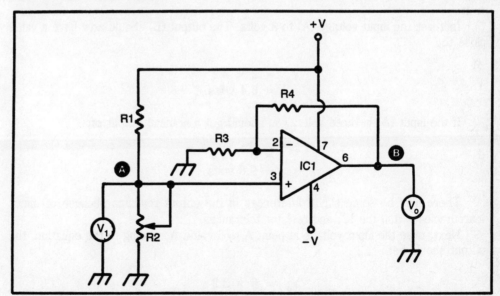

Fig. 4-19. This circuit demonstrates the operation of the non-inverting amplifier. PROJECT #32

IC1	741 op amp IC (8-pin DIP)
R1	1 kΩ ½ watt resistor
R2	1 kΩ potentiometer, linear taper
R3	10 kΩ ½ watt resistor (2)
R4	22 kΩ ½ watt resistor
	4.7 kΩ ½ watt resistor

Table 4-3. Parts List for the Non-Inverting Amplifier Demonstration Circuit in Fig. 4-19.

Initially breadboard the circuit of Fig. 4-19 using a 10 kΩ resistor for R3 and a 22 kΩ resistor for R4.

You should now be able to predict that the output voltage of this circuit will equal the input voltage multiplied by the gain factor;

$$V_o = V_i \times G$$

The gain factor (G) is, of course, determined by the resistors in the feedback network (R3 and R4);

$$
\begin{aligned}
G &= 1 + (R4/R3) \\
&= 1 + (22{,}000/10{,}000) \\
&= 1 + 2.2 \\
&= 3.2
\end{aligned}
$$

For any given input voltage, the output should be predicted by this equation;

$$V_o = V_i \times 3.2$$

Adjust potentiometer R2 for an input voltage of one volt at point A. Check the output at point B. You should get a reading of 3.2 volts at the output, or something very close to it.

Increase the input voltage (A) to 2 volts. The output (B) should now have a value close to;

$$
\begin{aligned}
V_o &= 2 \times 3.2 \\
&= 6.4 \text{ volts}
\end{aligned}
$$

If the input (A) is three volts, you should get a nominal output of;

$$
\begin{aligned}
V_o &= 3 \times 3.2 \\
&= 9.6 \text{ volts}
\end{aligned}
$$

There may be some slight differences in the output readings because of minor inaccuracies within the IC, and resistor tolerances.

Next, raise the input voltage at point A to 6 volts. According to the equation, the output should be;

$$
\begin{aligned}
V_o &= 6 \times 3.2 \\
&= 19.2 \text{ volts}
\end{aligned}
$$

If you measure the voltage at the output (point B), you will get a reading that is less than the supply voltage (15 volts). Once again the op amp is saturated. It can never output a higher voltage than its supply voltage. The output signal will be clipped whenever the input is greater than the supply divided by the gain.

Experiment with other input voltages. Can you predict the output voltage? Try substituting different valued resistors for R3 and R4 and calculate the gain. Do your experimental results confirm your calculations?

DIFFERENCE AMPLIFIERS

Nobody would call the projects described so far in this chapter very exciting; however, they are so useful, it is valuable to gain a thorough understanding of them. Moreover, it is difficult to follow what is going on in more interesting op amp circuits, if you are not clear about the workings of the inverting amplifier and the non-inverting amplifier.

I have already told you that the op amp was originally designed to perform mathematical operations. In most of its applications, the op amp is performing a mathematical function. In the inverting and non-inverting amplifiers discussed in the last few pages, the mathematical function was simple multiplication. A variable value (the input voltage) is multiplied by a constant value (the gain), and the result appears at the output.

The op amp's most fundamental mathematical operation is subtraction. This function is performed by the difference amplifier, which was briefly mentioned earlier in this chapter.

Refer to Fig. 4-2. This circuit was called a differential (or difference) amplifier. Because there is no feedback path, the full open-loop gain of the op amp is used. Remember that the open-loop gain of an ideal op amp is infinite, and practical op amps have extremely high open-loop gains. The open-loop difference amplifier operates in a special way that will be discussed later.

Simply put, a difference amplifier subtracts the voltage at the inverting input from the voltage at the non-inverting input and multiplies the difference by the amplifier's gain factor at the output.

Most practical difference amplifiers reduce the open loop gain with closed-loop feedback resistors, as shown in Fig. 4-20.

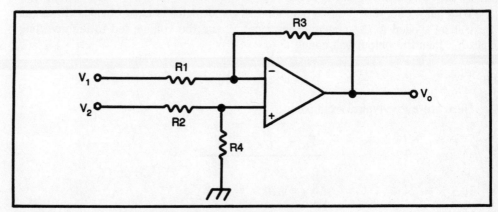

Fig. 4-20. The basic difference amplifier uses both inputs.

Generally, the two feedback loops (inverting and non-inverting) will be given equal component values. That is;

$$R1 = R2$$
$$R3 = R4$$

This exact equality is not absolutely necessary, although it is usually convenient; however, the feedback ratios *must* be equal;

$$\frac{R3}{R1} = \frac{R4}{R2}$$

These ratios define the closed-loop gain of the circuit. They need to be equal to give balanced gain for the two inputs. The gain can be determined from either feedback loop;

$$G = \frac{R3}{R1} = \frac{R4}{R2}$$

Take a moment and try a few examples on paper before actually breadboarding a test circuit.

To keep things simple, use the same resistance value for all four resistors, for example 22 kΩ. This makes the gain equal to;

$$G = \frac{22000}{22000}$$
$$= 1$$

If all four resistors have the same value, the circuit will exhibit unity gain. The exact resistance value used is irrelevant. Remember, the gain is defined by the resistance ratios, not by the resistances themselves.

With unity gain, this circuit's operation as a subtractor is most obvious. If we call the voltage applied to the non-inverting input V_a and the voltage fed to the inverting input V_b, then the output will equal;

$$V_o = V_a - V_b$$

Here are a few typical examples;

V_a –	V_b =	V_o
5	3	2
3	5	−2
4	4	0
4	0	4

0	3	−3
3	−2	5
−3	2	−5
−3	−2	−1
−3	−4	1
−3	−3	0

Do not be confused by a negative polarity. Remember, the inverting input always reverses the polarity, so the result is algebraic subtraction. If $V_a = +3$ and $V_b = −2$, as in one of the above examples, we are subtracting a negative value. Two negative signs on the same value algebraically cancel each other;

$$3 − (−2)$$
$$= 3 + 2$$
$$= 5$$

By using a non-equal resistance ratio, gains above and below unity can be achieved. For simplicity, throughout the following examples, assume the following equalities;

$$R1 = R2$$
$$R3 = R4$$

Remember, the ratios *must* be identical;

$$\frac{R3}{R1} = \frac{R4}{R2}$$

For the next example assign a value of 33 kΩ to R1 (and R2), and a value of 100 kΩ to R3 (and R4). In this case the gain value will work out to;

$$G = \frac{100,000}{33,000}$$
$$= 3.030303$$

For all intents and purposes, we can round off the gain to simply 3.

When a non-unity gain is used, the output is equal to the difference between the inputs multiplied by the gain. That is;

$$V_o = (V_a − V_b) \times G$$

Running through the same series of input voltages used in the unity gain example, notice that the output in this example (gain of 3) takes on the following values;

V_a	V_b	V_o
5	3	6
3	5	−6

4	4	0
4	0	12
0	3	−9
3	−2	15*
−3	2	−15*
−3	−2	−3
−3	−4	3
−3	−3	0

(The values marked * may be clipped due to saturation.)

For the next example, make R1 (R2) larger than R3 (R4);

$$R1 = 68 \text{ k}\Omega = R2$$
$$R3 = 22 \text{ k}\Omega = R4$$
$$G = 22{,}000/68{,}000$$
$$= 0.3235294$$

We can round this off to 0.3. Notice that this time there is less than unity gain, or attenuation. Looking at the sample inputs one more time for this example, there are the following output values;

V_a	V_b	V_o
5	3	0.6
3	5	−0.6
4	4	0
4	0	1.2
0	3	−0.9
3	−2	1.5
−3	2	−1.5
−3	−2	−0.3
−3	−4	0.3
−3	−3	0

A practical difference amplifier demonstration circuit you can breadboard and experiment with is shown in Fig. 4-21. A partial parts list is given in Table 4-4.

R5, R6, and R7 form a voltage divider to apply a positive or negative input voltage to the inverting input. R8, R9, and R10 form a similar voltage divider for the non-inverting input.

Experiment with different values for resistors R1 through R4. Remember to keep the ratios equal:

$$\frac{R3}{R1} = \frac{R4}{R2}$$

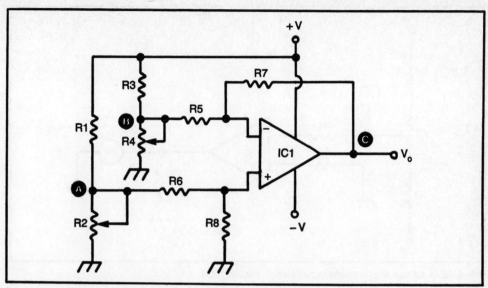

Fig. 4-21. A practical difference amplifier demonstration circuit. PROJECT #33

Table 4-4. Parts List for the Difference Amplifier Circuit in Fig. 4-21.

IC1	741 op amp (or similar)
R1, R3	1 kΩ resistor
R2, R4	1 kΩ potentiometer (linear taper)
R5, R6, R7, R8	10 kΩ resistor

Generally it will be most convenient, if you keep R3 equal to R4 and R1 the same as R2.

If you have a couple of oscillators (you can use one of the signal generator circuits described elsewhere in this book), and an oscilloscope, you might want to try out your difference amplifier with ac inputs. Some very peculiar waveforms can result from subtracting two out-of-phase (and probably different frequency) ac signals.

COMPARATORS

Breadboard the circuit shown in Fig. 4-22. The parts list is given in Table 4-5. Note that there are no feedback resistors for either input. In fact, the only resistors included in this circuit are the voltage dividers to provide independent variable voltages for each input.

Strictly speaking, this is a difference amplifier, but as you experiment with it, you should quickly realize that it is not a very good one. If the two inputs are not equal (or very, very close to equal), the output saturates, regardless of the exact amount of difference. Clearly this is not a practical difference amplifier, but it is still a quite useful circuit.

Functionally, it is known as a comparator. It compares two input signals and tells you which one is larger, assuming both signals have the same polarity. Comparator circuits are normally used in single polarity applications. For convenience, assume only positive

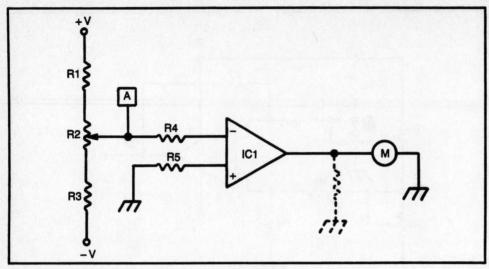

Fig. 4-22. A comparator demonstration circuit. PROJECT #34

input signals. The way the input voltage dividers are set up in Fig. 4-22 prevents any negative inputs.

Continue to refer to the non-inverting input signal as V_a and the inverting input signal as V_b.

Ignoring any specific numerical values, there are three possible combinations;

$$
\begin{aligned}
V_a &= V_b \\
V_a &> V_b \\
V_a &< V_b
\end{aligned}
$$

This is obvious enough. Either the two outputs are equal, or one is larger than the other. Let's see how the comparator responds to each of these possible situations.

First, remember the formula for determining the output voltage;

$$ V_o = (V_a - V_b) \times G $$

If the calculated value exceeds the supply voltage, the output signal will be clipped. The output signal will essentially equal the supply voltage when saturated. (Actually the output voltage will be slightly less than the supply voltage, but we can round things off here.)

Assuming an ideal op amp, the open-loop gain will be infinity. For any practical device, it will be very high, but not infinite.

IC1	741 op amp (or similar)
R1, R3	47 kΩ resistor
R2	100 kΩ potentiometer
R4, R5	22 kΩ resistor

Table 4-5. Parts List for the Comparator Demonstration Circuit in Fig. 4-22.

If the two input signals are identical, they cancel each other, leaving a difference of zero to be multiplied by the gain. Multiplying anything, even a very large value, by zero leaves zero. If the output of a comparator is zero, then the two input voltages are equal.

Now, what happens if V_a is larger than V_b, even if only by a small amount? Remember, we are assuming that both input voltages are positive. If V_a is larger than V_b, then the difference value will be positive. Even a tiny positive value multiplied by a large gain will be positive and very large. Multiplying even a small positive value by the large open-loop gain of a practical op amp will still result in a very large value, much higher than the supply voltage. Even a small positive difference will saturate the op amp's output in the positive direction. The output will essentially equal the V+ supply voltage.

On the other hand, if V_a is smaller than V_b (and both signals are positive), then the difference value will be negative and the output will be saturated towards the negative supply (V−).

In effect, there are only three possible outputs, each uniquely defining the relationship of the two input voltages;

Output	Input Condition
0	$V_a = V_b$
large positive value (V+)	$V_a > V_b$
large negative value (V−)	$V_a < V_b$

The differences between the output conditions are very clearcut and obvious. Further, they are easy to detect by other circuitry.

Figure 4-23 shows a modification to the comparator demonstration circuit of Fig. 4-22. The output state is indicated by a pair of LEDs. If both LEDs are dark, the output is zero ($V_a = V_b$). If LED1 is lit and LED2 is dark, then the output is positive ($V_a > V_b$). A negative output ($V_a < V_b$) will light LED2 while leaving LED1 off.

You might, in experimenting with this circuit, find a point where one of the LEDs is dimly lit. The output is not completely saturated. This can happen because the open-loop gain in a practical circuit is finite. If the two inputs are unequal by only a very small amount, the output value may not be fully saturated to the clipping point. This "range of uncertainty" is fortunately very small and can almost always be reasonably ignored without much concern about unreliable operation.

Figure 4-24 shows a graph of a comparator output. This graph really tells the whole story for this type of circuit.

SUMMING AMPLIFIERS

So far you have experimented with op amp circuits that perform the mathematical operations of multiplication and subtraction. Can an op amp perform other mathematical operations too?

In this section you will learn about summing amplifiers which essentially perform addition, with or without gain.

You may find it a little surprising to learn that only one of the op amp's input pins is used in a summing amplifier. The multiple inputs to be added are all fed to a single input on the op amp through isolation resistors.

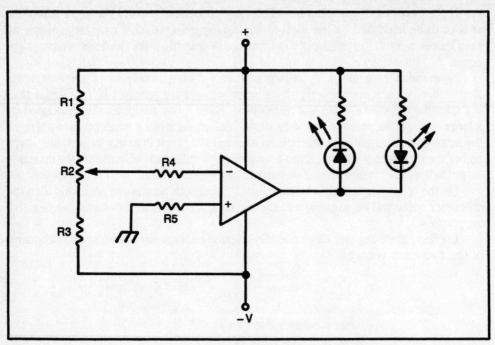

Fig. 4-23. This improved comparator demonstration circuit uses LEDs to indicate the output state.
PROJECT #35

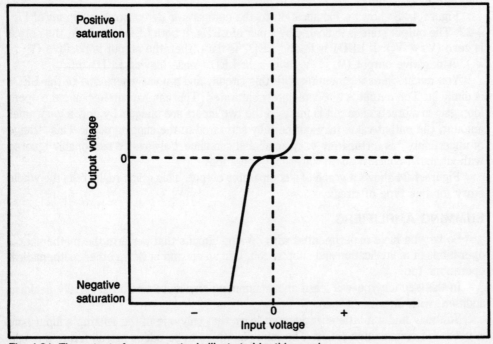

Fig. 4-24. The output of a comparator is illustrated by this graph.

Table 4-6. Parts List for the Inverting Summing Amplifier Circuit in Fig. 4-25.	IC1	741 op amp (or similar)
	R1, R2, R3	10 kΩ resistor (see text)
	R4	100 kΩ resistor
	R5	47 kΩ resistor

A simple inverting, summing amplifier circuit is shown in Fig. 4-25. For simplicity, the input voltage sources are not shown in this diagram. You can use three variable voltage dividers like the ones used in the earlier projects of this chapter, or almost any voltage sources that do not exceed the input limits of the op amp.

You should be able to tell that this is just a multiple input, inverting amplifier. Each input signal has its own input resistor (R1 through R3), while a single feedback resistor (R4) is shared by all the inputs. Three inputs are shown here, but the circuit can easily be adapted for any number of inputs.

Resistor R5 is used for offset correction. It is not always necessary, but it is probably a good idea to include it. The value of R5 should be equal to the parallel combination of the other four resistors;

$$1/R5 = 1/R1 + 1/R2 + 1/R3 + 1/R4$$

R5 may be made variable for fine adjustment of the output offset voltage.

For experimental breadboarding purposes, you can accept a certain degree of output offset. As long as R5 is relatively small, it will perform satisfactorily. You might want to experiment to see for yourself the effects of different values.

Each input functions like an ordinary inverting amplifier circuit. For example, for input V_1, ignore resistors R2 and R3 (and the input voltages through these resistors) as if they did not exist. The gain for V_1 is simply;

$$G_1 = -R_4/R_1$$

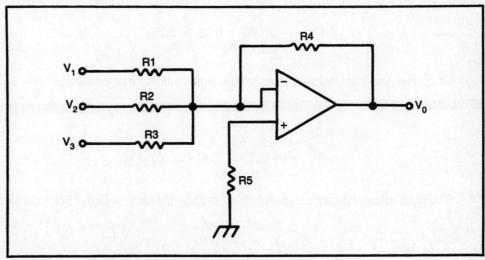

Fig. 4-25. An inverting summing amplifier circuit. PROJECT #36

The output (ignoring inputs V_2 and V_3) is;

$$V_0 = -(R4/R1) \times V_1$$

This is all exactly the same as for a single-input, inverting amplifier.

The same thing applies to inputs V_2 and V_3 except R2 or R3 replaces R1.

The combined output is simply the sum of the outputs due to the individual inputs;

$$V_0 = -((R4/R1) \times V_1 + (R4/R2) \times V_2 + (R4/R3) \times V_3)$$

If all the input resistors are made equal;

$$R = R1 = R2 = R3$$

then the equation can be simplified;

$$V_0 = -(R4/R) \times (V_1 + V_2 + V_3)$$

Breadboard this circuit with various resistor values. No parts list is given for this project, because all of the passive components (everything except the op amp itself) can be varied.

To begin with, give all of the gain-determining resistors (R1 through R4) an equal value, say 100 kΩ.

Since R1 = R2 = R3, we can use the shorter form of the output equation;

$$
\begin{aligned}
V_0 &= -(R4/R) \times (V1 + V2 + V3) \\
&= -(100{,}000/100{,}000) \times (V_1 + V_2 + V_3) \\
&= -1 \times (V_1 + V_2 + V_3) \\
&= -(V_1 + V_2 + V_3)
\end{aligned}
$$

when all the gain determining resistors are equal in value we have unity gain. The input voltages are simply added together and inverted at the output. For example, if all three inputs are fed a signal of 0.75 volt, the output voltage will be nominally equal to;

$$
\begin{aligned}
V_0 &= -(0.75 + 0.75 + 0.75) \\
&= -2.25 \text{ volts}
\end{aligned}
$$

Of course, the input voltages may have unequal values. For example;

$$
\begin{aligned}
V_1 &= 1.25 \text{ volts} \\
V_2 &= 3.40 \text{ volts} \\
V_3 &= 2.35 \text{ volts} \\
V_0 &= -(1.25 + 3.4 + 2.35) \\
&= -7.0 \text{ volts}
\end{aligned}
$$

The input voltages do not necessarily have to all be the same polarity. For example;

$$
\begin{aligned}
V_1 &= +2 \text{ volts} \\
V_2 &= -3 \text{ volts} \\
V_3 &= +4 \text{ volts}
\end{aligned}
$$

$$V_o = -(2 + (-3) + 4)$$
$$= -(2 - 3 + 4)$$
$$= -3 \text{ volts}$$

Any combination of input voltages may be summed in this manner. If the sum of inputs exceeds the op amp's supply voltage, the output will be clipped.

A summing amplifier may also have nonunity gain. Leave R1 = R2 = R3 = 100 kΩ, but change R4 to a 1 MΩ resistor. Now the output equation looks like this;

$$V_o = -(R4/R) \times (V_1 + V_2 + V_3)$$
$$= -(1,000,000/100,000) \times (V_1 + V_2 + V_3)$$
$$= -10(V_1 + V_2 + V_3)$$

The input voltages are summed as before, but the total is multiplied by ten (gain).

Less than unity gain is also possible. Simply make R4 less than R.

For straight summing, the input resistors should have equal values, but in some applications, it may be desirable to weight some of the inputs to count for more or less than normal. This is called weighted averaging. To achieve this effect select the appropriate values for the individual input resistors.

As an example, use the following component values;

$$R1 = 27 \text{ k}\Omega$$
$$R2 = 47 \text{ k}\Omega$$
$$R3 = 100 \text{ k}\Omega$$
$$R4 = 100 \text{ k}\Omega$$

Since this time the input resistors have unequal values, use the longer form of the general output equation;

$$V_o = -((R4/R1) \times V_1 + (R4/R2) \times V_2 + (R4/R3) \times V_3)$$
$$= -((100,000/27,000) \times V_1 + (100,000/47,000) \times$$
$$V_2 + (100,000/100,000) \times V_3)$$
$$= -(3.7 \times V_1 + 2.1 \times V_2 + 1 \times V_3)$$

Input signal V_1 has much more influence on the output than V_3, while V_2 is somewhere in between. Each input signal has its own individual gain. This is called weighting.

To see how a weighted summing amplifier works, try various input voltages to each of the inputs. For example, consider the following input voltages;

$$V_1 = 2.0 \text{ volts}$$
$$V_2 = -1.5 \text{ volt}$$
$$V_3 = 2.5 \text{ volts}$$

In this case the output voltage works out to a nominal (ignoring rounding off, resistor tolerances and any offset) value of;

$$V_o = -(3.7 \times 2 + 2.1 \times -1.5 + 2.5)$$
$$= -(7.4 + (-3.15) + 2.5)$$
$$= -6.75 \text{ volts}$$

Try other input combinations too.

Experiment a lot with this circuit. Try as many combinations of resistors as you can.

You might also want to experiment with using ac signals as input sources. With ac signals a summing amplifier functions as a mixer. For this application it is usually most desirable to use potentiometers for the individual input resistors. This will allow you to adjust the level for each input independently. You could also make the feedback resistor (R4) variable to give you a master gain control (affecting all inputs).

Non-inverting summing amplifiers are also possible, but the gain equations tend to be very awkward. The inverting version is almost always used. If the polarity inversion is undesirable for the specific application, just follow the inverting summing amplifier with an inverting voltage follower to re-invert the output signal.

OTHER MATHEMATICAL FUNCTIONS

The op amp can perform a great many mathematical functions. It is an incredibly versatile device. So far we have used the op amp for multiplication, subtraction, and addition. In this section circuits for several other mathematical operations will be illustrated.

Logarithmic Amplifier

Do you remember old-fashioned slide rules? These mechanical calculating devices have been pretty much replaced by pocket calculators. The slide rule permitted the user to perform many mathematical operations fairly easily. The secret of the slide rule lay in the use of logarithms.

The logarithm of a number is the exponent that indicates the power to which a specific base number must be raised to produce the given number. Common logarithms use a base of ten.

Logarithms can be a little confusing and intimidating when you first encounter them. Things become a little clearer when you see a few examples.

The common logarithm of 100 is 2. This is the same as saying that the base (10) raised by a power of 2 equals 100;

$$\text{Log } 100 = 2$$
$$10^2 = 100$$

In general:

$$\text{Log}_B X = y$$
$$B^y = X$$

For common logarithms B is always 10. If no base value is specified in a log equation, a base of 10 is assumed.

Not all logarithms are nice neat whole numbers like 2. Most include digits to the right of the decimal point. Here are a few more common logarithms;

$$\log 1 = 0$$
$$\log 2 = 0.3010$$
$$\log 3 = 0.0477$$
$$\log 4 = 0.60206$$
$$\log 5 = 0.6987$$
$$\log 10 = 1.0000$$
$$\log 12 = 1.0792$$
$$\log 20 = 1.3010$$
$$\log 25 = 1.3979$$
$$\log 30 = 1.4771$$
$$\log 1000 = 3.0000$$
$$\log 10,000 = 4.0000$$
$$\log 100,000 = 5.0000$$

Raising ten to the logarithm reproduces the original number;

$$10^0 = 1$$
$$10^{0.3010} = 2$$
$$10^{0.4771} = 3$$
$$10^1 = 10$$
$$10^2 = 100$$
$$10^3 = 1000$$

and so forth.

Raising any number to the power of zero (X^0) always results in 1, so the logarithm of 1 is 0, no matter what base is used. Negative logarithms correspond to numbers between one and zero. The logarithm is not defined for zero or negative numbers.

$$\log 0.1 = -1.0000$$
$$\log 0.2 = -0.6990$$
$$\log 0.005 = -2.3010$$

Each logarithm consists of two parts—the characteristic and the mantissa. The characteristic appears to the left of the decimal point, and the mantissa to the right. Published log tables generally only give the mantissa, because these values will repeat for different characteristics, according to simple rules. The characteristic indicates how many times the number can be divided by a whole number power of the base.

Look back at the list of examples presented earlier. Specifically, consider the logs of 2 and 20;

$$\log 2 = 0.3010$$
$$\log 20 = 1.3010$$

2 cannot be divided by 10, so the characteristic is 0. 20 equals 2 times 10, so there is a characteristic of 1. The mantissa (.3010) is the same for both.

Other bases are used in logarithms, besides 10. For instance, the natural logarithm uses *e* as its base. *e* is a mathematical constant with a value of approximately 2.718.

Any number may be used as a base for logarithms, but 10 (common logarithms) and *e* (natural logarithms) are the most frequently used.

The opposite of a logarithm (log) is the antilogarithm (antilog). An antilogarithm takes a logarithmic value and returns the original number. For example;

$$\log 2 = 0.3010$$
$$\text{antilog } 0.3010 = 2$$

Logarithms might seem like a lot of unnecessary fuss and bother, but they can actually simplify a lot of complex mathematical functions with relative ease. They can be used to perform multiplication and division on very large and very small numbers. Would you want to multiply 53,781,449.021 times 107,553,872.714 directly? Logarithms are also used to convert voltage and power values into decibels (dB). There are numerous other applications too.

As you've undoubtedly anticipated, the op amp can be used to calculate logarithms and antilogarithms. The basic log amplifier circuit is shown in Fig. 4-26. A resistor is used as the input component, as in an ordinary inverting amplifier. But the feedback element here is an npn transistor. The base is grounded.

The collector / emitter curve of many transistors is very close to a true logarithmic curve, making these devices ideal for use in logarithmic amplifiers. The collector / emitter current through the transistor will be equal to the input current, thanks to the nature of the op amp. As a result, the output voltage will be proportional to the logarithm of the input voltage. A power transistor will often be used in this application to reduce the series feedback resistance and to improve the circuit's current handling capabilities. For light duty applications, a smaller transistor may be used.

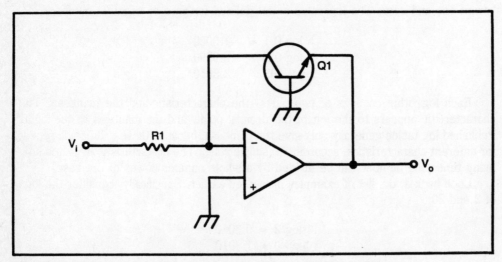

Fig. 4-26. A logarithmic amplifier uses a transistor as the feedback element.

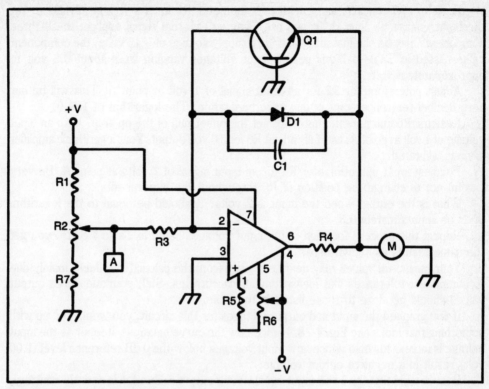

Fig. 4-27. A practical logarithmic amplifier circuit. PROJECT #37

A practical logarithmic amplifier circuit is shown in Fig. 4-27. Typical component values for this project are listed in Table 4-7. Because this application is somewhat critical and output offset can be a problem, the 741's offset adjustment pins (#1 and #5) are used. Potentiometer R6 is used to control the offset.

The offset adjust can also be used to calibrate the circuit to any desired reference point. The offset null is adjusted for an output of zero with an input signal corresponding to one unit. Remember, the log of 1 is always 0. The size of this unit, which can be almost anything the user desires, corresponds to the 0 dB reference level used in the circuit.

Table 4-7. Parts List for the Logarithmic Amplifier in Fig. 4-27.

	741 op amp IC
D1	1N4001 diode (or similar)
Q1	npn transistor (2N2222, or similar)
C1	0.1 μF capacitor
R1	47 kΩ resistor
R2	50 kΩ potentiometer
R3	47 kΩ resistor
R4	2.2 kΩ resistor
R5	330 Ω resistor
R6	10 kΩ potentiometer
R7	3.3 kΩ resistor

Resistors R1 and R7, along with potentiometer R2 form a voltage divider to set the input voltage at point A. If you are using an external signal source, these three components may be eliminated. Assuming a supply voltage of ± 15 volts, the component values listed in Table 4-7 will permit input voltages ranging from about 0.5 volt to approximately 8 volts.

Adjust potentiometer R2 for an input signal of 1 volt at point A. This will be our zero decibel reference point in our experimentation. The logarithm of 1 is 0.

Resistor R5 and potentiometer R6 set the offset null of the op amp. With an input voltage of 1 volt at point A, carefully adjust R6 for a 0 volt output. Your logarithmic amplifier is now calibrated.

Readjust input potentiometer R2 for an input signal of 2 volts at point A. Be very careful not to change the position of R6 throughout the experiments.

What is the output when the input is 2 volts? It should be equal to the logarithm of 2, or approximately 0.3.

Repeat this process for each of the input voltages listed in Table 4-8. Do you get the same results as shown here?

Your measured values may deviate slightly from the calculated values, mainly due to component tolerances and measurement inaccuracies. Still, your measured output values should be close to those listed in the table.

If you graphed the input and output voltages for this circuit, you would end up with something that looks like Fig. 4-28. Notice how the curve becomes steeper as the input voltage is increased. Also notice how input voltages below the 0 dB reference level (1.00 volt) result in a negative output voltage.

Bear in mind that the 1 volt input equals 0 volt output calibration is entirely arbitrary. You can calculate a logarithmic amplifier to almost any reference level you may choose.

Before moving on to the next project, you may want to try out the logarithmic amplifier on ac signals, if you have an oscilloscope and a signal generator. Observe how the waveshape is altered by the logarithmic amplifier.

Table 4-8. Some Typical Input and Output Values for the Logarithmic Amplifier in Fig. 4-27.

Input Voltage (A)	Output Voltage	Input Voltage (A)	Output Voltage
0.50	−0.30	4.75	0.68
0.75	−0.12	5.00	0.70
1.00	0.00	5.25	0.72
1.25	0.10	5.50	0.74
1.50	0.18	5.75	0.76
1.75	0.24	6.00	0.78
2.00	0.30	6.25	0.80
2.25	0.35	6.50	0.81
2.50	0.40	6.75	0.83
2.75	0.44	7.00	0.84
3.00	0.48	7.25	0.86
3.25	0.51	7.50	0.87
3.50	0.54	7.75	0.89
3.75	0.57	8.00	0.90
4.00	0.60		
4.25	0.63		
4.50	0.65		

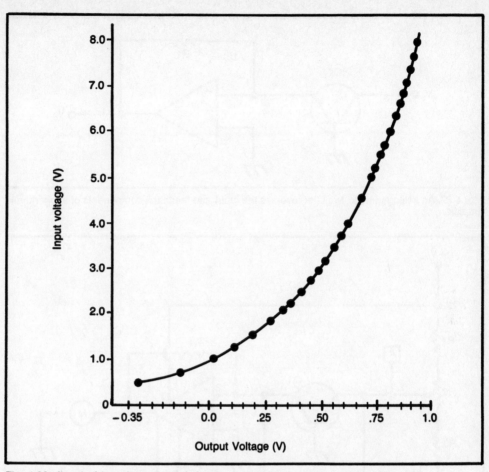

Fig. 4-28. A typical input/output graph for the logarithmic amplifier circuit of Fig. 4-27.

Antilogarithm Amplifier

The opposite of a logarithm is the antilogarithm. To repeat our earlier example;

$$\log 2 = 0.3010$$
$$\text{antilog } 0.3010 = 2$$

To create an antilogarithm amplifier, we just have to take a logarithm amplifier and reverse the input and feedback components. That is, the transistor is now the input element, and the resistor is the feedback element. The basic antilogarithm amplifier is illustrated in Fig. 4-29.

A practical antilogarithm amplifier circuit for you to breadboard is shown in Fig. 4-30. A typical parts list for this project is given in Table 4-9.

Once again, use a simple resistive voltage divider (R1, R2, and R3) to set the input voltage. Assuming a supply voltage of ±15 volts, the component values listed in Table 4-9 will permit signal voltages ranging from approximately −1.67 volts up to about +3.89 volts at point A.

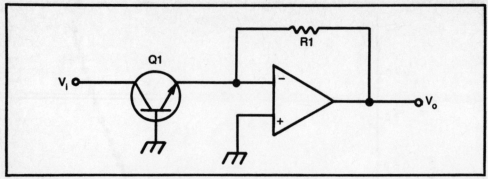

Fig. 4-29. An antilogarithmic amplifier reverses the input and feedback components of a logarithmic amplifier.

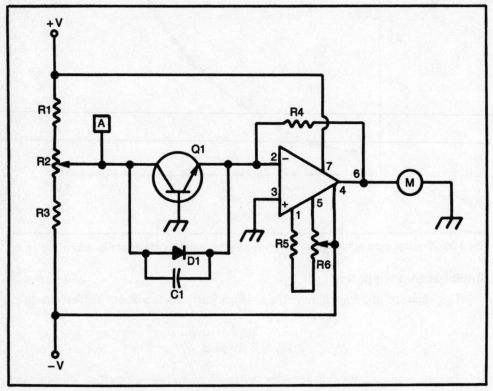

Fig. 4-30. A practical antilogarithm amplifier. PROJECT #38

Remember, negative logarithms are for values less than one, but greater than zero.

Adjust potentiometer R2 for an input voltage of 0 volts at point A. Since the logarithm of 1 is 0, it follows that the antilogarithm of 0 should be 1. With a 0 volts input, adjust the offset null control (R6) for an output of exactly +1.00 volt. Your antilogarithmic amplifier is now calibrated.

Now reset R2 so that the input voltage (A) is 0.3 volt. Can you guess what the output voltage will be before you look at the voltmeter at the output (B)?

Table 4-9. Parts List for the Antilogarithmic Amplifier in Fig. 4-30.

Breadboard system	
	741 op amp IC (need 2)
D1	1N4001 diode (or similar) (need 2)
Q1	npn transistor (2N2222, or similar) (need 2)
C1	0.1 μF capacitor (need 2)
R1	100 kΩ resistor
R2	50 kΩ potentiometer (need 2)
R3	120 kΩ resistor
R4	47 kΩ resistor (need 3)
R5	330 Ω resistor
R6	10 kΩ potentiometer (need 2)
	2.2 kΩ resistor
	3.3 kΩ resistor

Refer back to Table 4-8. Notice that the logarithmic amplifier had an output of 0.30 volt when the input was 2 volts;

$$\log 2 = 0.30$$

The antilogarithm is the mirror image of the logarithm. Therefore, if the logarithm of 2 is 0.30, then the antilogarithm of 0.30 should be 2. You should read an output of 2.00 volts (or something very close).

Experiment with a number of other input voltages. Also try recalibrating the circuit (via R6) for different reference points and see how that affects the operation of the circuit.

Multiplication And Division Circuits

Earlier we said that inverting amplifiers and non-inverting amplifiers perform multiplication. This is true enough, as far as it goes. The input voltage is multiplied by the gain factor, which is a constant.

In some applications, we might need to multiply two variable values (input voltages). The logarithm and antilogarithm amplifiers discussed in the last page will do the trick nicely. They can also perform division, but that comes later.

Mathematically, logarithms exhibit many interesting characteristics. For instance, if you add the logarithms of two numbers and then take the antilogarithm of their sum, you will get the product of the two original numbers. In algebraic terms, this can be expressed as follows;

$$\text{antilog} (\log A + \log B) = A \times B$$

The use of logarithms permits multiplication via simple addition.

To confirm that this system works, let's try a very simple example. Suppose we need to multiply 2 times 3. Now, we all know the answer is 6, but let's pretend we don't know that and want to use the logarithm method to find the result;

$$C = A \times B$$
$$C = \text{antilog} (\log A + \log B)$$

$$= \text{antilog } (\log 2 + \log 3)$$
$$= \text{antilog } (0.30103 + 0.47712)$$
$$= \text{antilog } 0.77815$$
$$= 6$$

Of course, this is an extremely simple example. The logarithm method is more useful in complex problems, such as;

$$C = 3607.814 \times 90011.0043$$
$$C = \text{antilog } (\log 3607.814 + \log 90011.0043)$$
$$= \text{antilog } (3.5572441 + 4.9542956)$$
$$= \text{antilog } 8.5115397$$
$$= 324,742,960.21$$

Op amps can do all this work for you. You can combine four basic op amp circuit stages to perform multiplication by the logarithm method. You need two logarithmic amplifiers, a summing amplifier, and an antilogarithmic amplifier. The block diagram of a complete op amp multiplier is illustrated in Fig. 4-31.

A practical two-input, multiplier circuit for you to breadboard is shown in Fig. 4-32. The parts list is given in Table 4-10. This is by far the most complex circuit presented so far in this book. It consists of five op amp stages, identified for your convenience in Fig. 4-33.

Please do not let the apparent complexity of this project scare you. Each of the five stages is just one of the simple op amp circuits you have already worked with earlier in this chapter. They are simply being combined here to perform a more sophisticated function. As a matter of fact, most complex electronics systems are made up of simpler stages. If you have a good grasp of the basic circuits, you can design or analyze almost any circuit.

Breadboard the circuit of Fig. 4-32, but instead of connecting the output of IC4 to point F, temporarily ground point F. This effectively applies an input of 0 to the antilogarithmic amplifier (IC5). Carefully adjust potentiometer R21 to calibrate this stage for an output of 1.00 volt for an input of 0.00 volts.

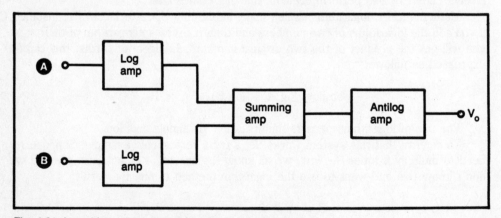

Fig. 4-31. Logarithms can be used for electronic multiplication.

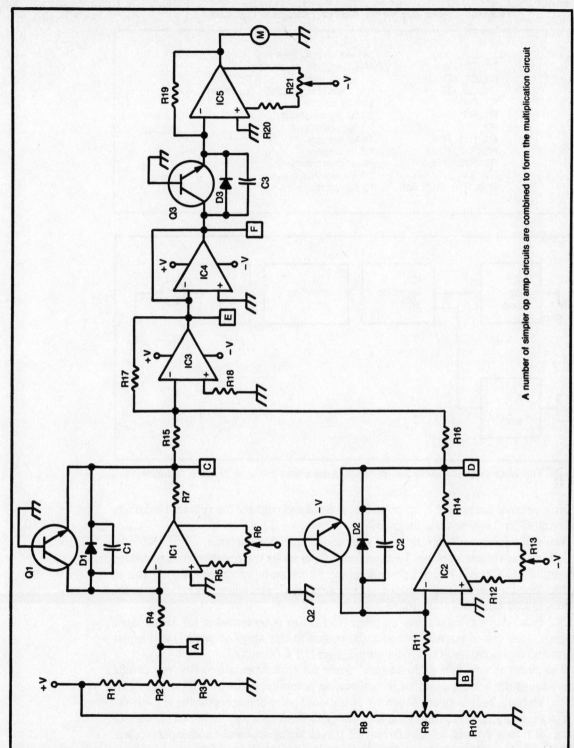

A number of simpler op amp circuits are combined to form the multiplication circuit

Fig. 4-32. A practical multiplier circuit. PROJECT #39

Table 4-10. Parts List for the Multiplier Circuit in Fig. 4-32.

	741 op amp IC (need 5)
D1, D2, D3	1N4001 diode (or similar)
C1, C2, C3	0.1 µF capacitor
Q1, Q2, Q3	npn transistor (2N2222, or similar)
R1, R8	100 kΩ resistor
R2, R9	50 kΩ potentiometer
R3, R10	3.3 kΩ resistor
R4, R11, R19	47 kΩ resistor
R5, R12, R20	330 Ω resistor
R6, R13, R21	10 kΩ potentiometer
R7, R14	2.2 kΩ resistor
R15, R16, R17, R18	10 kΩ resistor

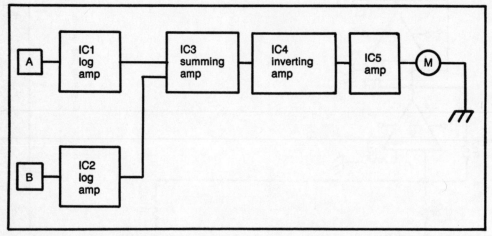

Fig. 4-33. This block diagram makes the operation of the circuit in Fig. 4-32 easier to follow.

Now remove the jumper from point F to ground and connect the rest of the circuit, as illustrated in the schematic diagram.

You still have to calibrate the two logarithmic amplifier sections.

IC1 is a logarithmic amplifier. Its input (point A) is set by the resistive voltage divider made up of R1, R2, and R3. Set potentiometer R2 for an input voltage of 1.00 volt at point A. Monitor this op amp's output voltage at point C, and adjust potentiometer R6 for a calibrated output of 0.00 volts.

IC2 is an identical logarithmic amplifier stage. Set potentiometer R9 for an input voltage of 1.00 volt at point B. Monitor the output of this stage at point D and adjust calibration potentiometer R13 for an output signal of 0.00 volts.

The circuit is now fully calibrated and ready for experimentation. Be very careful not to change the setting of any of the calibration potentiometers (R6, R13, and R21). It would probably be best to use screwdriver-adjusted potentiometers for these controls.

For the first step in experimenting with this multiplication circuit, leave potentiometers R2 and R9 at their present settings so that a 1.00 volt signal appears at both inputs (points A and B). The logarithmic outputs (at points C and D) should both be 0.00 volts, of course.

The next stage (IC3) is a summing amplifier with unity gain. It simply adds together the two logarithmic outputs. In this particular case, the logarithmic signals are both 0, so the summed output (at point E) should also be zero.

The next stage (IC4) is an inverting voltage follower. Its function is just to reverse the polarity inversion of the summing amplifier. In our current example, with a signal of 0 volts, this stage has no particular effect. The input to the antilogarithmic amplifier stage (IC5) is still 0 volts at point F. Assuming everything was calibrated correctly, the final output should be 1.00 volt. This, of course, is the product of the two original input signals (A and B);

$$1 \times 1 = 1$$

This was, admittedly, a very trivial example just to test the system.

For the next experiment, adjust R2 for an input voltage of 2.00 volts at point A. Set R9 for an input voltage of 1.50 volts at point B. The output of the entire circuit should be equal to;

$$2.00 \times 1.50 = 3.00 \text{ volts}$$

Trace your way through the circuit, as described above, and confirm that everything is functioning the way you would expect. IC1 converts its 2.00 volt input (point A) to its logarithm (0.30 volt) at point C. Meanwhile, IC2 is taking the logarithm of 1.50 volt and putting out approximately 0.18 volt at point D.

These two logarithmic voltages (C and D) are combined in the summing amplifier (IC3). Remember that since the inverting input of this op amp is being used, the output polarity is reversed;

$$
\begin{aligned}
E &= -(C + D) \\
&= -(0.30 + 0.18) \\
&= -0.48 \text{ volt}
\end{aligned}
$$

The following stage (IC4) is nothing more than a unity gain inverting voltage follower to correct for the polarity inversion of IC3. IC4's output at point F should be +0.48 volt.

This voltage is now fed to the input of the antilogarithmic amplifier stage (IC5). This stage calculates the antilogarithm of 0.48 and puts out an output of 3.00 volts, which is the product of the original input voltages (A and B).

As always, your exact measured values may vary slightly because of component tolerances, intrastage loading, and minor measurement errors. Still, the final result should be quite close to the calculated value.

Experiment with other input voltages.

Watch out that no stage in this circuit is ever overloaded, because that will throw off the results. In this particular circuit, the stage that is most likely to be overloaded is the final antilogarithmic amplifier (IC5).

Division can be performed in a similar manner. In this case we take the antilogarithm of the *difference* (rather than the sum) of the logarithms of the two original numbers;

$$A/B = \text{antilog} (\log A - \log B)$$

As a simple example, divide 15 by 3 using the logarithmic method. The result should be 5, of course.

$$
\begin{aligned}
C &= \text{antilog (log 15} - \text{log 3)} \\
&= \text{antilog (1.1760913} - 0.4771213) \\
&= \text{antilog } 0.69897 \\
&= 5
\end{aligned}
$$

The method works as predicted.

The block diagram for an op amp divider circuit is shown in Fig. 4-34. If you have grasped the principles of this chapter, you should have no difficulty in designing a practical version of this circuit. It is just a matter of putting the proper stages (simpler circuits) together in the correct order.

Exponents

Sometimes it is necessary to raise an input signal to a specific power. This process amounts to multiplying the number by itself a specified number of times. For example, consider 5 raised to the fourth power;

$$
\begin{aligned}
5^4 &= 5 \times 5 \times 5 \times 5 \\
&= 625
\end{aligned}
$$

This is a simple enough example, but consider the following problems;

$$
\begin{aligned}
1753^{13} &= ? \\
8.09^3 &= ? \\
7057.223^{9.17} &= ?
\end{aligned}
$$

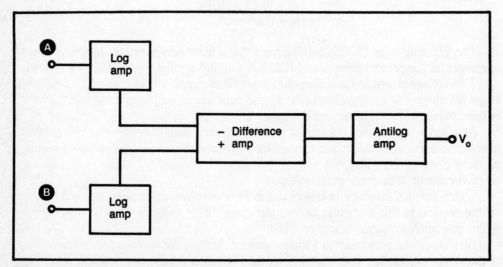

Fig. 4-34. Logarithmic amplifiers can also be used to perform division. PROJECT #40

Logarithms can be brought to the rescue again. To raise a number A, to the nth power, we can use this logarithmic formula;

$$A^n = \text{antilog } (n \times \log A)$$

Notice that n is used directly. We do not take its logarithm.

Check out this formula by solving for 5 to the fourth power again;

$$
\begin{aligned}
5^4 &= \text{antilog } (4 \times \log 5) \\
&= \text{antilog } (4 \times 0.69897) \\
&= \text{antilog } 2.79588 \\
&= 625
\end{aligned}
$$

This technique can also be applied electronically using op amps. Since the exponential power (n) will often be a constant in most applications, we can use the gain of a simple non-inverting amplifier to perform the multiplication.

A block diagram for a simple A^n exponent amplifier circuit is shown in Fig. 4-35. A practical circuit for you to breadboard is illustrated in Fig. 4-36. The parts list is given in Table 4-11.

The constant gain amplifier at the second stage could be replaced with a multiplication network (like Fig. 4-31). The output of the logarithmic amplifier in Fig. 4-35 is fed to input A of the multiplier, and a voltage corresponding to the desired exponential power is fed to input B. The complete block diagram for this version of the exponent circuit is shown in Fig. 4-37. It offers greater versatility than the simpler network of Fig. 4-35, but at somewhat increased complexity. Notice that this circuit requires three logarithmic amplifiers, two antilogarithmic amplifiers, and a summing amplifier. In addition, while it is not shown here, an inverting voltage follower stage will probably be needed after the summing amplifier, if this stage is designed in the inverting mode.

Sine Amplifiers

Op amps can also be used to perform trigonometric functions. All trigonometric functions are simply ways of expressing the ratios between the sides and angles of a

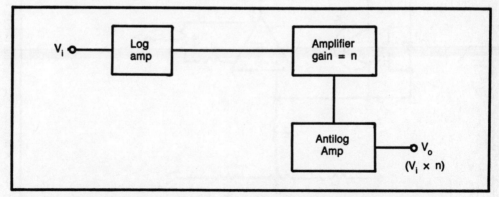

Fig. 4-35. Another application for logarithmic amplifiers is to calculate exponential values.

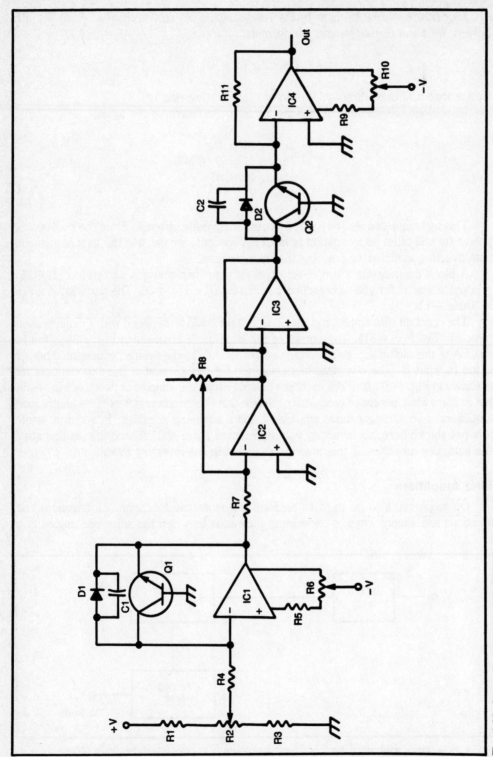

Fig. 4-36. A practical exponential circuit. PROJECT #41

Table 4-11. Parts List for the Exponential Circuit in Fig. 4-36.

IC1, IC2, IC3, IC4	741 op amp (or similar)
Q1, Q2	npn transistor (2N2222, or similar)
D1, D2	diode (1N4001, or similar)
R1, R3, R4, R11	47 kΩ resistor
R2	50 kΩ potentiometer
R5, R9	330 Ω resistor
R6, R10	10 kΩ trimpot
R7	2.2 kΩ resistor
R8	25 kΩ potentiometer
C1, C2	0.1 μF capacitor

right triangle. If the input voltages to an op amp circuit can be scaled to represent the sides of a right triangle, we will have a division circuit that yields that trigonometric function.

A simple sine amplifier circuit is shown in Fig. 4-38. The output voltage will be proportional to the input voltage and the sine of the angle defined by the position of the potentiometer shaft. A major drawback of this circuit is that it requires a special sine potentiometer, which may be difficult to come by. It is likely to be rather expensive, even if you can find one. But you might get lucky at an electronics surplus house. Check the mail order catalogs. The resistance at the wiper must be proportional to the sine of the wiper angle.

Absolute Value Circuit

In a number of applications, the magnitude of a voltage is important, but not the polarity. For instance, you may need to detect five volt signals of either polarity. This could be done using two separate detectors, of course—one for +5 volts, and one for −5 volts. But that is scarcely an elegant solution, and it may not always be practical.

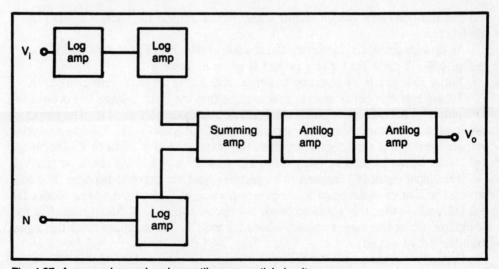

Fig. 4-37. A more advanced and versatile exponential circuit.

103

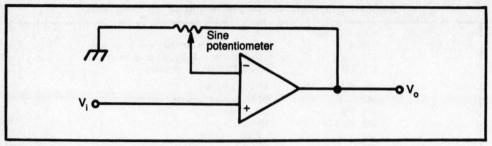

Fig. 4-38. A sine amplifier. PROJECT #42

What is needed here is a circuit to take the absolute value of the input voltage. Essentially the polarity sign is discarded and ignored.

In equations, absolute value is usually indicated by two bars on either side of the affected number;

$$|X| = \text{absolute value of X}$$

The absolute value function always has a positive value, regardless of the polarity of the original number. Here are some typical examples;

$$
\begin{aligned}
|5| &= 5 \\
|-7| &= 7 \\
|4.32| &= 4.32 \\
|-0.1| &= 0.1 \\
|19| &= 19 \\
|-19| &= 19 \\
-|3| &= -3
\end{aligned}
$$

Did that last one catch you off guard? If the sign is outside the bars, it is *not* part of the function.

An op amp circuit for extracting the absolute value from any input signal is shown in Fig. 4-39. A parts list for this project is given in Table 4-12.

Notice that IC1 is an inverting amplifier, and IC2 is a non-inverting amplifier.

To see how this circuit works, first assume that the input voltage (V_i) is positive. The output of IC1 will go negative and reverse bias diodes D1 and D2. The output of IC1 is effectively blocked from the circuit output (V_o). Meanwhile, IC2 has a positive output. Since this is a unity gain amplifier, the output of IC2 is equal to V_i. Diodes D3 and D4 are forward biased by this positive signal, which is fed to the circuit output (V_o).

If the input signal (V_i) happens to be negative, just the opposite happens. IC1 now provides a positive signal equal to the inverted value of V_i, forward biasing diodes D1 and D2, and allowing this signal to reach the circuit output (V_o). Meanwhile, IC2 has a negative output that reverse biases diodes D3 and D4. These diodes block this signal from the circuit output.

Regardless of the polarity of the input voltage, the output of this circuit will always be positive with a magnitude equal to the absolute value of the input signal.

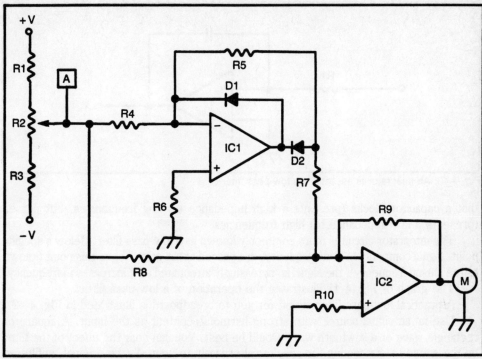

Fig. 4-39. This circuit determines the absolute value of the input. PROJECT #43

FILTERS

The circuit shown in Fig. 4-40 could have been included in the section on mathematical functions. Its technical name is an integrator. Integration is a function used in calculus. You could use this circuit in the same manner as the circuits described in the last section.

In the real world of electronics, the integrator is rarely used this way. In most of its applications, an ac signal is used as the input to this type of circuit. The integrator behaves in a funny way with ac signals. It is frequency sensitive in a predictable way. It passes low frequencies better than it does high frequencies. This is because a capacitor is used as the feedback element. From basic electronics theory, you should remember

Table 4-12. Parts List for the Absolute Value Circuit in Fig. 4-39.

Breadboard system

	741 op amp IC (need 2)
D1, D2	1N914 diode (or similar)
R1, R3	1 kΩ resistor
R2	10 kΩ potentiometer
R4, R5, R8, R9	10 kΩ resistor
R6, R7	4.7 kΩ resistor
R10	2.7 kΩ resistor
hook-up wire	
voltmeter(s)	

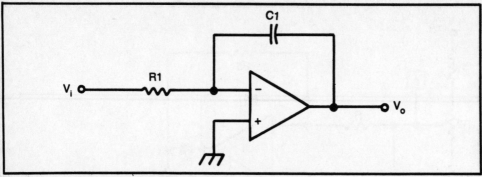

Fig. 4-40. An integrator is essentially a low-pass filter.

that a capacitor blocks (presents a high impedance to) low frequencies, but passes (presents a low impedance to) high frequencies.

The integrator circuit is more commonly known as a low-pass filter. Below a specific point, signal components (low frequency) are passed at full gain. Above this point (known as the cut-off frequency), the signal is increasingly attenuated as it increases in frequency.

The graph of Fig. 4-41 illustrates the operation of a low-pass filter.

A practical low-pass filter circuit for you to breadboard is illustrated in Fig. 4-42.

Use an ac signal source with strong harmonic content as the input. A square or rectangle wave or a sawtooth wave would be best. You can hear the effect of the filter on the sound by connecting the speaker alternately to point A (the original, unfiltered tone) and point B (the filtered, output tone). If you have an oscilloscope you can also observe the effect on the waveshape.

This circuit is not a true integrator, like the circuit in Fig. 4-40. Practical integrators tend to be rather complex, but the idea is the same.

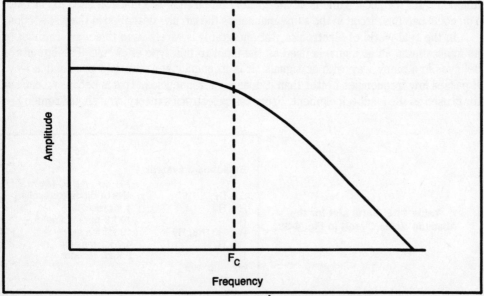

Fig. 4-41. This graph illustrates the frequency response of a low-pass filter.

106

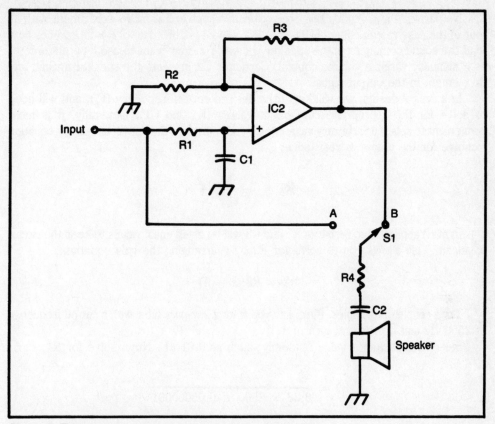

Fig. 4-42. This circuit is a practical low-pass filter. PROJECT #44

Essentially, Fig. 4-42 is a simple non-inverting amplifier with a RC network added to the input. the RC network forms a passive low-pass filter.

The gain for the passed band (low frequencies) is defined by resistors R2 and R3 in the usual manner for non-inverting amplifiers;

$$G = 1 + (R3/R2)$$

The cutoff frequency of the filter is determined by the values of R1 and C1, according to this formula;

$$F_c = \frac{1}{2 \pi R_1 C_1}$$

π, or pi, is a mathematical constant with an approximate value of 3.14. The equation can be rewritten as;

$$F_c = \frac{1}{6.28 R_1 C_1}$$

No parts list is given for this project because you will want to experiment with all four of the passive components (R1, R2, R3, and C1). The value of R4 determines how loud the sound coming from the speaker will be. You may want to use a potentiometer as a manually variable volume control. Capacitor C2 protects the speaker against any dc element in the output signal.

In a typical design, we will know the desired cut-off frequency (F_c), and will need to solve for the appropriate component values (R1 and C1). Generally, it is most convenient to select an arbitrary value for C1 and rearrange the cut-off frequency equation to solve for the unknown resistance;

$$R1 = \frac{1}{6.28 F_c C_1}$$

In most applications, resistors R1 and R3 will be given equal values to keep the circuit balanced. This allows you to solve for R2 by rearranging the gain equation;

$$R2 = R3(G - 1)$$

Try a couple of examples. First, say you want a low-pass filter with a cut-off frequency of 2500 Hz and a passband gain of 4.

Select a capacitance value randomly, such as 0.01 μF. Now, solve for R1;

$$R1 = \frac{1}{6.28 \times 2500 \times 0.00000001}$$
$$= \frac{1}{0.000157}$$
$$\cong 6369 \text{ ohms}$$

Round this off to 6.2 kΩ (6200 ohms), which is a standard 5% value. Because the attenuation slope is fairly gradual, the exact cut-off frequency is rarely very critical. Rounding off the calculated component values should not have any noticeable effect on the operation of the circuit.

R3 should have the same value as R1. R3 = R1 = 6.2 kΩ. Now determine the value of the feedback resistor (R2);

$$R2 = R3(G - 1)$$
$$= 6200(4 - 1)$$
$$= 6200 \times 3$$
$$= 18,600 \text{ ohms}$$
$$= 18.6 \text{ k}\Omega$$

As it turns out, 18 kΩ is a standard resistor value, so use that.

How much error has our rounding off introduced? Ignoring component tolerances, the actual gain is;

$$G = 1 + (R2/R3)$$
$$= 1 + (18000/6200)$$
$$= 1 + 2.9$$
$$= 3.9$$

This is certainly close enough to the desired gain of 4.

What about the actual cut-off frequency? Plugging in the selected component values:

$$F_c = \frac{1}{6.28R_1C_1}$$

$$= \frac{1}{6.28 \times 6200 \times 0.00000001}$$

$$= \frac{1}{0.0003894}$$

$$= 2568 \text{ Hz}$$

This is also quite close to the desired cut-off frequency of 2500 Hz. In other words, the component values selected in this example would do a good job.

Sometimes you may want to design two or more similar filters, without doing all the work from scratch for each one. As an example, say you need a companion low-pass filter with the same passband gain, but a cut-off frequency of 5000 Hz. This is twice the nominal cut-off frequency of the original filter.

To change the cut-off frequency in a filter, determine the ratio of the old frequency to the new frequency;

$$F_r = F_o/F_n$$

Then just multiply this factor either by all of the frequency-determining resistors, *or* all the frequency-determining capacitors, but not both.

In this example the ratio works out to;

$$F_r = 2500/5000$$
$$= 1/2$$

Because you do not want to alter the gain, change the capacitance value(s). In this simple filter circuit, there is only one frequency determining capacitor (C1). In some more advanced filter circuits there may be two or more frequency determining capacitors or resistors.

Since you only have to change C1, you only need to solve a single equation;

$$C1_n = F_rC1_o$$
$$= 1/2 \times 0.01$$
$$= 0.005 \ \mu F$$

This is a standard capacitance value.

With this new capacitance value, this revised filter will have an actual cut-off frequency of;

$$F_c = \frac{1}{6.28 \times 6200 \times 0.000000005}$$

$$= \frac{1}{0.0001946}$$

$$\cong 5139 \text{ Hz}$$

This is reasonably close to the desired cut-off frequency of 5000 Hz.

You could have changed R1 instead of C1, but then the gain determining resistors in the feedback network would also need to be changed.

Refer back to the basic integrator circuit of Fig. 4-40 for a moment. What do you suppose would happen if you reversed the positions of the capacitor and the resistor. The circuit now performs the mathematical function known as differentiation. It is called a differentiator.

The differentiator is also frequency sensitive, but in this case, it is the low frequencies that are blocked, and the high frequencies which receive full gain. Not surprisingly, this circuit is also known as a high-pass filter.

The action of a high-pass filter is illustrated in the graph of Fig. 4-43.

A practical high-pass filter circuit for you to breadboard is shown in Fig. 4-44. Notice that it is very similar to the low-pass filter circuit of Fig. 4-42. The only difference is that the positions of R1 and C1 are reversed. The same equations apply for both circuits.

Low-pass and high-pass filters can be combined to create two additional filter types. The first of these uses a low-pass filter and a high-pass filter in series, as shown in Fig. 4-45.

The cut-off frequencies of these two filters should overlap. That is, the cut-off frequency of the low-pass filter should be higher than the cut-off frequency of the high-pass filter.

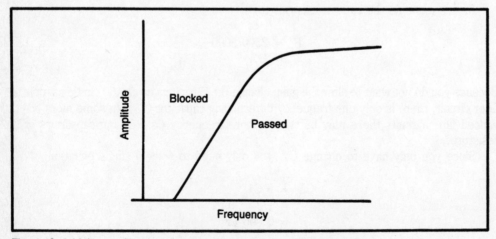

Fig. 4-43. A high-pass filter has the opposite response of a low-pass filter.

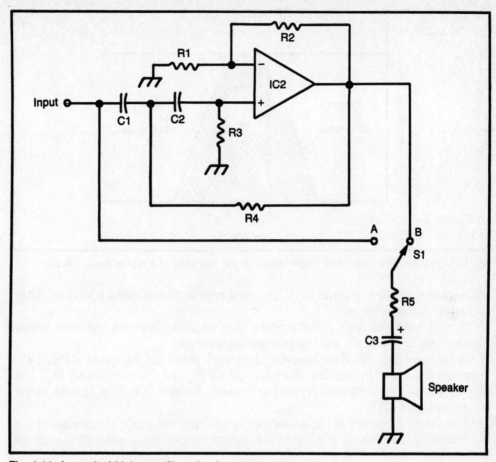

Fig. 4-44. A practical high-pass filter circuit. PROJECT #45

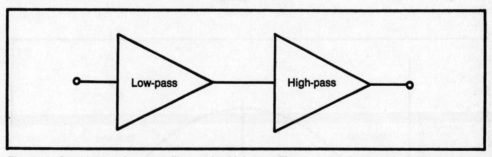

Fig. 4-45. Combining a low-pass filter and a high-pass filter in series produces a bandpass filter.

Only those frequencies which are passed by *both* of the component filters will reach the output. Any frequency blocked by either of the component filters will be blocked from the output of the composite filter. If the cut-off frequencies do not overlap, nothing at all will reach the output.

The frequency response graph for this type of filter is shown in Fig. 4-46. Only a specific band of frequencies that is common to the passbands of both component filters

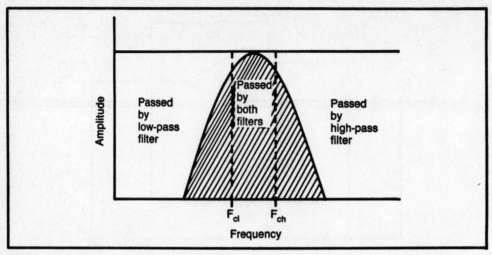

Fig. 4-46. This frequency response graph illustrates the operation of a typical bandpass filter.

will be passed by the composite filter. This new type of filter is called a bandpass filter for rather obvious reasons.

Special bandpass filter circuits rather than separate low-pass/high-pass series combinations are generally used in practical applications.

A bandpass filter has three important frequency points, as illustrated in Fig. 4-47. There are two cut-off frequencies—the lower cut-off (F_l) and the upper cut-off (F_h). The third significant frequency point is mid-way between the two. It is simply known as the center frequency (F_c).

The center frequency is the geometric, rather than the algebraic, average of the two cut-off frequencies. It is equal to the square root of the product of the cut-off frequencies;

$$F_c = \sqrt{F_l F_h}$$

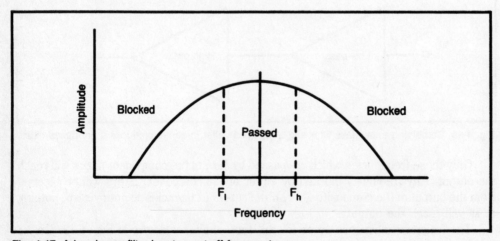

Fig. 4-47. A band-pass filter has two cut-off frequencies.

112

consider a bandpass filter with a lower cut-off frequency of 1000 Hz and an upper cut-off frequency of 2500 Hz. The center frequency is;

$$F_c = \sqrt{1000 \times 2500}$$
$$= \sqrt{2,500,000}$$
$$= 1581 \text{ Hz}$$

Another important specification for a bandpass filter is the bandwidth, or BW. This is the size of the passband and is equal to the difference between the upper and lower cut-off frequencies;

$$BW = F_h - F_l$$

For the above example, the bandwidth is;

$$BW = 2500 - 1000$$
$$= 1500 \text{ Hz}$$

There is one final specification that is often cited for bandpass filters. This is the Q, or quality factor. Essentially, Q is a measurement of the sharpness of the roll-off as the frequency moves away from the center frequency in either direction. The ratio between the bandwidth and the center frequency define the Q of the circuit;

$$Q = F_c/BW$$

Increasing the bandwidth will decrease the Q.

The Q for a practical bandpass filter circuit may be anywhere from less than 1 to several hundred.

A typical active bandpass filter circuit using an op amp is shown in Fig. 4-48. This circuit is called a multiple-feedback bandpass filter because there is more than one feedback path (through R2 and through C1 and C2).

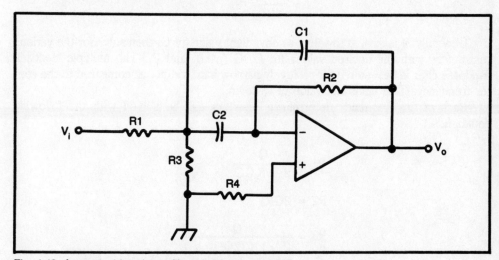

Fig. 4-48. A practical bandpass filter circuit. PROJECT #46

This circuit is suitable for moderate amounts of gain and has a Q between 15 and 20.

The formula for determining the gain of this circuit is a little more complicated than for any of the previous circuits in this chapter;

$$G = \frac{R2}{R1(1 + (C1/C2))}$$

This is the *maximum* gain, and is valid only at (or close to) the center frequency.

The equation for finding the center frequency is also rather complex, due to the relatively large number of frequency determining components;

$$F_c = \frac{1}{2\pi} \sqrt{\frac{1}{R2C1C2} \times \left(\frac{1}{R1} + \frac{1}{R3}\right)}$$

The constant $1/2\pi$ is equal to about 0.159.

Designing a multiple-feedback bandpass filter can be made much easier if equal capacitor values are used. That is, C1 = C2. The center frequency equation becomes;

$$F_c = 0.159 \times \sqrt{\frac{1}{R2 \times 2C} \times \left(\frac{1}{R1} + \frac{1}{R3}\right)}$$

Similarly, the gain equation is simplified to;

$$G = \frac{1}{R1\,(1 + (C/C))}$$

$$= \frac{1}{R1\,(1 + 1)}$$

$$= \frac{R2}{2R1}$$

Generally, it is easiest to select a convenient value for C, then solve for the various resistances with the desired values for Q, G (gain), and F_c. The multiple-feedback bandpass filter is best suited for relatively narrow bandwidths, as compared to the center frequency. This holds the value of Q down.

Each of the frequency determining resistors can be solved with the following equations;

$$R1 = \frac{Q}{2\pi F_c GC}$$

$$R2 = 2GR1$$

$$R3 = \frac{Q}{2\pi F_c C(2Q^2 - G)}$$

Here is a design example for a bandpass filter with the following specifications;

$$F_c = 2000 \text{ Hz}$$
$$BW = 400 \text{ Hz}$$
$$G = 2.5$$

The first step is to determine the Q for the circuit;

$$Q = F_c/BW$$
$$= 2000/400$$
$$= 5$$

Next, arbitrarily select a likely value for C. I will use 0.01 μF. Both capacitors (C1 and C2) will have the same value.

Plugging the known values into the equation for R1;

$$R1 = \frac{5}{6.28 \times 2000 \times 2.5 \times 0.00000001}$$

$$= \frac{5}{0.000314}$$

$$= 15,924 \text{ ohms}$$

A standard 15 kΩ resistor will be close enough. Next, for R2;

$$R2 = 2 \times 2.5 \times 15000$$
$$= 75,000 \text{ ohms} = 75 \text{ kΩ}$$

Finally, solve for resistor R3;

$$R3 = \frac{5}{6.28 \times 2000 \times 0.100000001 \times ((2 \times 5^2) - 2.5)}$$

$$= \frac{5}{0.0001256 \times (50 - 2.5)}$$

$$= \frac{5}{0.0001256 \times 47.5}$$

$$= \frac{5}{0.005966}$$

$$= 838 \text{ ohms}$$

A standard 820 ohm resistor will certainly be close enough.

The fourth and final major filter type can be simulated by connecting a low-pass filter and a high-pass filter in parallel, as shown in Fig. 4-49. Only those frequency

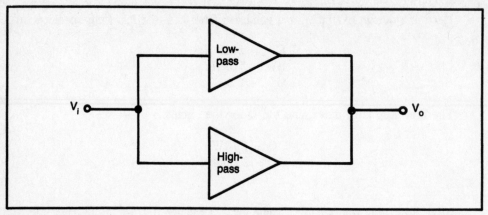

Fig. 4-49. Combining a low-pass filter and a high-pass filter in parallel produces a band-reject filter.

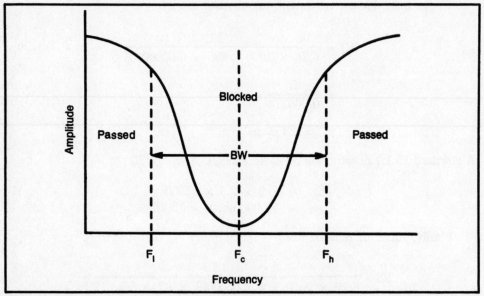

Fig. 4-50. Because of the appearance of its frequency response graph, the band-reject filter is also known as a notch filter.

components rejected by *both* filters will be deleted from the output. Any frequency passed by either component filter will be passed by the composite filter.

As the frequency response graph of Fig. 4-50 illustrates, this type of filter passes all but a specified band of frequencies, which is rejected. This is called a band-reject filter, or, because of the appearance of it's frequency response graph, a notch filter.

The band-reject filter is the opposite of a bandpass filter.

A typical band-reject filter circuit is shown in Fig. 4-51. Solving for the component values is not particularly difficult, because certain rules of equality must be followed in order for the circuit to work;

$$R1 = R2$$

$$R3 = R1/2$$
$$C1 = C2$$
$$C3 = 2 \times C1$$

The center frequency, sometimes called the null frequency is determined by the following formula;

$$F_c = \frac{1}{2 \pi R_1 C_1}$$

The remaining three components (R4, R5, and C4) are selected for the desired circuit Q, based on the values of the frequency determining components;

$$R4 = R5 = 2QR1$$
$$C4 = C1/Q$$

Band-reject filters generally have narrow bandwidths, and are most frequently used to block noise or interference signals.

SIGNAL SOURCES

All of the projects presented so far in this chapter operate on a signal from some external source. Op amps can also be used to generate ac signals of various waveforms.

Sine Wave Oscillator

The simplest possible ac waveform is the sine wave. This waveform, which is illustrated in Fig. 4-52 is comprised of just a single frequency component—the fundamental frequency. Ideally, it is perfectly pure with no harmonic content.

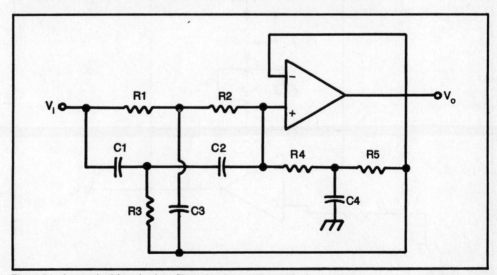

Fig. 4-51. A practical band-reject filter circuit. PROJECT #47

117

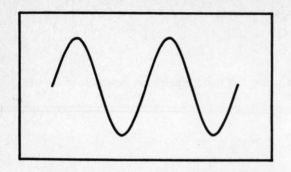

Fig. 4-52. The simplest ac waveform is the sine wave.

It is difficult to generate a perfectly pure, distortion free sine wave. Fortunately, we can come reasonably close to the ideal with an oscillator circuit built around an op amp.

A typical op amp sine wave oscillator circuit is shown in Fig. 4-53. The feedback network is a twin-T circuit. Resistors R1 and R2, along with capacitor C1 form one T. The other T is made up of C2, C3, R3, and R4. This second T is shown upside down in the schematic.

For the circuit to oscillate, the following conditions must be true;

$$R2 = R1$$
$$R3 = R1/4$$
$$R4 \cong R1/2$$
$$C1 = 2 \times C2$$
$$C3 = C2$$

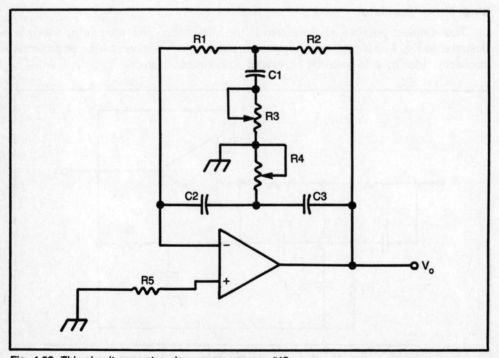

Fig. 4-53. This circuit generates sine waves. PROJECT #48

The output frequency will be equal to;

$$F = \frac{1}{2\pi R_1 C_2}$$

The twin-T network is detuned slightly by adjusting the value of R4. This will usually be a multiturn potentiometer. To calibrate the circuit, R4 is first set for its maximum resistance, then is slowly decreased in value until the circuit breaks into oscillations. If R4 is set at too low a resistance, the sine wave will be distorted at the output.

No parts list is given for this project, because the component values will be selected for the desired output frequency. The sample oscillator will develop a sine wave with a frequency of 600 Hz.

The first step is to select a reasonable value for the capacitor. I'll try a 0.01 μF capacitor for C2 and C3. (Remember, these two components must have equal values.)

Now, by algebraically rearranging the frequency equation, find the appropriate value for R1;

$$R1 = \frac{1}{2\pi F C_2}$$

$$= \frac{1}{6.28 \times 600 \times 0.00000001}$$

$$= \frac{1}{0.0000377}$$

$$= 26,526 \text{ ohms}$$

A 27 kΩ resistor should be close enough for most purposes.

Now it's a simple matter to find the values for the other components in the circuit;

$$
\begin{aligned}
R2 &= R1 = 27 \text{ k}\Omega \\
R3 &= R1/4 = 27000/4 \\
   &= 6750 \\
   &\cong 6.8 \text{ k}\Omega \\
R4 &= R1/2 = 27000/2 \\
   &= 13.500 \text{ ohms}
\end{aligned}
$$

(Use a 15 k to 25 k potentiometer for R4.)

$$
\begin{aligned}
C1 &= 2C2 = 2 \times 0.01 \\
   &= 0.02 \ \mu\text{F} \\
C3 &= C2 = 0.01 \ \mu\text{F}
\end{aligned}
$$

The major disadvantage of this circuit is that the frequency and purity of the output waveform is dependent upon the interlocking values of all of the components. There is no easy way to make the output frequency variable.

Square Wave Generator

The op amp can also be used to generate a square wave, like the astable multivibrators described in Chapters 2 and 3.

A square wave generator can be created by forcing an op amp alternately into positive and negative saturation. With the right feedback network, the switching between output stages will be very rapid. In practical devices, a slight slurring will be introduced. The sides of the squarewave will not quite be 90° straight lines. This is due to the slew rate of the op amp IC. The slew rate determines how fast the output can respond to changes in the input signal. In most cases, the slew rate will be very short, and probably unnoticeable in many applications. When the shape of the output square wave is very critical, a high quality op amp with a very short slew rate should be used.

Figure 4-54 shows what may well be the simplest possible square wave generator circuit. Besides the op amp itself, only three resistors and a single capacitor are required.

This circuit delivers a true square wave with a duty cycle of 50%.

Resistor R1 and capacitor C1 define the time constant of the circuit, but the output frequency is also affected by the positive feedback network comprised of resistors R2 and R3. The general equations are rather complex, but they can be simplified for specific R3/R2 ratios;

$$\text{If } R3/R2 = 1.1$$

$$\text{then } F = 0.5/R1C1$$

$$\text{If } R3/R2 = 10$$

$$\text{then } F = 5/R1C1$$

For a non-expert circuit designer, it would probably be best to stick to one of these R3/R2 ratios to keep the design equations as simple as possible.

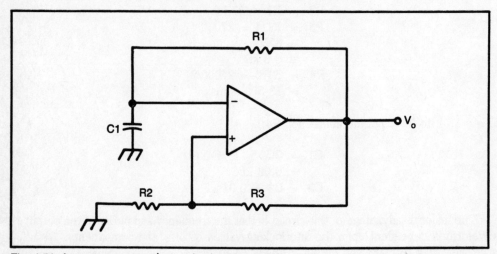

Fig. 4-54. A square wave generator circuit. PROJECT #49

As an example, design a square wave generator with an output frequency of 1200 Hz.

First, choose the R3/R2 ratio. A ratio of 10 is the most convenient to use with standard resistance values. Arbitrarily select a value for R2, such as 22 kΩ, and then solve for R3;

$$
\begin{aligned}
R3 &= R2 \times R3/R2 \\
&= R2 \times 10 \\
&= 22{,}000 \times 10 \\
&= 220{,}000 \\
&= 220 \text{ k}\Omega
\end{aligned}
$$

Because you are using a R3/R2 ratio of 10;

$$F = 5/R1C1$$

I already know I want a value of 1200 Hz for F. I need to find the necessary values for R1 and C1. The best procedure is to select a suitable value for C1, then rearrange the frequency equation to solve for R1;

$$R1 = 5/FC1$$

If I assign a value of 0.22 μF to C1, then R1's value should be;

$$R1 = \frac{5}{1200 \times 0.00000022}$$

$$
\begin{aligned}
&= 5/0.000264 \\
&= 18.940 \text{ ohms}
\end{aligned}
$$

A standard 18 kΩ resistor should be close enough.

This circuit can be made even more useful by adding a potentiometer, as shown in Fig. 4-55. This allows the output frequency to be changed manually while the circuit is operating. The value of R1 in this case is equal to the series combination of fixed resistor $R1_a$ and the adjusted value of potentiometer $R1_b$. The fixed resistor is included to prevent the value of R1 from ever becoming zero. The fixed value of $R1_a$ and the maximum setting of $R1_b$ sets the range of output frequencies. For example, the following component values will give output frequencies ranging from about 833 Hz up to approximately 5 kHz;

$R1_a$	10 kΩ
$R1_b$	50 kΩ potentiometer
R2	22 kΩ
R3	220 kΩ
C1	0.1 μF

Figure 4-56 shows how this basic circuit can be adapted to create a variable-width rectangle wave generator. The user can manually adjust the duty cycle.

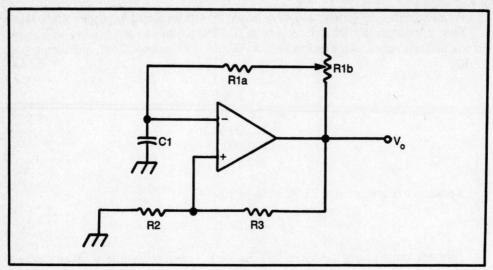

Fig. 4-55. The circuit in Fig. 4-54 can easily be adapted for a variable frequency output. PROJECT #50

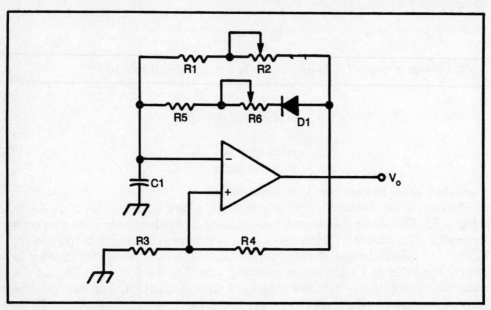

Fig. 4-56. This modification of the circuit in Fig. 4-54 generates variable width rectangle waves. PROJECT #51

On negative half-cycles, diode D1 blocks the flow of current through R5 and R6. The time constant is determined by R1, R2, and C1. On positive half-cycles, the diode conducts, and the time constant is defined by C1 and the parallel combination of R1—R2 and R5—R6;

$$T_+ = C1 \times \frac{(R1 + R2) \times (R5 + R6)}{(R1 + R2) + (R5 + R6)}$$

The length of the total cycle is simply the sum of the two half-cycle time constants;

$$T_t = T + T_-$$

The output frequency is the reciprocal of the time for a total cycle;

$$F = 1/T_t$$

Notice that changing the duty cycle will affect the output frequency in this circuit.

Triangle Wave Generator

Another popular waveform is the triangle wave, shown in Fig. 4-57. The op amp can generate this waveform too.

A triangle wave has the same harmonic content as a square wave, except the harmonics are weaker. A triangle wave can be created by passing a square wave through an integrator (or low-pass filter). This is what happens in the circuit of Fig. 4-58. IC1, and its associated components make up an integrator. IC2 and its associated components serve as a simple square wave generator. Notice that both square wave and triangle wave outputs are provided.

The square wave will swing back and forth between the op amp's positive and negative saturation voltages. The amplitude of the triangle wave is controlled by the ratio of R2/R1. These components also determine the output frequency, making adjustment a little tricky.

Both waveforms will always have the same frequency. This is the formula for finding the output frequency;

$$F = \frac{1}{4R_3C_1} \times \frac{R1}{R2}$$

This circuit could be called a function generator. A function generator is a signal generator circuit with more than one type of output waveform.

Sawtooth Wave Generator

You can obtain a fair approximation of a sawtooth wave by tapping off an output across the timing capacitor in a rectangle wave generator. The circuitry is illustrated in Fig. 4-59. This circuit functions in basically the same way as the rectangle wave generator of Fig. 4-56. Fixed resistors are shown here for simplicity.

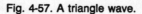
Fig. 4-57. A triangle wave.

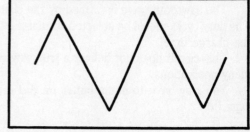

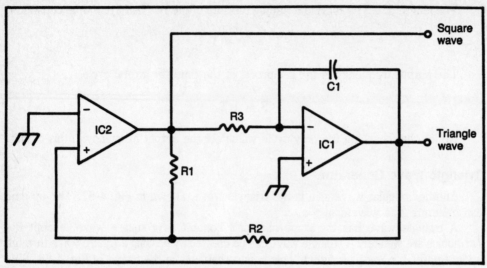

Fig. 4-58. This circuit generates triangle waves. PROJECT #52

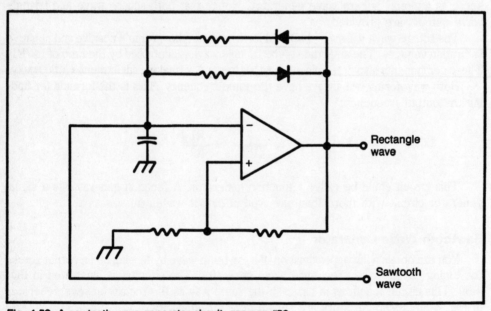

Fig. 4-59. A sawtooth wave generator circuit. PROJECT #53

The sawtooth wave is formed by the charging and the discharging of capacitor C1. The duty cycle should be selected so that the discharge time is short in comparison with the charge time.

This circuit does not deliver a true sawtooth wave, but it will be close enough for many applications.

You may have to use a buffer on the sawtooth output to avoid loading down the capacitor.

CHAPTER SUMMARY

Despite the length of this chapter, we have barely scratched the surface of op amp applications. There are countless other applications. Many more sophisticated applications are basically variations on the circuits shown here.

While there are many, many circuits that had to be left out, the circuits presented in this chapter will keep you busy experimenting for quite some time.

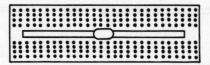

5

The LM339 Quad Comparator

THIS CHAPTER WILL DISCUSS A DEVICE THAT IS CLOSELY RELATED TO THE OP AMP—THE LM339 quad comparator.

Chapter 4 provided experiments with the op amp as a comparator, but the op amp is a general purpose device. For best performance and maximum convenience in this specific type of application, it makes sense to use a dedicated device designed especially for comparator applications.

THE CHIP

The LM339 quad comparator IC is shown in Fig. 5-1. It contains four identical, but independent, comparator sections. The only pins the sections share are the power supply connections (V+—pin #3 and ground—pin #12). All of the other pins are inputs or outputs for individual comparator sections.

This chip, unlike the 741 and most other standard op amps, requires only a single polarity supply voltage. Moreover, the voltage powering this device can vary over a wide range. Any voltage from +2 to +32 volts will do.

The arrangement of the pins might seem a little odd. The outputs are separated from the inputs by the supply pins. This is done for a definite reason. If an output lead is too close to the input leads, the comparator could develop uncontrollable oscillations.

Since there are four comparator sections in a single package, many applications will leave some of the sections unused. All of the unused pins of any comparator should be grounded both inputs and outputs.

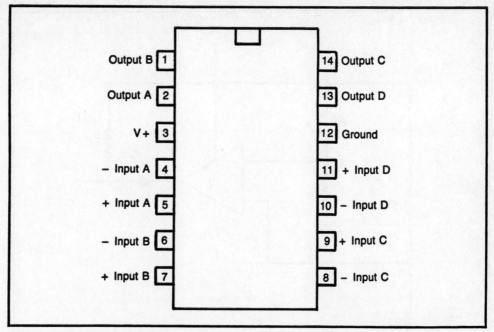

Fig. 5-1. The LM339 contains four independent comparator sections in a single housing.

Before moving on to specific circuits for the LM339, briefly review the basics of comparator operation. A comparator does exactly what its name implies. It compares two input voltages and produces an output that unambiguously indicates which of the input signals is larger. This can be a surprisingly useful electronic function.

The basic comparator circuit is shown again in Fig. 5-2. A variable (presumably unknown) input signal (V_{in}) is compared to (usually) a fixed reference voltage (V_{ref}). Whenever the input signal is even slightly greater than the reference signal, the output goes HIGH. Even a difference of just a few millivolts can trigger the circuit.

A simple comparator demonstration circuit for you to breadboard is shown in Fig. 5-3. A typical parts list is given in Table 5-1.

The two inputs are tapped from two voltage dividers. One (V_{ref}—point B) is fixed (R1 and R2). The other (V_{in}—point A) is variable via the potentiometer (R3, R4, and R5). With the component values shown in the parts list and a supply voltage of 9 volts, V_{ref} (point B) will be 4.5 volts. The variable voltage (V_{in}—point A) can range from a little over 2 volts to just under 7 volts. Resistor R6 limits the current through the LED (D1).

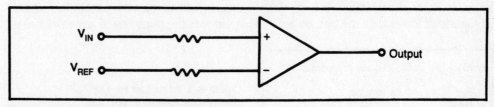

Fig. 5-2. The basic comparator circuit.

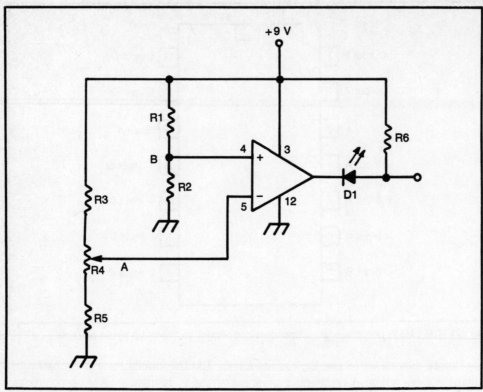

Fig. 5-3. A practical comparator demonstration circuit. PROJECT #54

If the voltage at point A (V_{in}) is larger than the voltage at point B (V_{ref}) the LED will light up, otherwise, it will remain dark.

HYSTERESIS

You may have detected a problem while experimenting with the demonstration circuit. If V_{in} is very close to V_{ref}, the output may tend to oscillate between states. In many applications you will be more concerned with fairly large differences in the voltages, and this small difference oscillation may not be a problem, or it may just be an inconsequential annoyance at worst. In some precision applications, any output oscillation could mean major problems.

Fortunately, a simple solution is possible. Add a little hysteresis with a feedback resistor, R_f, as shown in Fig. 5-4. Hysteresis means that the turn-off level in this circuit is somewhat lower than the turn-on level. This reduces the tendency of any small noise

IC1	LM339 quad comparator IC
D1	LED
R1, R2	10 kΩ resistor
R3, R5	4.7 kΩ resistor
R4	10 kΩ potentiometer
R6	470 Ω resistor

Table 5-1. Parts List for the
Comparator Circuit in Fig. 5-3.

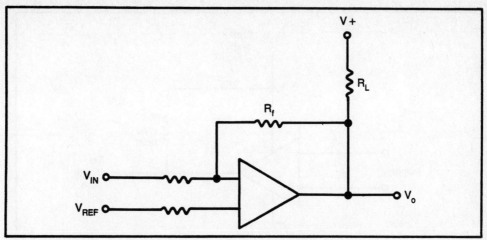

Fig. 5-4. This comparator circuit features hysteresis to eliminate "chatter".

signal causing input "chatter" and confusing the comparator. The feedback resistor is generally given a very large value. A minimum of 1 MΩ should be used here, and 10 MΩ is even better.

Besides adding hysteresis, the feedback resistor provides additional benefits for the circuit. It tends to speed up the comparator's switching time. In many cases it can substantially "clean up" noisy input signals, functioning somewhat like a Schmitt trigger. You should breadboard the circuit of Fig. 5-4 and compare its operation to the earlier circuit of Fig. 5-3. Use the same input and output components (R1 through R6, and D1), wired in the same way as in the earlier experiment.

LOADING

A nice feature of the LM339 is that its inputs can be driven from virtually any source without noticeable loading effects, almost no matter what the source impedance may be. The LM339's outputs are open collector npn transistors. An external pull-up resistor can be used to drive an output load at a different supply voltage than the comparator. These loading characteristics make this chip well suited for use with any of the major logic families, including CMOS, DTL, ECL, MOS, and TTL.

A digital driver comparator is shown in Fig. 5-5. For operation with TTL gates, power the comparator with a +5 volt source. The resistor's value should be about 10 kΩ. For use with CMOS devices, raise the resistor value to about 100 kΩ. The supply voltage can be whatever is being used by the CMOS chips.

The outputs of the LM339 comparator can sink up to 20 mA (0.02 amp). Multiple outputs can be hard-wired together for an OR output. (For more information on gates, refer to Chapter 8.)

LIMIT COMPARATOR

Figure 5-6 shows a circuit called a limit comparator. This type of circuit is also occasionally known as a window comparator. The output LED will light up (output goes HIGH) when the input voltage is within a specific range. If it is above the maximum

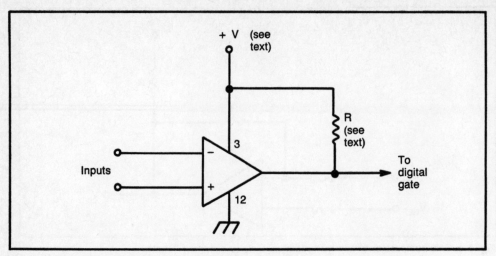

Fig. 5-5. The LM339 comparator can be used to drive digital gates. PROJECT #55

specified value, or below the minimum specified value, the LED will remain dark (output is LOW).

The voltage range of interest is determined by the ratios of the resistor values in the reference voltage divider network (R1, R2, and R3). Since R2 is between the upper limit comparator and the lower limit comparator, its value will define the extent of the ON range. A small value for R2 (compared to R1 and R3) will give a fairly narrow range of input voltages that will turn on the LED. If a larger value is used for R2, the ON range will be proportionately larger.

There is not much point in providing a parts list for a project like this. The two fixed-value resistors are marked in the schematic. These values are not critical; you can substitute anything close. The transistor may be any low-power npn device. The diode, of course, is a standard LED.

Experiment with different values for resistors R1, R2, and R3. I will offer two quick examples. First, use the following resistance values;

$$R_1 = 1 \text{ k}\Omega$$
$$R_2 = 2.2 \text{ k}\Omega$$
$$R_3 = 10 \text{ k}\Omega$$

Assuming a supply voltage of nine volts, we can use Ohm's Law to find the comparator limits. First, the current flow through the resistors (ignoring the drain of the comparator inputs, which should be very small) works out to;

$$I = E/R$$

$$= \frac{9}{1000 + 2200 + 10,000}$$

$$= \frac{9}{13,200}$$

130

$$= 0.00068 \text{ amp}$$
$$= 0.68 \text{ mA}$$

Now, we can find the voltage drop across each individual resistor;

$$E = IR$$
$$R_1 = 1 \text{ k}\Omega$$
$$E_1 = 0.00068 \times 1000$$
$$= 0.68 \text{ volt}$$
$$R_2 = 2.2 \text{ k}\Omega$$
$$E_2 = 0.00068 \times 2200$$
$$= 1.5 \text{ volt}$$
$$R_3 = 10 \text{ k}\Omega$$
$$E_3 = 0.00068 \times 10,000$$
$$= 6.8 \text{ volts}$$

Adding the three voltage drops together, we should get the original supply voltage;

$$V+ = E_1 + E_2 + E_3$$
$$= 0.68 + 1.5 + 6.8$$
$$= 8.98 \text{ volts}$$

The small error is due to rounding off in the equations.

The lower limit of the ON range is set by the voltage drop across R3, or 6.8 volts in this example. The upper limit is equal to the supply voltage minus the voltage drop across R1. In our example, this works out to;

$$V+ - E_1 =$$
$$9 - .068 =$$
$$8.32 \text{ volts}$$

For the component values used in this example, the LED will light up for any input voltage between 6.8 and 8.3 volts. The ON range is about 1.5 volts wide. For the second example, we will not show all the equations here, but the problem is solved in exactly the same way as in the preceding example. Once again, we use a +9 volt supply. This time, the following resistor values are used;

$$R_1 = 18 \text{ k}\Omega$$
$$R_2 = 47 \text{ k}\Omega$$
$$R_3 = 22 \text{ k}\Omega$$

This time, the LED will turn on for input voltages ranging from about 2.28 volts up to approximately 7.14 volts. The turn-on band in this example is about 4.86 volts wide. Notice that in each case, the turn-on range width is equal to the voltage drop across R2.

Breadboard the circuit of Fig. 5-6 using these and other resistor values. For maximum versatility, you might want to use potentiometers for R1, R2, and R3.

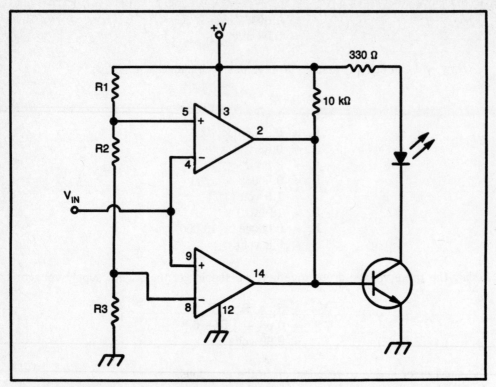

Fig. 5-6. This circuit is a limit comparator. PROJECT #56

MONOSTABLE MULTIVIBRATOR

The LM339 can also be used in a number of less obvious applications, such as monostable multivibrators (timers). Figure 5-7 shows the basic LM339 monostable multivibrator circuit. With no input signal, the inverting input of the comparator is biased to about 1.25 volts by the voltage divider made up of R1 and R2. A negative-going trigger pulse at the input forces the comparator's inverting input below ground potential. Protective diode D1 limits how far negative this input can go to a drop of about one volt.

The resulting positive-going output is fed back to the non-inverting input through feedback capacitor C2. The output will remain HIGH for a time period determined by the time constant of resistor R4 and capacitor C2. Using a 1 megohm resistor for R4 (a typical value) will give the following time constants for various values of C2;

$$
\begin{array}{ll}
C_2 = 100 \text{ pF} & T = 0.0003 \text{ second} \\
C_2 = 1000 \text{ pF} & T = 0.003 \text{ second} \\
C_2 = 0.01 \ \mu\text{F} & T = 0.03 \text{ second} \\
C_2 = 0.1 \ \mu\text{F} & T = 0.3 \text{ second}
\end{array}
$$

The LM339 monostable multivibrator is only suitable for relatively small time periods. It is scarcely a replacement for circuits built around timers like the 555 or the XR2420; however, in a large circuit that needs a short delay and has a spare comparator section available, the circuit of Fig. 5-7 will come in quite handy. A parts list appears in Table 5-2.

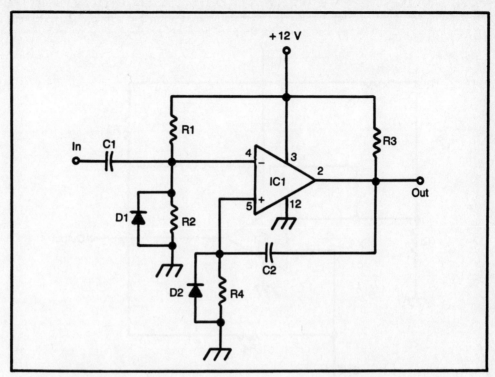

Fig. 5-7. The LM339 comparator can be used as a monostable multivibrator. PROJECT #57

ASTABLE MULTIVIBRATOR

The LM339 can also be forced to operate as a signal source in the astable multivibrator mode. Such a circuit is shown in Fig. 5-8. A parts list for this project is given in Table 5-2, but be sure to experiment with other component values. Using the component values shown here, the output signal will have a frequency between 2500 Hz and 3000 Hz. R4 and C1 are the principal frequency-determining components in this circuit.

LIGHT DETECTOR

Figure 5-9 shows an interesting application for the LM339 quad comparator IC. If you look at this circuit carefully, you should see that it is essentially the same as the limit comparator circuit of Fig. 5-6. The only difference here is that the input is tapped from a simple two-part voltage divider made up of a photocell (PC1) and a potentiometer (R4). Each of these components has a variable resistance. R4 varies with its manual

Table 5-2. Parts List for the Monostable Multivibrator Circuit in Fig. 5-7.

IC1	LM339 quad comparator
D1, D2	1N4148 diode (or similar)
R1	6.8 MΩ resistor
R2, R4	1 MΩ resistor
R3	1 kΩ resistor
C1	100 pF capacitor

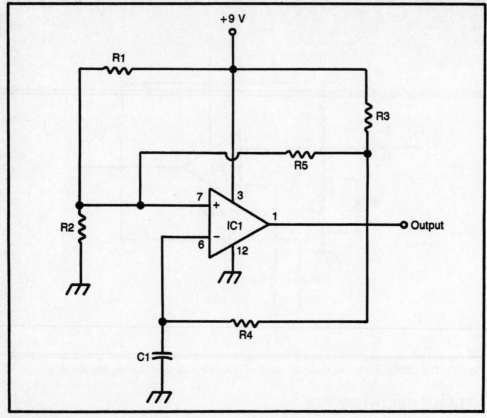

Fig. 5-8. An astable multivibrator circuit using the LM339 comparator. PROJECT #58

setting, so it acts like a range control. The resistance of PC1 depends on the intensity of the light striking it.

If the light striking the photocell is within a given range (determined by R1, R2, and R3), the LED will light up (output goes HIGH). For any specific setting of R4, the voltage presented to the input depends on the resistance of PC1. In all other respects, this circuit functions in exactly the same manner as the limit comparator discussed earlier in the chapter.

Experiment with various values of R1, R2, and R3. A fixed resistor may be used for R4, if you prefer to forego the manual range control.

BARGRAPH

Multiple comparators can be used together to build a bargraph display unit. As the input voltage increases, more LEDs will light up. The number of lit LEDs gives an indication of the approximate input voltage.

Figure 5-10 shows a simple four-stage bargraph circuit. It uses all four sections of a single LM339 quad comparator IC. If you like, you can easily expand the circuit by adding more comparator sections. Four stages are shown here because there are four sections in one chip. There is nothing critical about the number of stages.

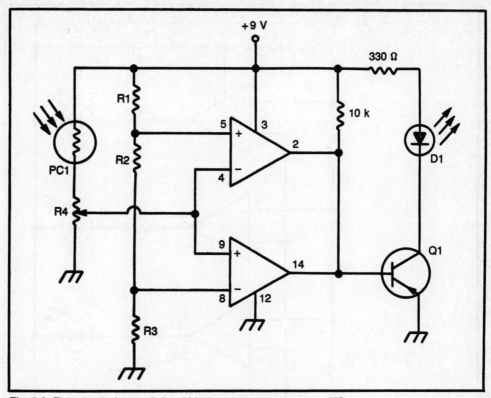

Fig. 5-9. This circuit detects light within a preset range. PROJECT #59

The value of resistor R1 determines the sensitivity of the circuit. You could use a potentiometer here as a calibration control. Resistors R2 through R5 should have identical values for equal steps per LED. You could use non-equal resistors to weight the scale.

Resistors R6 through R9 simply protect the LEDs from excessive current flow. Their values determine the brightness of their associated LEDs.

The only other thing to bear in mind is that the input signal is not referenced directly to ground. The input voltage is connected across the two points marked in the diagram.

A typical parts list for this project is given in Table 5-3. Feel free to experiment with any or all of the component values.

CAPACITANCE METER

Figure 5-11 shows a simple circuit for a capacitance meter built around two sections

Table 5-3. Parts List for the LED Bargraph Circuit in Fig. 5-10.

IC	LM339 quad comparator
D1 - D4	LED
R1	68 kΩ resistor
R2 - R5	2.2 kΩ resistor
R6 - R9	470 Ω resistor

135

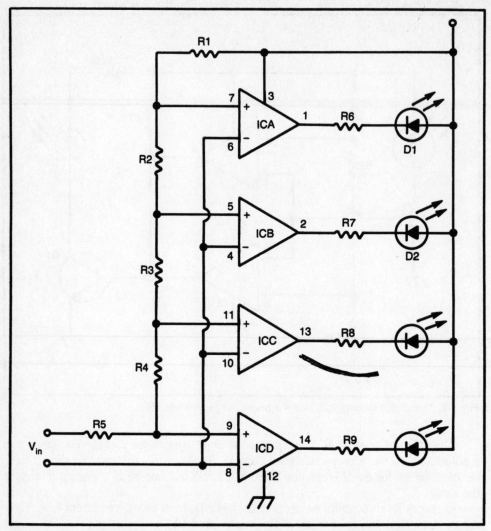

Fig. 5-10. Several comparator sections can be used together to form a bargraph display. PROJECT #60

of a LM339 quad comparator IC. The unknown capacitance is charged linearly by a constant current source.

The comparators are set up for a lower limit of 0.1 volt and an upper limit of 1.1 volts. The capacitance can be determined by measuring the time it takes the capacitor to linearly charge the one volt between the low and high comparators.

This circuit is shown here only as an illustration of a sophisticated application for the comparator. The circuitry as shown here is somewhat simplified. The complete project is beyond the scope of this book. For this reason, no parts list is provided here.

Incidentally, you should notice that in Fig. 5-11 the IC is shown as a "black box". The functional individual comparator stages are not drawn out. This is often done in schematics, especially for moderate to large scale systems. If you want to understand how the circuit works, just compare the pin numbers with a pin-out diagram of the IC

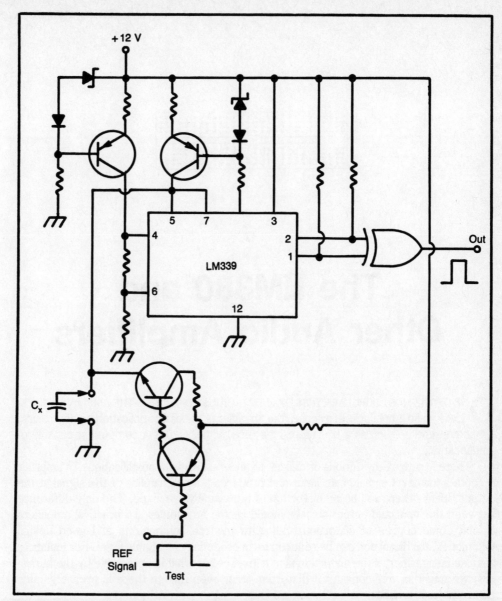

Fig. 5-11. This is a capacitance meter circuit. PROJECT #61

in question. The "black box" type IC schematic is used to simplify and unclutter the diagram.

SUMMARY

Essentially, the LM339 quad comparator is a specialized variation on the basic op amp. It is not so specialized that it does not have a variety of potential applications. There are several other comparator ICs available, but the LM339 is by far the most popular today.

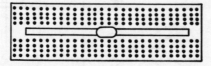

6

The LM380 and Other Audio Amplifiers

ONE OF THE MOST POPULAR TYPES OF ELECTRONICS PROJECTS IS THE AMPLIFIER, ESPE-cially audio amplifiers. In a sense, the amplifier is *the* basic application of electronics. An active device (such as a transistor or a tube) is defined as a component capable of amplification.

There is nothing mysterious or difficult to understand about amplification. An amplifier accepts a low-level signal at its input and produces a larger replica of the signal at the output. Ideally there will be no distortion of the signal waveshape. The only difference between the input and output signals should be the amplitude. *All* practical amplifiers exhibit some degree of distortion. But with modern components and good design techniques, the distortion can be reduced to an essentially negligible level. For instance, in an audio amplifier, if the distortion is at a level below what is detectable by the human ear, we might as well consider it distortion-free, even though there is probably some measurable distortion.

Most people can only hear distortions greater than one percent. Most commercial high-fidelity amplifiers offer distortion ratings far below one percent. Even in moderately priced equipment, 0.1 percent is typical today. The best quality amplifiers offer lower distortion ratings.

What is the point in setting the distortion specifications below one percent if the distortion is inaudible? Distortion effect in a sound system is cumulative. You also have to take into account any distortion introduced by the signal source and the loudspeakers. Loudspeakers, in particular, tend to introduce significant amounts of distortion. Even for very good speakers, three percent is not uncommon. It is certainly undesirable for the amplifier to add any unnecessary distortion on top of that.

Because of the popularity and widespread use of audio amplifiers, it is not surprising that IC manufacturers have designed numerous audio amplifier chips. Many of these devices are very good for low power applications. Because of thermal build-up, it would be unreasonable for a tiny IC chip to handle 200 watts per channel. There are ways, however, to force an amplifier IC to deliver more than its rated amount of power. We'll explore this later in some of the projects.

Some of the amplifier ICs available these days are extremely impressive regarding power output, package size, and performance.

For the most efficient and reliable performance, any IC amplifier should be used with adequate heatsinking. In most cases, the better the heatsinking, the greater the maximum output power will be. As a general rule of thumb, if an amplifier IC is to deliver more than 50 percent of its rated power, heatsinking should be considered mandatory. A lot of heat can build up inside a chip during amplification. Too much heat can damage or destroy the delicate silicon crystal.

Heatsinking is most important in a permanent installation, but it is not to be ignored, even in breadboarding.

Always leave adequate air space around any amplifier IC. This is most important in a permanent installation, which will probably be contained in an enclosed housing of some kind, but ventilation should be considered even while breadboarding.

When in doubt, try to err on the side of too much thermal protection, rather than too little.

THE LM380 AUDIO AMPLIFIER IC

The LM380 is an audio amplifier IC that has been around for a few years, and still enjoys considerable popularity.

This chip is widely available in two types of packaging. The pinout for the compact eight-pin DIP version is shown in Fig. 6-1, while the fourteen-pin version is illustrated in Fig. 6-2. On both versions of this chip, only six of the pins are active. The remaining

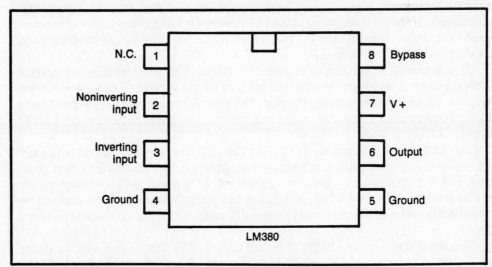

Fig. 6-1. The LM380 is available in an eight-pin DIP housing.

139

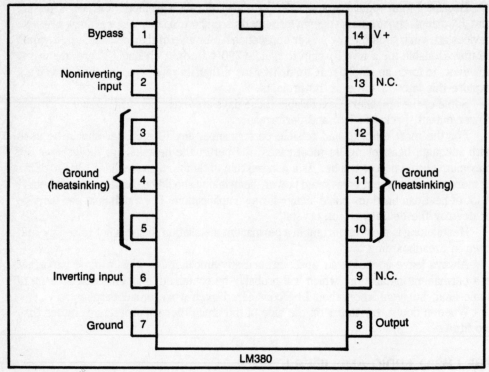

Bypass	1		14	V+
Noninverting input	2		13	N.C.
	3		12	
Ground (heatsinking)	4		11	Ground (heatsinking)
	5		10	
Inverting input	6		9	N.C.
Ground	7		8	Output

LM380

Fig. 6-2. The fourteen-pin version of the LM380 has increased on-board heatsinking.

pins should be shorted to ground, providing limited internal heatsinking. Obviously, the fourteen-pin version has more heatsinking pins than the eight-pin version, thus it can handle greater amounts of power without overheating.

Without external heatsinks, the LM380 can typically dissipate up to about 1.25 watts at room temperature. Higher output levels can be obtained with external heatsinking. For example, if the six heatsinking pins of a fourteen-pin LM380 are soldered to a six-square-inch copper foil pad on a PC board (two-ounce foil), the IC can produce up to 3.7 watts at room temperature.

The maximum power output is heat dependent. This chip features an internal automatic thermal shutdown circuit which will turn off the amplifier if excessive current flow ever causes the IC to start overheating. The internal circuitry is a fairly sophisticated circuit, made up of no fewer than twelve transistors. A simplified version of the LM380 internal circuitry is shown in Fig. 6-3.

The LM380 gain is internally fixed at 50 (34 dB). The output signal automatically centers itself around one-half of the supply voltage, effectively eliminating offset problems. Either a single polarity (positive) power supply or a dual polarity power supply may be used to drive the LM380. If a dual polarity supply is used, the output will be automatically centered around ground potential (0 volts) with no dc component to worry about.

The input stage of the LM380 is rather unique. The input signal may be either referenced to ground, or ac coupled, depending on the specific requirements of the individual application.

140

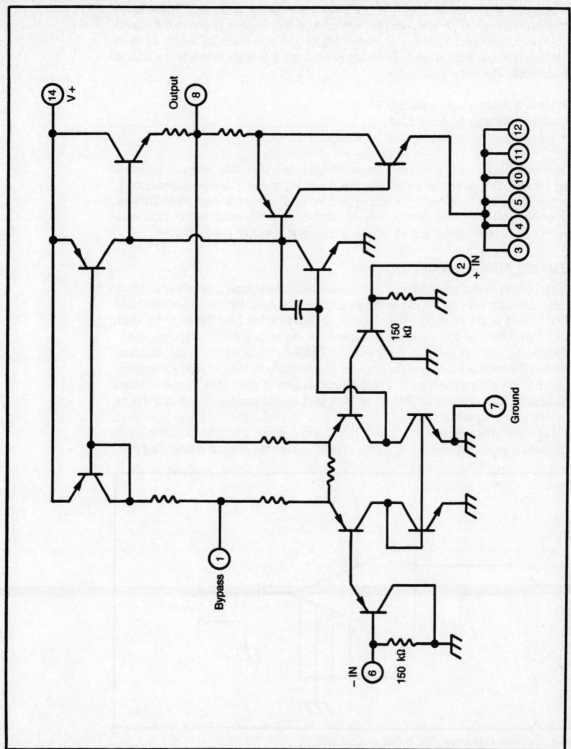

Fig. 6-3. The LM380 internal circuitry.

The inputs are internally biased with a 150 kΩ resistance to ground. Transducers (or previous stages) which are referenced to ground (no dc component in the signal) may be directly coupled to either the inverting or the non-inverting input. In most applications, only one input is used. There are several possible ways to handle the unused input terminal. They are;

- leave it floating (unconnected)
- short it directly to ground, or
- reference it to ground through a resistor or a capacitor

In most applications in which the non-inverting input is used, the inverting input will be left floating. You should be aware that this could make circuit layout rather critical. Stray capacitances in the circuit may lead to positive feedback and undesired oscillations. When working with amplifier circuits, you should always bear in mind that the difference between an amplifier circuit and an oscillator circuit is a rather small one.

THE BASIC AMPLIFIER CIRCUIT

The LM380 is designed for use with a minimum of external components, which certainly makes life easy for the circuit designer. The most basic form of an LM380-based amplifier circuit is shown in Fig. 6-4. Clearly, it would be hard for things to be much simpler than this. The only external component is the output decoupling capacitor.

Notice that the fourteen-pin version of the LM380 chip is shown in this diagram. we will use this version for each of the projects. If you decide to use the eight-pin version, just correct the pin numbering. It would be particularly a good idea to use external heatsinking on the eight-pin LM380. It will not hurt to add some external heatsinking to the fourteen-pin package too.

Of all those grounded pins in Fig. 6-4, pin #7 is the supply ground connection point. The remaining grounded pins (#3, 4, 5, 10, 11, and 12) are the internal heatsinking pins.

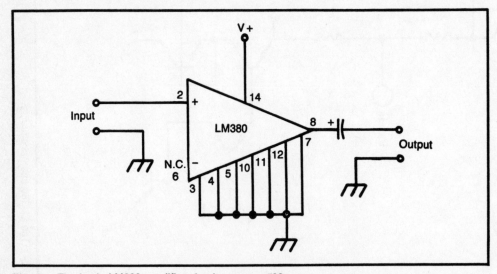

Fig. 6-4. The basic LM380 amplifier circuit. PROJECT #62

In many practical applications, several additional external components may be required for best performance or to add specific features.

If the LM380 chip is physically located more than two or three inches from the power supply filter capacitor, adding an extra decoupling capacitor is advisable. This capacitor should be mounted between the V+ terminal of the LM380 and ground. A supply line decoupling capacitor should always be mounted as physically close to the body of the IC as possible. A typical value for this component is 0.1 μF.

The LM380 audio amplifier IC is intended primarily for use with audio frequencies, but it can be used with signals outside the audible range too. If it is used in a high-frequency (several megahertz or more) application, the chip may tend to oscillate. Adding the extra resistor and capacitor shown in Fig. 6-5 between the output and ground will help suppress such high-frequency oscillations. Generally, the resistor will have a very small value— around 2.7 ohms is typical. In most cases, 0.1 μF will be a good value for the capacitor.

Since these oscillations occur at frequencies of 5 MHz to 10 MHz, they usually will not be of much significance in audio applications, as far as the signal is concerned. Such oscillations will cause the chip to dissipate extra power, which is not only wasteful, but could cause thermal problems. If the LM380 is being used in an RF sensitive environment, shielding and oscillation suppression components are advisable.

Notice that in Fig. 6-5, and in the rest of the LM380 schematics in this chapter, the heatsinking pins are not shown. This omission is intended to reduce diagram clutter. The heatsinking pins are always grounded in all applications, so the connections can be assumed.

Figure 6-6 shows a practical audio amplifier circuit built around the LM380. A parts list is given in Table 6-1.

The input to this circuit is provided by an inexpensive low-impedance microphone. Other low level signal sources may be used in place of this microphone, if you choose. The impedance matching transformer (T1) should be used for any low-impedance source. If the signal source has a high-output impedance, you may omit this transformer.

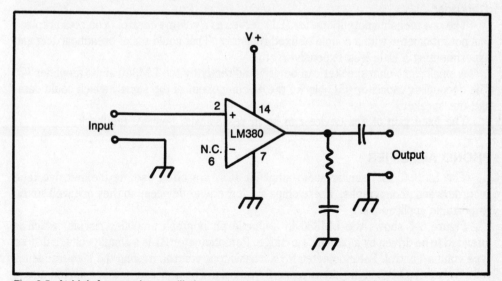

Fig. 6-5. At high frequencies, oscillation suppression components should be used.

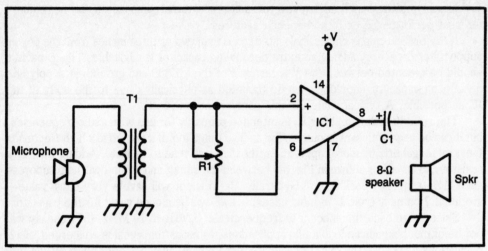

Fig. 6-6. An audio amplifier circuit. PROJECT #63

Table 6-1. Parts List for the Audio Amplifier Circuit in Fig. 6-6.

IC1	LM380 audio amplifier
C1	500 μF capacitor (electrolytic)
R1	1 MΩ resistor
T1	Impedance matching transformer
	Primary—500 Ω (or to match input source
	Secondary—200 kΩ
SPKR	8 Ω speaker

The input signal should not have too high an amplitude, or the amplifier may be overloaded.

The one megohm potentiometer (R1) serves as a volume control. You could replace this potentiometer with a couple of fixed resistors. That could make breadboarding and experimenting a little less expensive.

A small eight-ohm speaker can be driven directly by the LM380 audio amplifier IC. The decoupling capacitor (C1) blocks the dc component of the signal, which could damage the speaker.

The fixed gain of this device can be increased with positive feedback.

PHONO AMPLIFIER

The LM380, and similar audio amplifier ICs, are often used in inexpensive tape recorders and phonographs. These chips are low power devices, so they are well suited to portable applications.

Figure 6-7 shows the LM380 in a simple phonograph amplifier circuit, which is intended to be driven by a ceramic cartridge. Potentiometer R1 is a simple voltage divider type volume control. Potentiometer R3 is a basic tone control, making the high-frequency roll-off characteristics of the circuit manually variable. The user can, within a limited range, adjust the tonal quality of the sound to suit his or her individual taste.

144

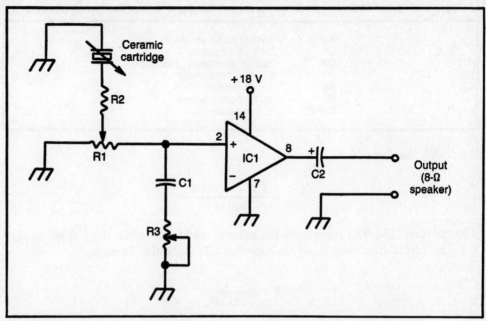

Fig. 6-7. This circuit is an amplifier for a ceramic cartridge phonograph. PROJECT #64

Most serious phonograph applications (anything beyond a crude toy), require frequency response shaping to provide the standard RIAA equalization characteristic. All commercial phonograph records are equalized according to the RIAA standards. If the complementary response shaping is not included in playback, the sound will not seem natural.

Figure 6-8 shows an LM380 phonograph amplifier circuit with RIAA equalization. A typical parts list for this project appears as Table 6-3. The mid-band gain can be de-

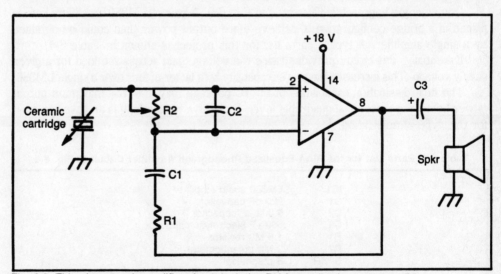

Fig. 6-8. This phonograph amplifier circuit includes RIAA equalization. PROJECT #65

Table 6-2. Parts List for the Ceramic Cartridge Phonograph Amplifier Circuit in Fig. 6-7.

IC1	LM380 audio amplifier
C1	0.05 μF capacitor
C2	500 μF electrolytic capacitor
R1	25 kΩ potentiometer
R2	75 kΩ resistor
R3	10 kΩ potentiometer
SPKR	8 Ω speaker

fined with this formula;

$$G_{mid} = \frac{R1 + 150,000}{150,000}$$

The constant (150,000) represents the internal resistance within the LM380 itself.

The corner frequency is set via capacitor C1, using this formula;

$$F_c = \frac{1}{2\pi C_1 R_1}$$

The component values listed in Table 6-3 will provide correct RIAA equalization, but you may want to experiment with other values in the breadboarded circuit to see how they affect the frequency response of the amplifier.

BRIDGED AMPLIFIER

A 1.25 watt to 3.7 watt output is pretty impressive for a tiny IC chip. But it's still pretty low power for most applications. There are some tricks a circuit designer can use to get more ''oomph'' out of a LM380.

One common approach is illustrated in Fig. 6-9. A pair of LM380 amplifiers can be placed in a bridge configuration to achieve more output power than could be obtained by a single amplifier. A typical parts list for this project is shown in Table 6-4.

Essentially, this circuit provides twice the voltage gain across the load for a given supply voltage. This increases the power capability by a factor of four over a single LM380.

The heat dissipation capabilities of the IC package may limit the maximum output power below the theoretical quadruple level. Extensive heatsinking is an absolute must for this type of application.

Table 6-3. Parts List for the RIAA-Equalized Phonograph Amplifier Circuit in Fig. 6-8.

IC1	LM380 audio amplifier
C1	220 pF capacitor
C2	0.002 μF capacitor
C3	500 μF electrolytic capacitor
R1	1.5 MΩ resistor
R2	2 MΩ potentiometer
SPKR	8 Ω speaker

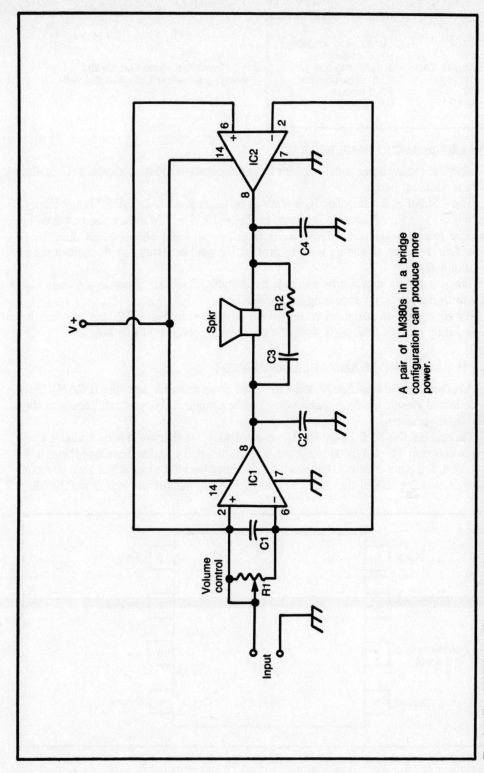

A pair of LM380s in a bridge configuration can produce more power. PROJECT #66

Fig. 6-9. Two LM380 amplifiers can be bridged for greater output power.

IC1, IC2	LM380 audio amplifier	
C1	50 pF capacitor	**Table 6-4. Parts List for the**
C2, C3, C4	0.1 μF capacitor	**Bridged Amplifier Circuit in Fig. 6-9.**
R1	2 MΩ potentiometer	
R2	2.7 Ω resistor	
SPKR	8 Ω speaker	

THE LM386 AUDIO AMPLIFIER IC

There are many other audio amplifier ICs on the market today. We could not possibly examine them all here.

The LM386 audio amplifier IC seems to be edging out the LM380 in popularity. The pinout diagram of this chip is shown in Fig. 6-10. The LM386 can be powered by a source from +4 volts to +12 volts. It can drive an eight-ohm speaker directly. A decoupling capacitor should be used to protect the speaker from any dc component in the output signal.

The gain of this amplifier is internally fixed at 20. The basic circuit is shown in Fig. 6-11, with the parts list appearing as Table 6-5.

By adding a few additional components, as shown in Fig. 6-12, the gain can be increased up to 200. The parts list for this circuit is given in Table 6-6.

THE HA-2400 PROGRAMMABLE AMPLIFIER

A rather unusual amplifier IC is the HA-2400 programmable amplifier (PRAM). This device is also known as a four-channel operational amplifier. (We just can't seem to stay away from op amps.)

Throughout this book I have tried to use only devices that are readily available from various sources. The HA-2400 is a little more exotic, and you may have a problem finding it. Still, it is such an interesting device that I have decided to include it here anyway. If you do manage to find this chip, you will find experimentation with it worthwhile.

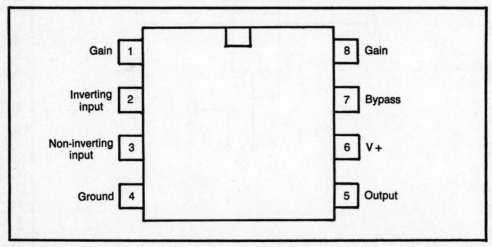

Fig. 6-10. The LM386 is another popular audio amplifier IC.

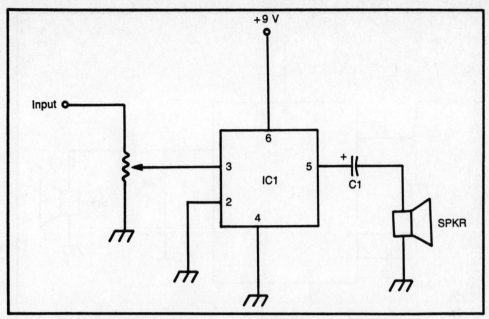

Fig. 6-11. The basic LM386 amplifier circuit has a fixed gain of 20. PROJECT #67

The HA-2400 pinout diagram is shown in Fig. 6-13. Figure 6-14 illustrates the internal circuitry of this IC.

Basically there are four op amp input stages, which are user selectable via a digitally controlled electronic switch. One of the four input stages is used to drive a fifth op amp, which serves as an output stage. Table 6-7 lists the various digital input combinations and their effects. When the enable pin (#14) is HIGH, one of the four input stages will be connected to the output stage. If the enable pin is LOW, all four input stages will be inactive. In a logic diagram "X" means "don't care". The indicated signal may be a 0 or a 1 without affecting the output in any way.

Any standard op amp application (see Chapter 4 for some examples) can be performed with the HA-2400, with the added advantage of programmability.

The output stage is internally wired as a non-inverting unity gain voltage follower. Feedback components can be connected from the chip output (pin #10) back to the appropriate input. The device as a whole will then function like a regular op amp, depending on which input stage is selected.

If the HA-2400 is being used with a gain less than 10, frequency compensation should be used to ensure closed-loop stability. This is done by connecting a small capacitor (2 pF to 15 pF) from pin #12 to ac ground. (The V+ supply is recommended by the manufacturer.)

Table 6-5. Parts List for the Low-gain LM386 Amplifier Circuit in Fig. 6-11.

IC1	LM386 audio amplifier
C1	200 μF electrolytic capacitor
R1	10 kΩ potentiometer (volume control)
SPKR	8 Ω speaker

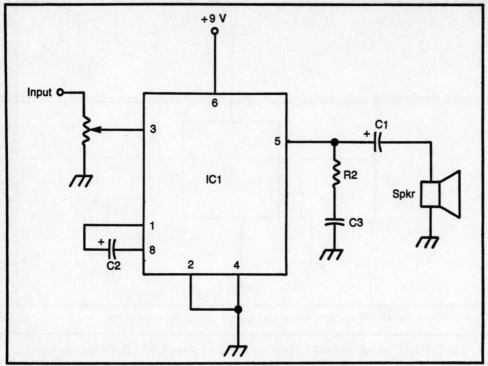

Fig. 6-12. The gain of the LM386 can be increased to 200. PROJECT #68

Each of the four input stages can be wired for different op amp applications, allowing even the function to be digitally selectable.

The circuit designer must bear in mind that the unselected input stages may still constitute a load at the amplifier output and the signal input. The analog input terminals of an OFF channel draw the same bias current as an ON channel. The input signal limitations must be observed, even when the channel is OFF.

When pin #14 (ENABLE) is made LOW (grounded), all four input channels are turned OFF. Under these circumstances, the output voltage (at pin #10) will tend to drift slowly towards the negative supply voltage (V−). This will not be a problem often, but you should be aware of it. If your specific application requires the HA-2400 to hold a zero-volt output when "OFF", wire one of the input channels as a non-inverting voltage follower with the non-inverting input grounded (input of 0 volts). Select this "dummy" channel instead of deactivating the ENABLE input of the chip. Of course this effectively

Table 6-6. Parts List for the High-gain LM386 Amplifier Circuit in Fig. 6-11.

IC1	LM386 audio amplifier
C1	200 μF electrolytic capacitor
C2	10 μF electrolytic capacitor
C3	0.1 μF capacitor
R1	10 kΩ potentiometer (volume control)
R2	12 Ω resistor
SPKR	8 Ω speaker

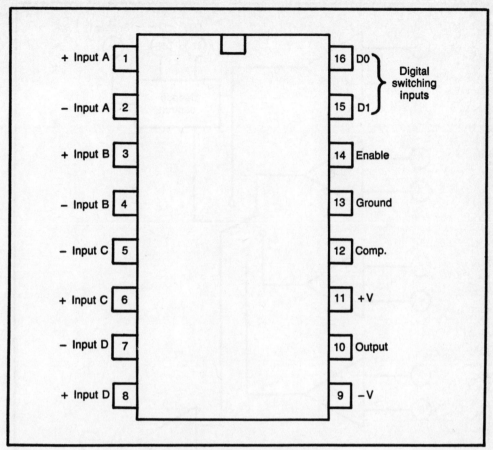

Fig. 6-13. The HA-2400 Programmable Amplifier is a novel device.

reduces the number of programmable channels to three, but if it is what the application requires, then you are stuck with it. Besides, three programmable channels is two more than most other devices offer.

It is usually not possible to wire the outputs of two or more HA-2400s together. This is because the output impedance remains low, even when the inputs are disabled. One trick you can use to get around this problem is to use the compensation pin (#12) as the output. The voltage at this pin will be about 0.7 volt higher than at the nominal output pin (#10), but the output impedance of pin #12 is very high. Consequently, two or more compensation outputs may be wired together if the application calls for it.

The HA-2400 is a very handy and economical device. The programmability obviously offers a tremendous amount of versatility in circuit design. Even in applications where only a single active channel is to be switched on and off, it will often be less expensive to use a HA-2400 than a separate op amp and analog switch.

Digital inputs should never be left floating. Any unused digital inputs must be shorted to ground (for a permanent LOW state), or to +5 volts (for a permanent HIGH state). If they are left floating, they will behave as if held HIGH, but will be unreliable.

The digital inputs are DTL and TTL compatible.

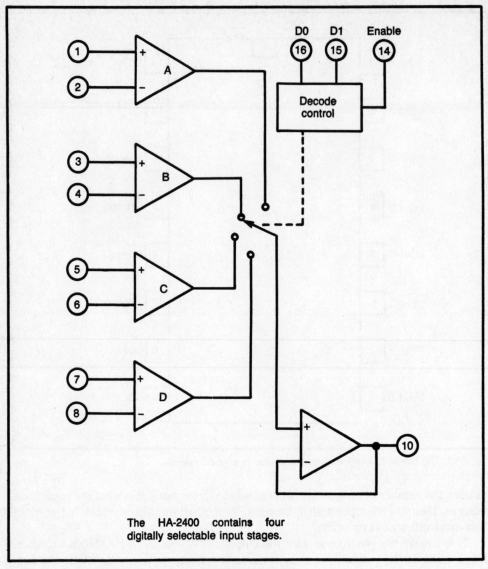

The HA-2400 contains four
digitally selectable input stages.

Fig. 6-14. The HA-2400 features four selectable input stages.

Table 6-7. This Table Summarizes the Operation of the HA-2400 PRAM.

Digital Inputs			Channel			
D0	D1	Enable	A	B	C	D
X	X	0	Off	Off	Off	Off
0	0	1	Off	Off	On	Off
0	1	1	On	Off	Off	Off
1	0	1	Off	Off	Off	On
1	1	1	Off	On	Off	Off

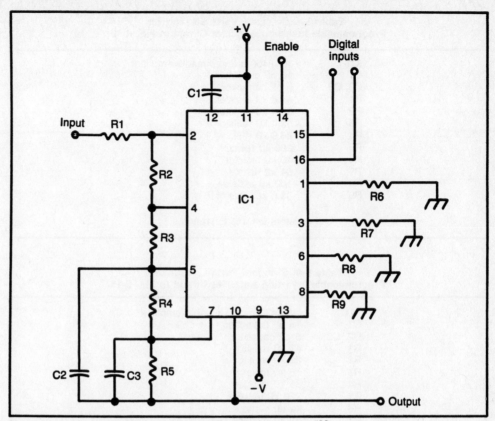

Fig. 6-15. A programmable inverting amplifier circuit. PROJECT #69

Figure 6-15 shows a typical application for the HA-2400 PRAM. This is an inverting amplifier with programmable gain. Two parts lists are given for this project. Table 6-8 lists the exact calculated component values for a high precision application. In Table 6-9 the component values are rounded off to the nearest standard values. The results should be close enough for most applications.

Depending on the states of the digital inputs, the input signal will be given a gain of 0 (disabled). -1, -2, -4, or -8. Remember, the negative sign merely indicates inversion of the signal polarity.

The same thing could also be accomplished with one input resistor and one feedback resistor per channel. But the circuit in Fig. 6-15 offers a lower parts count—only five resistors, instead of eight.

Figure 6-16 shows the HA-2400 PRAM being used as a sine wave oscillator with a programmable output frequency. Experiment with various component values.

The circuit shown in Fig. 6-17 is a multifunction circuit. It can perform various adder/subtractor functions, depending on the states of the digital inputs. The four possible functions that may appear at the output are;

$$-G_1X \quad \text{CHANNEL 1}$$
$$-G_2Y \quad \text{CHANNEL 2}$$

**Table 6-8. Precision Parts List for the
Programmable Inverting Amplifier Circuit in Fig. 6-15.**

IC1	HA-2400 programmable amplifier
C1	15 pF capacitor
C2, C3	5 pF capacitor
R1	44.6 kΩ resistor
R2	35.4 kΩ resistor
R3	53.4 kΩ resistor
R4	66.6 kΩ resistor
R5	200 kΩ resistor
R6	40 kΩ resistor
R7	64 kΩ resistor
R8	100 kΩ resistor
R9	86.6 kΩ resistor

All resistors are 1% tolerance

**Table 6-9. Standard Parts List for the
Programmable Inverting Amplifier Circuit in Fig. 6-15.**

IC1	HA-2400 programmable amplifier
C1	15 pF capacitor
C2, C3	5 pF capacitor
R1	47 kΩ resistor
R2	33 kΩ resistor
R3	56 kΩ resistor
R4	68 kΩ resistor
R5	220 kΩ resistor
R6	42 kΩ resistor
R7	62 kΩ resistor
R8	100 kΩ resistor
R9	82 kΩ resistor

$$-(G_3X + G_4Y) \qquad \text{CHANNEL 3}$$
$$-(G_5X - G_6Y) \qquad \text{CHANNEL 4}$$

where G_i stands for the appropriate gain, which will, of course, be dependent on the resistance values used in the active channel. The minus sign again indicates that the signal is inverted at the output.

These are just a few of the many, many applications for this fascinating IC. Experiment. Go back and reread Chapter 4. Surely you'll get some ideas of potential applications for the HA-2400 programmable amplifier IC.

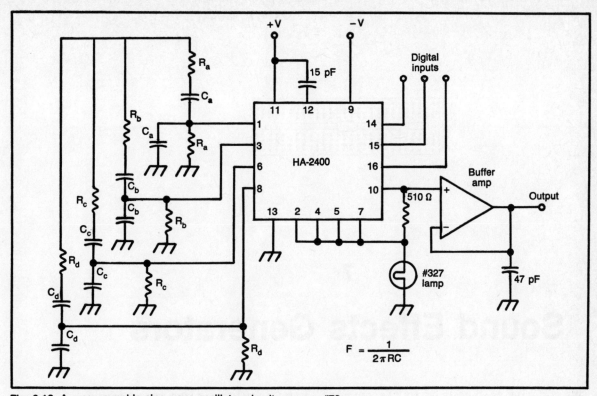

Fig. 6-16. A programmable sine wave oscillator circuit. PROJECT #70

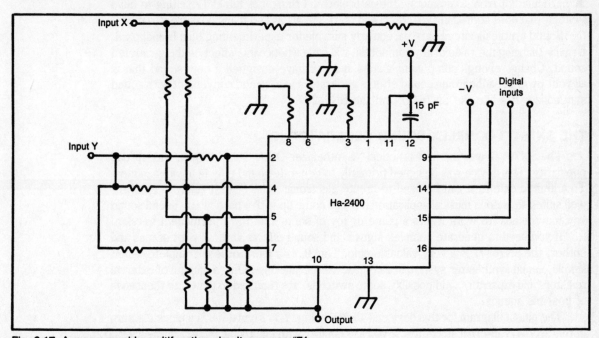

Fig. 6-17. A programmable multifunction circuit. PROJECT #71

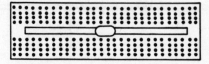

7

Sound Effects Generators

IF YOU HAVE READ SOME OF MY EARLIER BOOKS, YOU MAY HAVE REALIZED THAT I AM particularly partial to sound synthesis projects. I think it is fun and exciting to build a circuit that does something so direct, and there are always so many possible variations.

Sound synthesis circuits are particularly suitable for experimenting on a breadboard. Usually changing the value of any component will have a noticeable effect on the generated sound. Change enough component values and you have designed a new sound that is all your own. Breadboarding sound effects generators is easy and convenient with sound synthesizer ICs like the SN76477 and the SN94281.

THE SN76477 COMPLEX SOUND GENERATOR IC

The SN76477 was the first practical "Synthesizer-On-A-Chip" to gain widespread popularity. This device was designed primarily to generate sound effects in video games. To a limited extent, it can be used to create electronic music, but it really is not very well suited to serious musical applications. If you come up with a particularly useful sound you may be able to work it into a game or toy of some kind for a permanent version.

If you need to generate complex signals and sound effects without a lot of fuss and bother, the SN76477 is a very valuable chip. This IC is a more or less complete, albeit simple, sound synthesizer system in a compact 28-pin package. Only a handful of external resistors and capacitors, and possibly some switches, are required to generate thousands of possible sounds.

The pinout diagram for this device is shown in Fig. 7-1. Figure 7-2 is a block diagram of the SN76477 internal structure. If you are familiar with electronic music synthesizers,

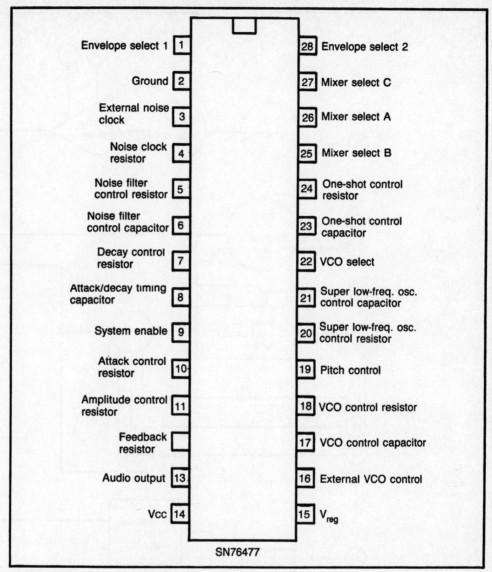

Envelope select 1 — 1	28 — Envelope select 2
Ground — 2	27 — Mixer select C
External noise clock — 3	26 — Mixer select A
Noise clock resistor — 4	25 — Mixer select B
Noise filter control resistor — 5	24 — One-shot control resistor
Noise filter control capacitor — 6	23 — One-shot control capacitor
Decay control resistor — 7	22 — VCO select
Attack/decay timing capacitor — 8	21 — Super low-freq. osc. control capacitor
System enable — 9	20 — Super low-freq. osc. control resistor
Attack control resistor — 10	19 — Pitch control
Amplitude control resistor — 11	18 — VCO control resistor
Feedback resistor —	17 — VCO control capacitor
Audio output — 13	16 — External VCO control
Vcc — 14	15 — V_{reg}

SN76477

Fig. 7-1. The SN76477 Complex Sound Generator IC is a fascinating device for breadboard experiments.

you should recognize most of the functions as standard synthesizer modules. In case you are not familiar with the terminology, a VCO is a Voltage-Controlled Oscillator. The output frequency is controlled by an input voltage. SLF refers to the Super Low Frequency Oscillator. The purpose and operation of the various sections will be explained in the next few pages.

Pin Functions

Because most of the pin functions on this IC are likely to be unfamiliar to most readers, we will examine the SN76477 pin by pin.

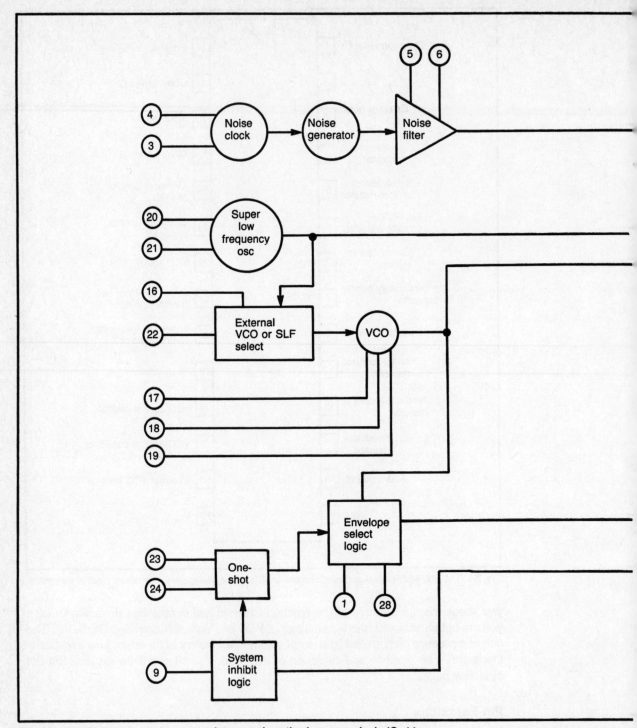

Fig. 7-2. The SN76477 contains a complete sound synthesizer on a single IC chip.

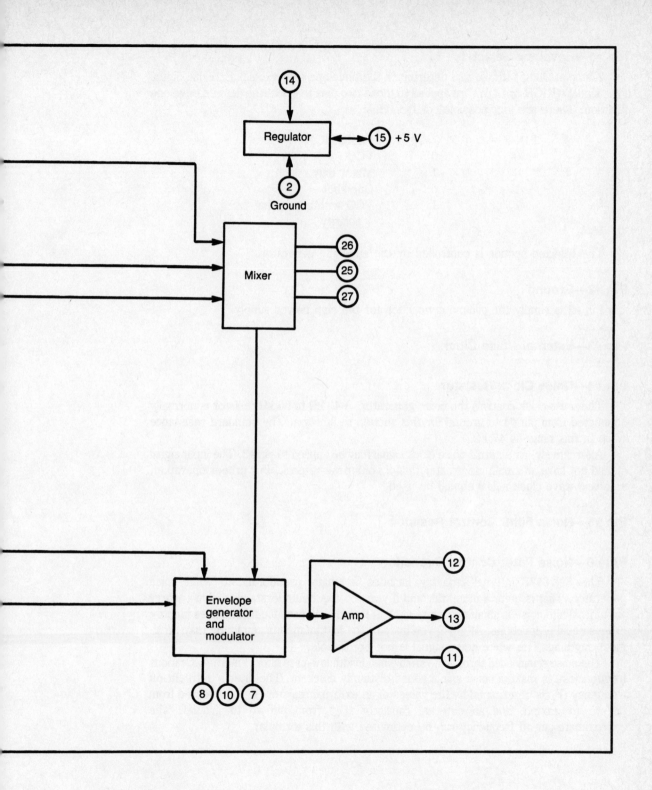

Pin #1—Envelope Select 1

This pin, along with pin #28 determines the envelope select logic. External digital logic signals (HIGH or LOW) are applied to these two pins to select the desired envelope function. There are four possible combinations;

PIN #1	PIN #28	FUNCTION
0	0	VCO
0	1	Mixer only
1	0	One-shot
1	1	VCO with alternating polarity

The selected section is controlled by the envelope generator.

Pin #2—Ground

Pin #2 is simply the ground connection for the chip power supply.

Pin #3—External Noise Clock

Pin #4—Noise Clock Resistor

The noise clock controls the noise generator. A 43 kΩ to 50 kΩ resistor is normally connected from pin #4 to ground for this section to function. The standard resistance value in this range is 47 kΩ.

Alternatively, an external noise clock signal may be applied to pin #3. The input signal should not have an amplitude greater than 5 volts peak-to-peak. For proper operation, a square wave clock signal should be used.

Pin #5—Noise Filter Control Resistor

Pin #6—Noise Filter Control Capacitor

The SN76477 internal circuitry includes a binary pseudorandom white-noise generator. That is quite a mouthful, and if you don't quite understand it, don't worry about it. White noise is similar to white light. It includes all possible frequencies in more or less equal proportions. At any given instant, the instantaneous amplitude may be almost anything. The white noise signal is not predictable.

The noise signal is fed through a variable bandwidth low-pass filter. Filtering at various frequencies can make a noise signal sound distinctly different. The filter's 3 dB cut-off frequency (F_c) is determined by the values of an external resistor (R_{nf}) connected from pin #5 to ground, and an external capacitor (C_{nf}) from pin #6 to ground. The approximate cut-off frequency can be estimated with this formula;

$$F_c = 1.28/(R_{nf}C_{nf})$$

Pin #7—Decay Control Resistor

Pin #8—Attack/Decay Timing Resistor

Pin #10—Attack Control Resistor

Pins #7, 8, and 10 are used to set the timing values for the envelope generator. Envelopes are not difficult to understand. Most real world sounds don't just switch on, instantly jumping from zero to the maximum amplitude, and then switch instantly back off to zero again. Rather, they generally take some finite time to build up to the maximum level (attack), and then again, to drop back down to zero (decay). If we graphed the instantaneous amplitude of a single sound, we would have a picture of its envelope. Several simple envelopes are illustrated in Fig. 7-3.

The envelope generator allows control of how the amplitude changes with time. A common timing capacitor (C_{ad}) is used for both the attack and decay times. It is connected between pin #8 and ground. A resistor (R_a) from pin #10 to ground also influences the attack time. The attack time in seconds is about equal to;

$$T_a = R_a C_{ad}$$

Similarly, the decay time is determined by C_{ad} (pin #8) and a second resistor (R_d) which is placed between pin #7 and ground;

$$T_d = R_d C_{ad}$$

Pin #9—System Enable

Pin #9 is used to inhibit or enable the chip's operation. A logic 0 (LOW) enables the system, while a logic 1 (HIGH) disables it. The inhibit/enable pin can be used to hold the output in a no-sound condition. It can also be used to trigger the on-board one-shot. The one-shot is triggered by a negative-going pulse. Pin #1 must be held LOW

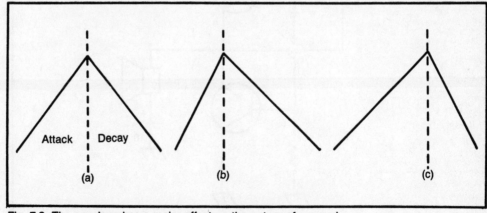

Fig. 7-3. The envelope has a major effect on the nature of a sound.

for the entire duration of the sound. The one-shot will function only when the proper envelope select logic inputs are present at pins 1 and 28. "One-shot" is just another name for a monostable multivibrator.

Pin #11—Amplitude Control Resistor

A resistor connected from pin #11 to ground sets the overall amplitude of the output signal, by setting the operating currents for the internal circuitry of the op amp type output stage. Typically, the amplitude resistor will have a value in the 47 kΩ to 220 kΩ range. Lower resistances should be avoided, because the op amp will tend to become saturated. This is especially noticeable during the decay portion of the sound envelope.

Pin #12—Feedback Resistor

Pin #13—Audio Output

Pins #12 and 13 are used as part of an external output amplifier. The SN76477 is not designed to drive a speaker directly, so an external amplifier is required.

A simple amplifier circuit that is often used with the SN76477 is shown in Fig. 7-4. This amplifier will drive a small 8-ohm speaker with about 300 to 400 mW (0.3 to 0.4 watt). This is more than sufficient for experimentation and many practical applications.

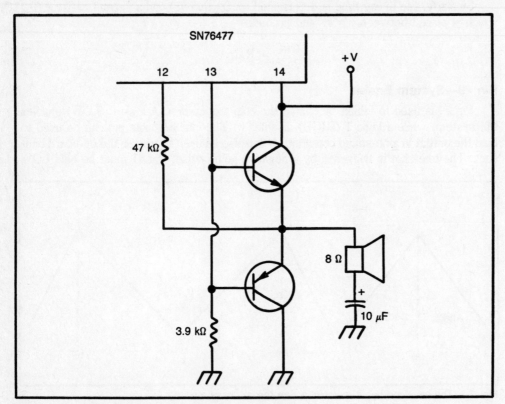

Fig. 7-4. The SN76477 requires an external output amplifier.

Pin #13 is the actual output point for the chip. A feedback resistor is connected to pin #12. The output circuitry at pin #13 is in an emitter-follower configuration. There is no internal load resistor, so an external pull-down resistor must be connected from pin #13 to ground, as shown in the diagram. The value should be between 2.7 kΩ and 10 kΩ. A 3.9 kΩ resistor is indicated in Fig. 7-4.

The feedback resistor, which is connected to pin #12, compensates for external inaccuracies and any chip-to-chip variations. In a sense, this resistor allows you to "fine-tune" the chip's operation. The peak output voltage can be approximated with this formula;

$$V_o = 3.4 \ R_f/R_{amp}$$

where R_f is the feedback resistor connected to pin #12, and R_{amp} is the amplitude resistor at pin #11.

The dynamic output of the SN76477 is internally limited to 2.5 volts peak-to-peak. If you try to achieve a larger output voltage, severe clipping distortion will result. Of course, that might provide the sound you are looking for. That is one of the fun things about sound synthesis circuits. Doing something wrong occasionally turns out right. If you intentionally try to distort the output, be careful not to overload the chip which could cause damage.

Pin #14—V_{cc}

The supply voltage is normally, but not always, applied to pin #14. (See also the description of pin #15, below). The supply voltage at pin #14 can be anything from +7.5 volts to +12 volts, although +9 volts is the recommended maximum.

Pin #15—V_{reg}

The functioning of pin #15 is rather unusual. It can be used in two *very* different ways. Pin #15 can be used either as a regulated voltage output *or* a regulated voltage input.

The SN76477 contains an internal +5.0 volt regulator. This regulated voltage is available at pin #15 when the chip is powered from pin #14. The regulated +5.0 volts may be used as a fixed control voltage source or a logic HIGH signal for the chip's other inputs. The internal regulator can supply up to 10 mA (0.01 amp) of current.

Alternatively, an external +5.0 volt regulated power supply can be used to drive the chip. The external regulated voltage is fed to pin #15, and the regular supply voltage pin (#14) is left unused.

Pin #16—External VCO Control

An external control voltage may be applied to pin #16 to control the pitch (frequency) of the VCO.

Pin #17—VCO Control Capacitor

Pin #18—VCO Control Resistor

The nominal frequency of the VCO is set by a resistance from pin #18 to ground and a capacitance from pin #17 to ground. The nominal frequency is the minimum frequency produced when the control voltage (whether from an internal or an external source) is zero.

The formula for approximating the nominal output frequency of the SN76477's VCO is;

$$F_n = 0.64/R_{vco}C_{vco}$$

The frequency range for the VCO is about 10:1.

Pin #19—Pitch Control

Pin #19 is labelled the pitch control for the VCO. This probably isn't the best name in the world, but it is the one provided by the designers of the SN76477.

More specifically, pin #19 is used to determine the duty cycle, which indirectly affects the frequency. Since we're talking about duty cycles, the output of the VCO is in the form of a rectangle wave.

The duty cycle is determined by this formula;

$$DC = 50 \times V_{16}/V_{19}$$

where V_{16} is the voltage at pin #16 and V_{19} is the voltage at pin #19. The formula gives the duty cycle in percent. A constant 50 percent duty cycle (square wave) can be achieved by holding pin #19 HIGH (5 volts).

Pin #20—Super Low-Frequency Oscillator Control Resistor

Pin #21—Super Low-Frequency Oscillator Control Capacitor

The VCO discussed above is the main tone source in the SN76477. This chip also contains a second oscillator, which is designed primarily for low frequencies. This is called the Super Low-Frequency Oscillator, or SLF. It is designed specifically for output frequencies from 0.1 Hz to 30 Hz, but it can be forced into operation at frequencies up to 20 kHz. Combining this with the main VCO allows a number of sophisticated FM (frequency modulation) effects.

The frequency of the SLF is determined by an external resistance from pin #20 to ground (R_{lf}) and an external capacitance from pin #21 to ground. The approximate SLF frequency can be found with this formula;

$$F_{lf} = 0.64/R_1C_{lf}$$

The Super Low-Frequency Oscillator produces two separate waveforms. A square wave is fed to the mixer. The second SLF signal is a triangle wave, which is fed to the VCO when pin #22 is HIGH.

Pin #22—VCO Select

Pin #22 is used to select the control voltage source for the VCO. If this pin is held LOW, an external control voltage, applied to pin #16, drives the VCO. Alternatively, holding pin #22 HIGH allows the SLF to control the VCO.

164

Pin #23—One-Shot Control Capacitor

Pin #24—One-Shot Control Resistor

Pins #23 and 24 are used to set the timing period of an internal one-shot stage, or monostable multivibrator. The timing capacitor (C_{os}) is placed between pin #23 and ground. The timing resistor (R_{os}) is connected between pin #24 and ground. The timing period for the one-shot (in seconds) is approximately equal to;

$$T = 0.8\, R_{os} C_{os}$$

The one-shot is used for non-continuous sounds. A typical example might be a gunshot.

Pin #25—Mixer Select B

Pin #26—Mixer Select A

Pin #27—Mixer Select C

Pins #25, 26, and 27 are logic inputs that control the external mixer stage. The states of these control pins determine which of the several internal signals within the SN76477 will appear at the output.

The mixer select pins are not in sequence. Pin #26 is mixer control A, pin #25 is mixer control B, and pin #27 is mixer control C.

There are eight possible combinations of digital inputs for these three control pins. Each combination results in a different output, or combination of outputs;

CONTROL PIN A B C	OUTPUT(S)
0 0 0	VCO
0 0 1	SLF
0 1 0	Noise
0 1 1	VCO & Noise
1 0 0	SLF & Noise
1 0 1	VCO, SLF & Noise
1 1 0	VCO & SLF
1 1 1	Inhibit (no output)

As you can see, the SN76477 is designed to create a wide variety of different sounds.

Pin #28—Envelope Select 2

Pin #28 is used in conjunction with pin #1, and was explained in the discussion of that pin.

While the SN76477 has a lot of pins with fairly uncommon functions, it is extremely easy to use. For your convenience, I will summarize the way the pins are used here.

The following pins are used by connecting a resistor from the pin to ground;

    4 Noise Clock
    5 Noise Filter Control
    7 Decay Control
   10 Attack Control
   11 Amplitude Control
   18 VCO Control
   20 SLF Control
   24 One-shot Control

The following pins are used by connecting a capacitor from the pin to ground;

    6 Noise Filter Control
    8 Attack/Decay Timing
   17 VCO Control
   21 SLF Control
   23 One-shot Control

Notice that the passive components controlling the various parameters of the sound are all connected from the appropriate pin to ground.

The following pins are digital inputs accepting a logic LOW (0 volt) or logic HIGH (5 volts) signal to determine the operation of a specific internal function;

    1 Envelope Select 1
    9 System Enable
   22 VCO Select
   25 Mixer Select B
   26 Mixer Select A
   27 Mixer Select C
   28 Envelope Select 2

The following pins accept an external control voltage or clock signal;

    3 External Noise Clock
   16 External VCO Control
   19 Pitch Control

That leaves just a handful of uncategorized pins (#2, 12, 13, 14, and 15). The uses of these pins were described in the pin-by-pin descriptions.

You now have enough information to start experimenting with the SN76477 Complex Sound Generator IC. If you follow the rules discussed here, almost any circuit you set up will work, although some combinations will not produce any sound. If that happens, don't worry about it; just try something else. I will present a few specific circuits to get you started; however, we should consider a few limitations of this chip.

Limits

For the best results, each of the various programming resistors and capacitors should be kept within certain ranges. Each of the components should have values within the limits given in Table 7-1.

The SN76477 complex sound generator IC is a great device for the experimenter, because there are so many things you can do with it. Feel free to try out any idea that might occur to you. This device is pretty hard to damage, as long as you do not exceed any of the input voltage limitations. Do not apply more than six volts to any of the input pins, except the power supply pin #14.

If you do something "wrong", usually the worst that will happen is that you will get a terribly obnoxious sound, or perhaps no sound at all. If that happens, just try something else. You will never build all of the possible circuits for the SN76477.

Always remember that the SN76477 cannot do everything, and it was never intended to. It generally falls short of the requirements for serious electronic music applications, but it can provide many versatile sound sources.

SN76477 CIRCUITS

There is not much to be said about any of the following circuits, except that they are intended primarily as suggestions. By all means, experiment with other component values. It is so easy with a solderless breadboard. You just might come up with a new

**Table 7-1. Limiting Values of External
Resistors and Capacitors with the SN76477 IC.**

RESISTORS	
PIN #	ACCEPTABLE RANGE
4	40 kΩ - 50 kΩ
5	7.5 kΩ - 1 MΩ
7	7.5 kΩ - 1 MΩ
10	7.5 kΩ - 1 MΩ
18	7.5 kΩ - 1 MΩ
20	7.5 kΩ - 1 MΩ
24	7.5 kΩ - 1 MΩ
CAPACITORS	
6	150 pF - 0.01 μF
8	0.01 μF - 10 μF
17	100 pF - 1 μF
21	500 pF - 100 μF
23	0.1 μF - 50 μF

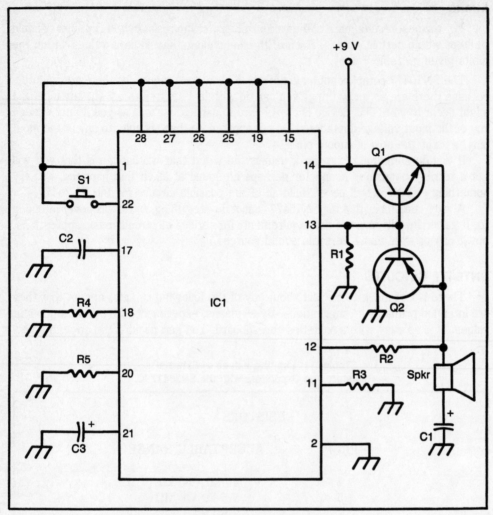

Fig. 7-5. This circuit produces a space "phaser" sound. PROJECT #72

application. I've said it throughout this book, but it's a particularly good idea here—experiment, experiment, experiment!

Figure 7-5 shows a circuit for producing a "space-phaser" sound, or perhaps the sound of a laser gun. A typical parts list is given in Table 7-2. Remember that using different component values will give you drastically different sounds that may sound nothing at all like a "space phaser".

The circuit shown in Fig. 7-6 produces a sound that resembles a steam engine train, if the component values listed in Table 7-3 are used.

An explosion effect is generated by the circuit shown in Fig. 7-7. A typical parts list for this circuit is given in Table 7-4. You can use this same circuit to simulate a gunshot, by reducing the value of R5 to less than 100 k. Don't reduce this resistor below about 60 k or so, or you'll end up with a pretty wimpy sounding gun. Standard resistance values in the suitable range are 68 k, 82 k, and 91 k.

Table 7-2. Parts List for the "Space Phaser" Circuit in Fig. 7-5.

IC1	SN76477 complex sound generator IC
Q1	npn transistor (2N3904, or similar)
Q2	pnp transistor (2N3906, or similar)
R1	3.9 kΩ resistor
R2	47 kΩ resistor
R3	120 kΩ resistor
R4	39 kΩ resistor
R5	180 kΩ resistor
C1	10 μF electrolytic capacitor
C2	0.02 μF capacitor
C3	1 μF capacitor
S1	Normally Open SPST push switch
SPKR	small 8 Ω speaker

Figure 7-8 shows a circuit that produces two related sound effects. When the switch is open, you will hear a sound like a speeding car. Adjust the values of R4 and R5 to change the apparent speed. When switch S1 is closed, you will hear the car crash. A typical parts list for this project appears as Table 7-5. In all of these projects, you should experiment with the component values to improve the desired effect, or to get an entirely different sound.

Before leaving the SN76477 I want to give you a few tips on less obvious tricks for getting the most out of this powerful chip. The noise source is a pseudo-random digital circuit. The clock rate will influence the nature of the sound in some fairly subtle, but definite ways. Ordinarily, the clock frequency is set by a simple fixed resistor connected between pin #4 and ground. But you can get fancier, if you like. For example, try connecting a transistor to pin #4, as illustrated in Fig. 7-9. This arrangement allows for dynamic control of the noise clock frequency via the signal applied to the base of the transistor.

In the diagram, the base is connected through a large value resistor to pin #8, which is the connection point for the envelope timing capacitor. The voltage at this point varies as the capacitor charges and discharges. The sound quality of the noise will vary along with the envelope, producing some fascinating "swooshing" effects.

This same trick of substituting a transistor for a resistor can be used for any of the programming resistors. Remember, a transistor is basically a voltage variable resistance element. The very name comes from *trans*fer res*istor*. In some cases, using a transistor in place of an ordinary programming resistor will produce some very novel and exciting sounds. In other cases, it won't be particularly effective. I will let you determine which pin functions can be helped by this technique through your own experimentation. After all, this is a very subjective decision. An effect that I find useless just may be precisely what you are looking for.

The SN76477 VCO is intended to only produce rectangle waves, but you can trick it into generating triangle waves. A partial circuit for accomplishing this is shown in Fig. 7-10. There is at least one major limitation to this approach. The signal amplitude is sensitive to changes in the control voltage applied to pin #16. In other words, the volume changes with frequency. This problem does not seem to occur with the regular square wave output, or when the internal voltage control (SLF) is used.

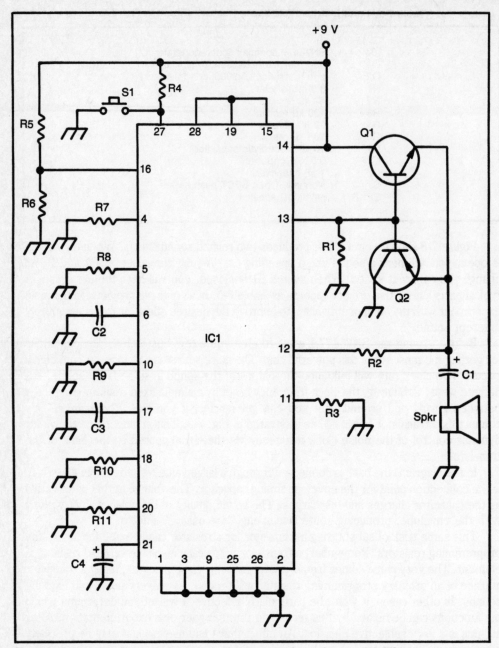

Fig. 7-6. This circuit simulates the sound of a steam engine train. PROJECT #73

THE SN94281 COMPLEX SOUND GENERATOR

Another popular complex sound generator IC is the SN94281. At the time of this writing, this chip is available from Radio Shack, and a number of other sources.

The SN94281 is a more recently developed device than the SN76477. It is even easier to use than its predecessor. Despite the fact that the SN94281 has only 16 pins,

Table 7-3. Parts List for the Steam Engine Circuit in Fig. 7-6.

IC1	SN6477 Complex Sound Generator IC
Q1	npn transistor (2N3904, or similar)
Q2	pnp transistor (2N3906, or similar)
R1	3.9 kΩ resistor
R2, R8, R10	47 kΩ resistor
R3	120 kΩ resistor
R4	4.7 kΩ resistor
R5	68 kΩ resistor
R6	27 kΩ resistor
R7	39 kΩ resistor
R9	100 kΩ resistor
R11	470 kΩ resistor
C1	10 μF electrolytic capacitor
C2	500 pF capacitor
C3	0.005 μF capacitor
C4	2.2 μF electrolytic capacitor
S1	Normally Open SPST push switch
SPKR	small 8 Ω speaker

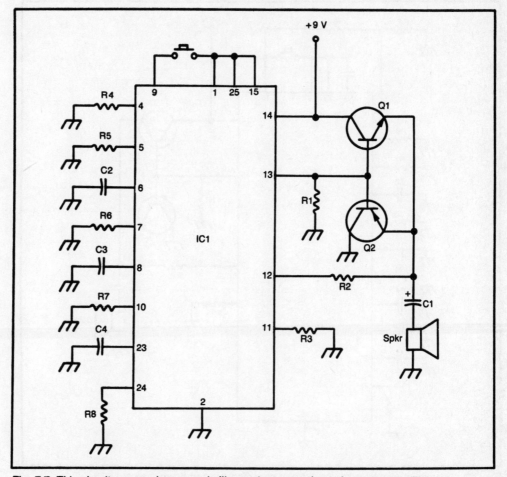

Fig. 7-7. This circuit can produce sounds like explosions and gunshots. PROJECT #74

Table 7-4. Parts List for the Explosion Effect Circuit in Fig. 7-7.

IC1	SN76477 complex sound effect generator
Q1	npn transistor (2N3904, or similar)
Q2	pnp transistor (2N3906, or similar)
R1	3.9 kΩ resistor
R2	47 kΩ resistor
R3	120 kΩ resistor
R4	47 kΩ resistor
R5	390 kΩ resistor (see text)
R6	680 kΩ resistor
R7	3.3 kΩ resistor
R8	330 kΩ resistor
C1	10 μF electrolytic capacitor
C2	400 pF capacitor
C3	0.68 μF capacitor
C4	0.01 μF capacitor
S1	Normally Open SPST push switch
SPKR	small 8 Ω speaker

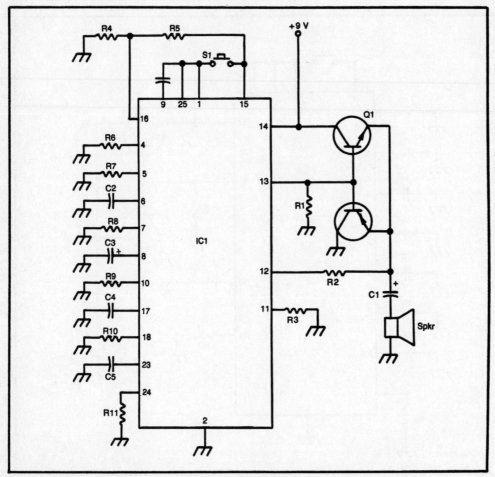

Fig. 7-8. This circuit simulates the sound of a speeding car and crash. PROJECT #75

172

Table 7-3. Parts List for the Steam Engine Circuit in Fig. 7-6.

IC1	SN76477 complex sound effect generator IC
Q1	npn transistor (2N3904, or similar)
Q2	pnp transistor (2N3906, or similar)
R1	3.9 kΩ resistor
R2, R4, R8	47 kΩ resistor
R3	120 kΩ resistor
R5, R6	68 kΩ resistor
R7	330 kΩ resistor
R9	4.7 kΩ resistor
R10	39 kΩ resistor
R11	220 kΩ resistor
C1, C3	10 μF electrolytic capacitor
C2	400 pF capacitor
C4	0.5 μF capacitor
C5	0.1 μF capacitor
S1	Normally Open SPST switch
SPKR	small 8 Ω speaker

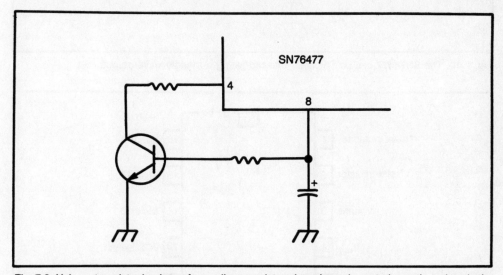

Fig. 7-9. Using a transistor in place of an ordinary resistor gives dynamic control over the noise clock.

as compared to the 28 pins of the SN76477, it is every bit as versatile, if not more so.

The pinout diagram of the SN94281 is shown in Fig. 7-11. This chip's internal circuitry includes both analog and digital circuitry. It can be used with just a few external resistors, capacitors, and switches. Alternatively, the SN94281 can be interfaced directly to a microcomputer for true programmability.

A built-in 125 mW (0.125 watt) amplifier is included on the chip itself. It can drive a small speaker directly, or it can be used as an input to a more powerful amplifier.

Figure 7-12 shows a typical sound effect circuit built around the SN94281. Using the component values listed in Table 7-6, the effect will resemble a steam locomotive. You might want to compare this circuit with the similar SN76477 circuit shown back in

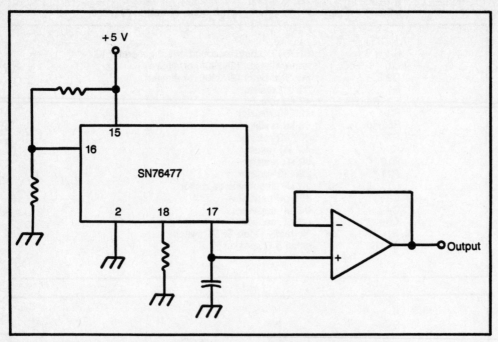

Fig. 7-10. The SN76477 can be "tricked" into producing a triangle wave output.

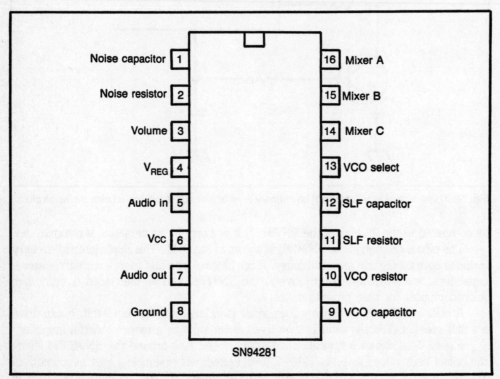

Fig. 7-11. The SN94821 is another complex sound generator IC.

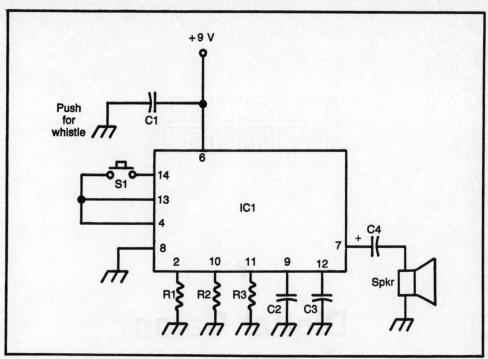

Fig. 7-12. An SN94281 simulates the sound of a train. PROJECT #76

Table 7-6. Parts List for the SN94281 Train Effect Circuit in Fig. 7-12.

IC1	SN94281 complex sound generator
C1	10 µF electrolytic capacitor
C2	0.001 µF capacitor
C3	0.1 µF capacitor
C4	50 µF electrolytic capacitor
R1	820 kΩ resistor
R2	470 kΩ resistor
R3	1 MΩ resistor
S1	Normally Open SPST push switch

Fig. 7-6. This circuit includes an extra feature. Momentarily closing the switch will cause a whistle to be sounded. Different component values and configurations can produce a wide variety of additional sounds and effects. This chip usually comes with an extensive specification sheet that explains the various pin functions.

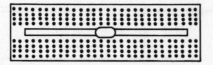

8

Digital Gates

IT IS UNFORTUNATE, BUT MANY PEOPLE INVOLVED WITH ELECTRONICS, EITHER PROFESsionally or as a hobby are still intimidated by digital electronics. Digital circuits are making more and more inroads into applications that were formally strictly in the analog domain. If you are going to work with electronics today in any capacity, you might as well resign yourself to the fact that sooner or later you are going to have to learn about digital electronics.

Actually, despite the widespread fear, and the complexity of full digital systems, such as computers, digital electronics is really pretty simple on the basic level. All signals may take on only one of just two unambiguous states—LOW (or 0) and HIGH (or 1). All the most sophisticated computer in the world can do is distinguish a 0 from a 1. It can do this many, many times a second, and many series of 1s and 0s can be encoded in a variety of ways, which can get quite complicated. Fundamentally any digital circuit is just doing something very simple over and over again. The complexity comes in the repetition and patterns of just a few basic functions.

This chapter will include a number of simple digital circuits ranging from educational demonstration circuits to practical applications. Somewhat more sophisticated digital functions will be covered in the next chapter.

THE BASIC GATES

The basic digital circuit is the gate. Any digital circuit can ultimately be reduced to gates. Complex systems may include hundreds, thousands, or even millions of gates. Sophisticated digital ICs include multiple gates in their internal circuitry. This is more practical than using physically separate gates, of course. Early computers were immense room-filling monsters because discrete components had to be used. The digital revolution could not have occurred without the introduction of the integrated circuit.

A gate is simply a circuit that accepts one or more digital inputs and produces one or more digital outputs. The output state(s) depends on the input signal(s) according to a specific and unambiguous set of rules.

There are several common gate types, each widely available in IC form.

The simplest possible gate is the buffer, shown in Fig. 8-1. It has one input and one output. The output state is always the same as the input state. This might sound pretty silly and useless, but remember the unity gain voltage follower, which is used in many linear circuits. The digital buffer serves a similar function. It essentially prevents a stage from loading down a preceding stage in a large system.

Figure 8-1 also includes the *truth table* for this device. The truth table is simply a convenient method for notating the output conditions for all possible input combinations.

Another one input/one output gate is the inverter, illustrated in Fig. 8-2. This is rather like an inverting voltage follower (see Chapter 4). The output is always the opposite of the input. If the input is a 0, the output is a 1, and vice versa.

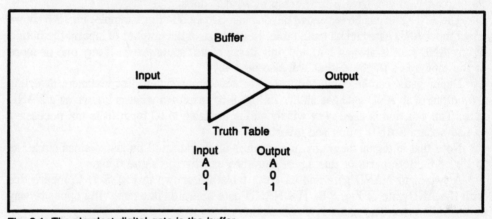

Fig. 8-1. The simplest digital gate is the buffer.

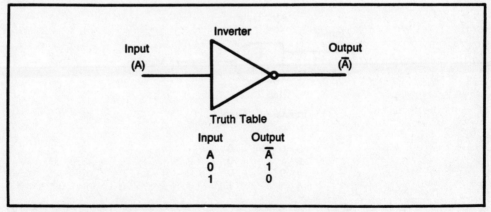

Fig. 8-2. The output of an inverter is always the opposite of the input.

Things get more interesting when we add a second input. With two digital inputs, there are four possible combinations;

$$0\ 0$$
$$0\ 1$$
$$1\ 0$$
$$1\ 1$$

There are no other possibilities.

The truth table for a two input/single output device must have four entries.

There are several possible output patterns for a two input gate. Certain patterns are so useful they have been assigned special names and are standard digital devices.

The two input AND gate is shown in Fig. 8-3, along with its truth table. The name gives a clue to its operation. The output is a 1 if, *and only if*, both input A and input B are 1s. If either (or both) of the inputs is a 0, the output will be a 0.

An AND gate demonstration circuit for you to breadboard is shown in Fig. 8-4. The parts list is given in Table 8-1. Try all possible input combinations. Play around with this circuit until you have a firm grasp of what it does.

The AND gate can be expanded beyond just two inputs. For example, Fig. 8-5 shows a four input AND gate and its truth table. Regardless of the number of inputs, the output of any AND gate is always 1 if, and only if, *all* of its inputs are 1. If any one or more of the inputs is a 0, the output will also be a 0.

Digital gates can be combined to create new gating types. For instance, inverting the output of an AND gate, as shown in Fig. 8-6, results in what is known as a NAND gate. This function is used very widely and is available in IC form. It is not necessary to use separate AND gates and inverters.

Note that in digital diagrams, inversion is often indicated by just a small circle, as in Fig. 8-6. Both parts of this figure illustrate exactly the same thing.

A two-input NAND gate and its truth table are shown in Fig. 8-7. Compare this with the AND gate of Fig. 8-3. The NAND gate operates in exactly the opposite way as an AND gate. The name is a contraction of "Not AND".

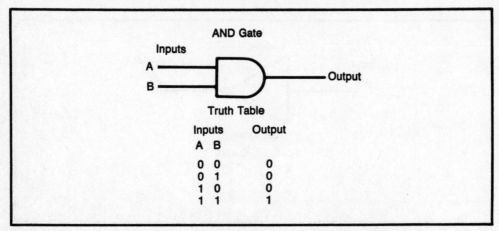

Fig. 8-3. The output of an AND gate is a 1 if, and only if, both inputs are 1s.

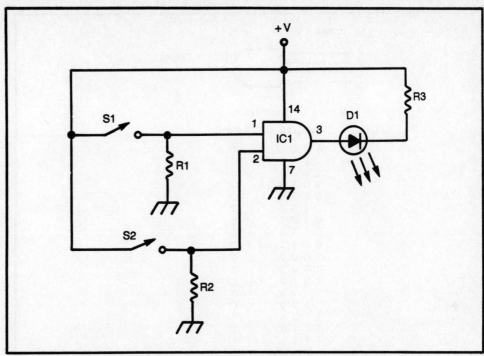

Fig. 8-4. This circuit demonstrates the operation of an AND gate. PROJECT #77

The output of a NAND gate is a 1 *unless* all inputs are 1s. As long as at least one input is a 0, the output will be a 1.

Figure 8-8 shows a NAND gate demonstration circuit. The parts list is given in Table 8-2.

Incidentally, if you invert an inverted signal, you will end up with the original, uninverted signal. Following a NAND gate with an inverter, as shown in Fig. 8-9, is the same as a simple AND gate.

The other basic multi-input digital gate is the OR gate. This device, and its truth table, are illustrated in Fig. 8-10. The output is 1 if input A OR input B is 1. The output is a 0, only if all inputs are 0s.

Like the AND gate, the OR gate can be expanded for any number of inputs. A three-input OR gate is shown in Fig. 8-11.

A demonstration circuit for the OR gate is shown in Fig. 8-12, with the parts list in Table 8-3.

Inverting the output of an OR gate, as illustrated in Fig. 8-13, produces a NOR (Not OR) gate. Like the NAND gate, the NOR gate is also a standard digital device, available

Table 8-1. Parts List for the AND Gate Circuit in Fig. 8-4.

IC1	CD4081 quad AND gate
D1	LED
R1, R2	1 MΩ resistor
R3	470 Ω resistor
S1, S2	SPST switch

179

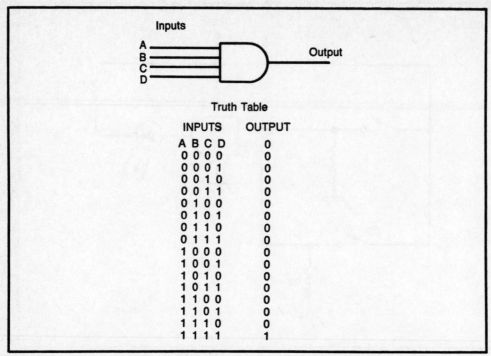

Fig. 8-5. An AND gate can be expanded to include any number of inputs.

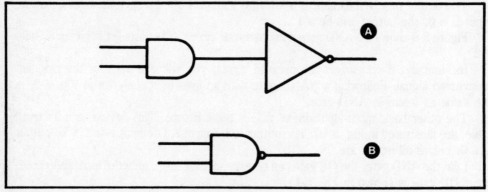

Fig. 8-6. Inverting the output of an AND gate produces a NAND gate.

in IC form. It is shown, along with its truth table in Fig. 8-14. The output is a 1 if, and only if, neither input A NOR input B is a 1. If any input is a 1, the output will be a 0. See Fig. 8-15 and Table 8-4.

There is also an important variant of the basic OR gate. This is the exclusive-OR, or X-OR gate, shown in Fig. 8-16. This gate is sometimes called an unequality detector. The output is a 1 if input A is a 1, OR input B is a 1, *but not both*. If both inputs are 0s, or if both inputs are 1s, the output will be a 0. Another way of looking at it is, if the inputs have unequal values, the output will go HIGH. If the same signal is applied to both inputs, the output will be LOW.

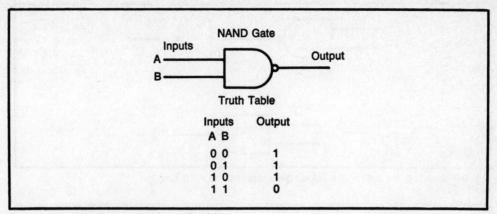

Fig. 8-7. The NAND gate and its truth table.

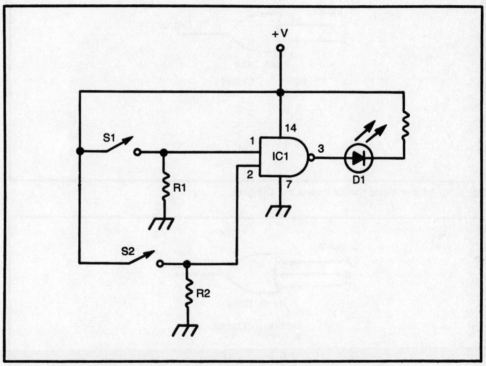

Fig. 8-8. This circuit demonstrates the operation of a NAND gate. PROJECT #78

Table 8-2. Parts List for the NAND Gate Circuit in Fig. 8-8.

IC1	CD4011 quad NAND gate
D1	LED
R1, R2	1 MΩ resistor
R3	470 resistor
S1, S2	SPST switch

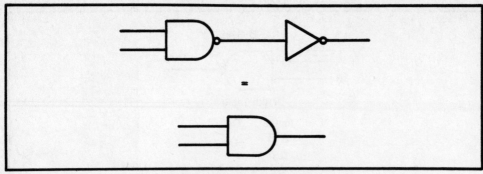

Fig. 8-9. Inverting the output of a NAND gate restores the AND function.

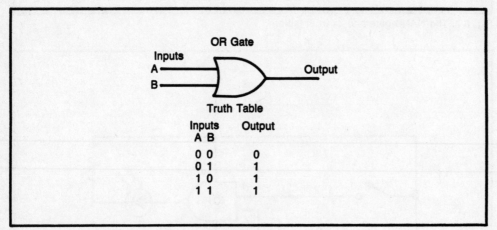

Fig. 8-10. Another basic type of gate is the OR gate.

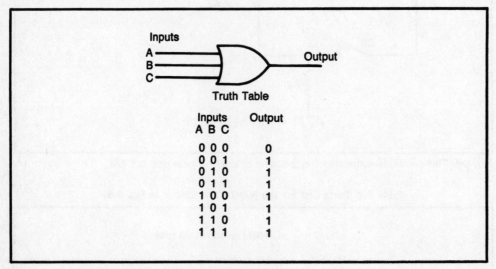

Fig. 8-11. An OR gate may have any number of inputs.

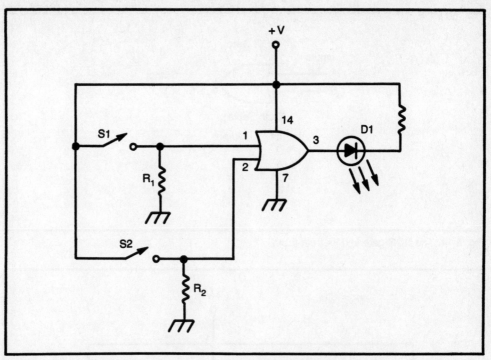

Fig. 8-12. This circuit demonstrates the operation of an OR gate. PROJECT #79

Table 8-3. Parts List for the OR Gate Circuit in Fig. 8-12.

IC1	CD4071 quad OR gate
D1	LED
R1, R2	1 MΩ resistor
R3	470 Ω resistor
S1, S2	SPST switch

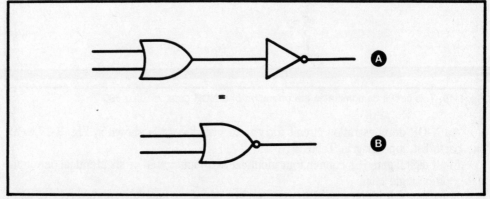

Fig. 8-13. Inverting the output of an OR gate produces a NOR gate.

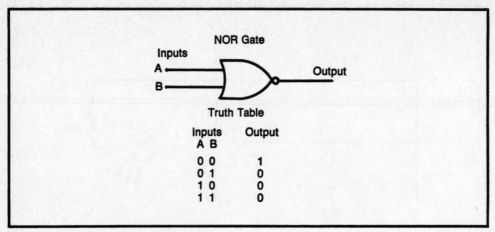

Fig. 8-14. The NOR gate and its truth table.

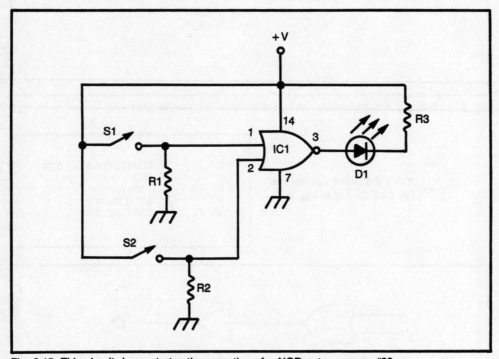

Fig. 8-15. This circuit demonstrates the operation of a NOR gate. PROJECT #80

An X-OR demonstration circuit for you to breadboard is shown in Fig. 8-17, with the parts list appearing in Table 8-5.

Most digital gate ICs contain four identical two-input gates or six identical one-input gates on a single chip.

Sometimes, it is convenient to use one type of gate to simulate another type of gate. For example, if you are building a circuit that requires three NAND gates and an inverter. You could use a quad NAND gate IC and a hex inverter IC. You would have one unused

Table 8-4. Parts List for the NOR Gate Circuit in Fig. 8-15.

IC1	CD4001 quad NOR gate
D1	LED
R1, R2	1 MΩ resistor
R3	470 Ω resistor
S1, S2	SPST switch

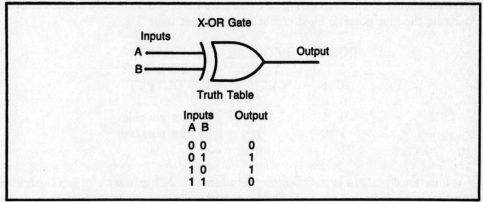

Fig. 8-16. The X-OR gate is a variation on the basic OR gate.

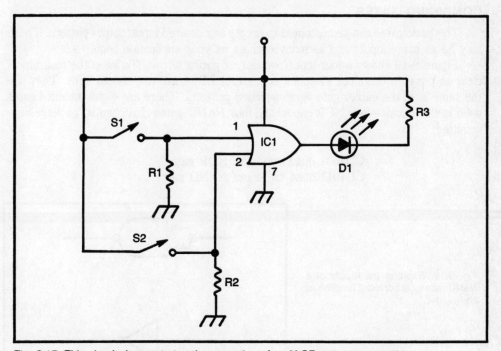

Fig. 8-17. This circuit demonstrates the operation of an X-OR gate. PROJECT #81

Table 8-5. Parts List for the X-OR Gate Circuit in Fig. 8-17.

NAND gate and five unused inverters left over. This is obviously wasteful and inefficient. You can build the same circuit with just the quad NAND gate IC, by employing the unused NAND gate as an inverter. All you have to do is short the two inputs together, as illustrated in Fig. 8-18. The two inputs to the gate will now always have identical values, reducing the four possible input combinations to just two;

INPUTS		REGULAR NAND OUTPUT	NAND INVERTER OUTPUT
A	B		
0	0	1	1
0	1	1	not possible
1	0	1	not possible
1	1	0	0

Functionally, there is no difference between a NAND gate with its inputs shorted together and a dedicated inverter. This same trick will also work with spare NOR gates.

COMBINING GATES

The basic gates can be combined to create any desired input/output pattern. There may be as many inputs and as many outputs as your application requires.

Figure 8-19 shows a four-input/two-output gating circuit. To keep the diagram as clear as possible the input switches and output LEDs are not shown here. They are the same as in the earlier gate demonstration projects. There are eight standard gates used in this circuit—four NOR gates, and four NAND gates. Just two IC packages are required;

CD4001 quad two-input NOR gate
CD4011 quad two-input NAND gate

Fig. 8-18. Shorting the inputs of a NAND gate together lets it function as an inverter.

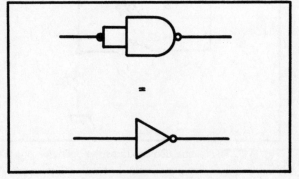

186

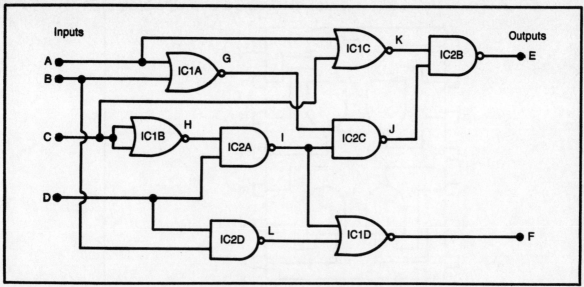

Fig. 8-19. Simple gates can be combined to produce complex gating functions. PROJECT #82

The pinout diagrams for these devices are shown respectively in Fig. 8-20 and Fig. 8-21. Pin numbers are often omitted from gate schematics to avoid diagram clutter. All of the gates in each IC package are 100 percent interchangeable. When specific pin numbers must be used, they will be indicated in the schematic. Otherwise, they really are not necessary.

You should also notice that there are no power supply connections indicated in Fig. 8-19. This omission is also standard practice to keep schematic diagrams as clear as

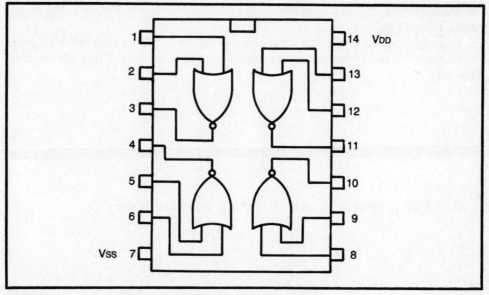

Fig. 8-20. The pin-out diagram of the CD4001 quad NOR gate.

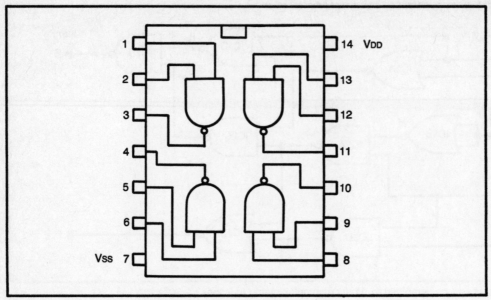

Fig. 8-21. The pin-out diagram for the CD4011 quad NAND gate.

possible. The power supply connections are always assumed. Since they are the same for any circuit using a given chip, there is no need to draw them out, especially in a circuit including a great many ICs.

Can you predict the input/output patterns of the circuit shown in Fig. 8-19 before physically breadboarding it and trying it out? This really is not very difficult, although it can be a bit tedious. Just trace the signals out through each gate. For your convenience, I have labeled each point in the diagram that has a different signal. This will make our discussion a little easier, since we can always identify exactly which point in the circuit we are referring to.

Tracing the signals is just a matter of determining the output for each individual gate. We will start with IC1A which combines original output signals A and B into intermediate signal G:

INPUTS		OUTPUT
A	B	G
0	0	1
0	1	0
1	0	0
1	1	0

Gate IC1B is wired as an inverter, and just inverts input signal C.

INPUT	OUTPUT
C	H
0	1
1	0

$$H = \overline{C}.$$

188

This signal is NANDed with input signal D by IC2A to form intermediate signal I;

INPUTS		OUTPUT
H	D	I
0	0	1
0	1	1
1	0	1
1	1	0

Gate IC2C NANDs intermediate signals G and I below. All of the above truth tables are combined.

ORIGINAL INPUTS				INTERMEDIATE SIGNALS			CURRENT OUTPUT
A	B	C	D	G	H	I	J
0	0	0	0	1	1	1	0
0	0	0	1	1	1	0	1
0	0	1	0	1	0	1	0
0	0	1	1	1	0	1	0
0	1	0	0	0	1	1	1
0	1	0	1	0	1	0	1
0	1	1	0	0	0	1	1
0	1	1	1	0	0	1	1
1	0	0	0	0	1	1	1
1	0	0	1	0	1	0	1
1	0	1	0	0	0	1	1
1	0	1	1	0	0	1	1
1	1	0	0	0	1	1	1
1	1	0	1	0	1	0	1
1	1	1	0	0	0	1	1
1	1	1	1	0	0	1	1

You can continue this simple procedure for the rest of the gates in the circuit. Because these extensive truth tables eat up a lot of page space, I will not show the rest of the intermediate signals here. The final input/output truth table is as follows;

INPUTS				OUTPUTS	
A	B	C	D	E	F
0	0	0	0	1	0
0	0	0	1	1	0
0	0	1	0	1	0
0	0	1	1	1	0
0	1	0	0	0	0
0	1	0	1	0	1
0	1	1	0	1	0
0	1	1	1	1	0

```
1 0 0 0     1 0
1 0 0 1     1 0
1 0 1 0     1 0
1 0 1 1     1 0
1 1 0 0     1 0
1 1 0 1     1 1
1 1 1 0     1 0
1 1 1 1     1 0
```

There is almost always more than one way to achieve any given gating problem. The circuit of Fig. 8-19 is not necessarily the best possible circuit for the job.

Output E is a logic 1 except for two of the sixteen possible input combinations;

0100

0101

Obviously the value of input D is irrelevant. A and C must both be 0s and B must be a 1 for an output of 0.

Similarly, output F is a 0 except for two of the sixteen possible input combinations;

0101

1101

Here input A is ignored. Inputs B and D must both be 1, and C must be a 0 for an output of 1.

Before reading on, try to design the simplest possible alternate circuit that will give the same input/output pattern as the circuit of Fig. 8-19.

The simplest alternative I could come up with is shown in Fig. 8-22. In this version

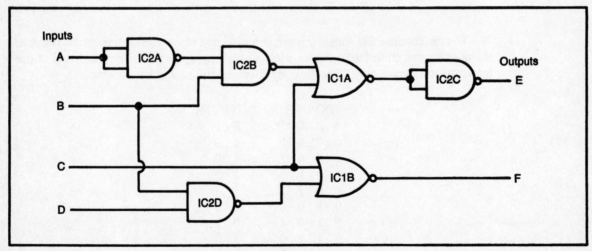

Fig. 8-22. A simplified version of the circuit shown in Fig. 8-19.

190

of the circuit I have saved two NOR gates (that could be used for other circuitry), and the signal paths are much more logical and easier to follow.

In many practical applications, you will know the desired input/output pattern, and you will need to devise an efficient gating circuit for that pattern. In other words, you start out with the truth table.

As an example, we will design a four input/three output gating circuit with the following truth table;

INPUTS				OUTPUTS		
A	B	C	D	E	F	G
0	0	0	0	0	1	1
0	0	0	1	0	1	1
0	0	1	0	0	0	1
0	0	1	1	0	0	1
0	1	0	0	1	0	0
0	1	0	1	1	0	0
0	1	1	0	0	0	1
0	1	1	1	0	0	1
1	0	0	0	0	1	1
1	0	0	1	0	1	1
1	0	1	0	1	0	0
1	0	1	1	1	0	0
1	1	0	0	0	0	1
1	1	0	1	0	0	1
1	1	1	0	0	0	1
1	1	1	1	0	0	1

Now, how can you start designing a practical circuit from this? The first step is to examine the truth table carefully for any readily apparent patterns. Two things should occur to you. First, compare outputs E and G. They always have the opposite state from one another. Once we obtain output E, we just have to invert that signal to get output G.

The other thing you should notice is that input D has no effect on any of the outputs. We don't need this signal at all. Unneeded signals get designed into digital systems more often than you may suspect!

We can now simplify the truth table considerably;

INPUTS			OUTPUTS	
A	B	C	E	F
0	0	0	0	1
0	0	1	0	0
0	1	0	1	0
0	1	1	0	0
1	0	0	0	1
1	0	1	1	0
1	1	0	0	0
1	1	1	0	0

Outputs E and F don't seem to relate to each other in any meaningful pattern, so we will deal with them separately.

First we will look at output E. This output signal is usually a 0. It becomes a 1 with two input combinations;

$$010$$
$$101$$

A and C must have the same state, while B must be at the opposite state. There are several ways to accomplish this pattern. Here is what I came up with;

$$((A\ NOR\ C)\ AND\ B)\ OR\ ((A\ NAND\ C)\ NOR\ B)$$

Can you come up with anything more efficient?

Now, look at output F. This signal is also 0 for most input combinations. It is a 1 for the following input combinations;

$$000$$
$$100$$

The value of A is irrelevant. For F to be a 1, both B and C must be 0. The simplified truth table for this output becomes;

INPUTS		OUTPUT
B	C	F
0	0	1
0	1	0
1	0	0
1	1	0

This is nothing more than a simple NOR gate pattern.

As you can see here, what appears to be a complex problem can often be broken down into something quite simple. Figure 8-23 shows the complete circuit I came up with for producing the desired truth table in this example. A couple of extra inverter stages have been added so we can build the entire circuit from NAND gates and NOR gates. The functions of the AND gates and OR gates are simulated with inversion.

If you follow the signals through Fig. 8-23 you will see that this circuit does indeed correspond to the truth table given above.

Any complex gating pattern can be achieved by combining basic gates.

SIGNAL GENERATORS

By using feedback, a digital gate can be forced into oscillation and serve as a signal generator.

A simple square wave generator, or clock circuit can be constructed from a pair of inverters, two resistors, and a capacitor, as shown in Fig. 8-24. Shorted input NAND gates seem to work better than actual dedicated inverters. The modified circuit is shown in Fig. 8-25.

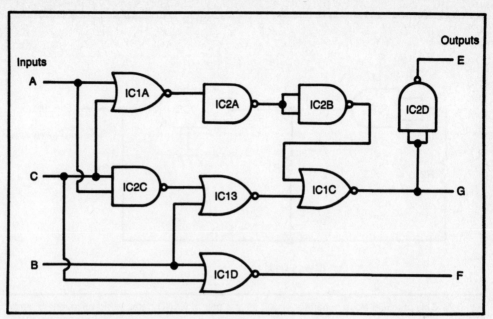

Fig. 8-23. The second complex gating circuit. PROJECT #83

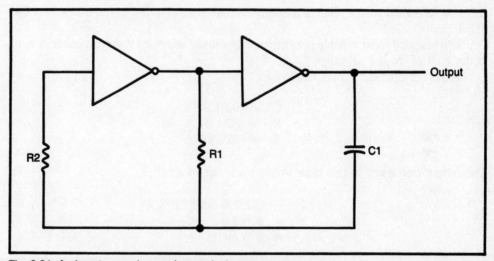

Fig. 8-24. An inverter can be used as a clock generator.

This very simple circuit uses just half of a CD4011 (or similar) quad NAND gate IC. A duplicate circuit could be built around the other half of the IC, just by changing the appropriate pin numbers. Refer back to the pin-out diagram of Fig. 8-21.

The output frequency from this circuit will be approximately equal to;

$$F \cong R_1C_1/2.2$$

C1 is in microfarads.

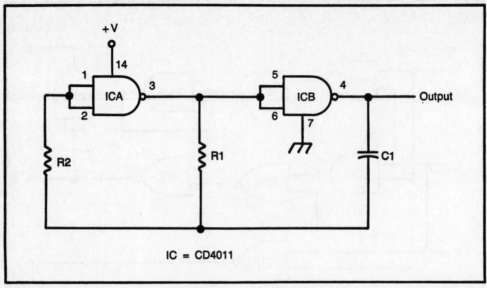

Fig. 8-25. This practical clock generator circuit uses a pair of NAND gates wired as inverters. PROJECT #84

Resistor R2 should have a value that is approximately equal to five to ten times the value of R1.

The best and most reliable performance is usually achieved if the capacitor is kept in the 0.01 μF to 0.1 μF range.

Typical component values might be;

$$C_1 = 0.01 \ \mu F$$
$$R_1 = 82 \ k\Omega$$
$$R_2 = 820 \ k\Omega$$

The output frequency in this case would work out to about;

$$F = (82,000 \times 0.01)/2.2$$
$$= 820/2.2$$
$$\cong 373 \ Hz$$

Figure 8-26 shows a simple but powerful modification to the circuit. An external digital signal is used to turn the oscillator on and off. When the input signal is a 1, the signal is generated. When the input signal is a 0, the output is cut off.

An alternate square wave signal generator circuit is shown in Fig. 8-27. This circuit is built around a single X-OR gate. This circuit is well suited for very high frequency operation. For example, using a 1 k resistor and a 0.001 μF capacitor will produce an output signal that is close to 2 MHz.

An entirely different approach to digital signal generation is illustrated in the circuit of Fig. 8-28. This circuit is known as a phase shift oscillator. All of the resistors should

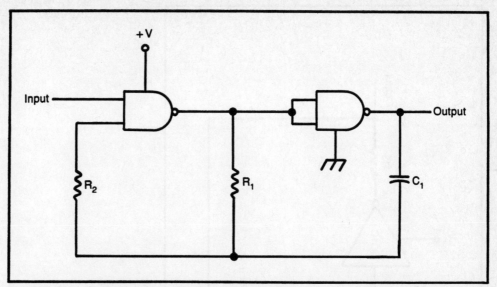

Fig. 8-26. This clock generator circuit can be gated on and off by an external logic signal. PROJECT #85

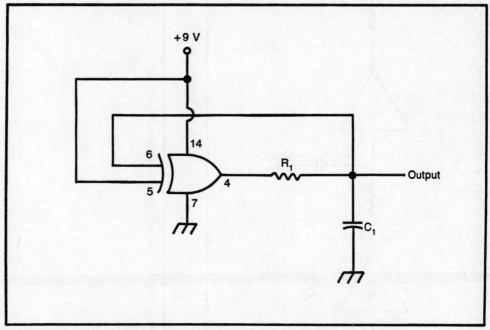

Fig. 8-27. This clock generator circuit is built around an X-OR gate. PROJECT #86

have equal values. All of the capacitors should also be equal. The output frequency formula is;

$$F = 1/3.3RC$$

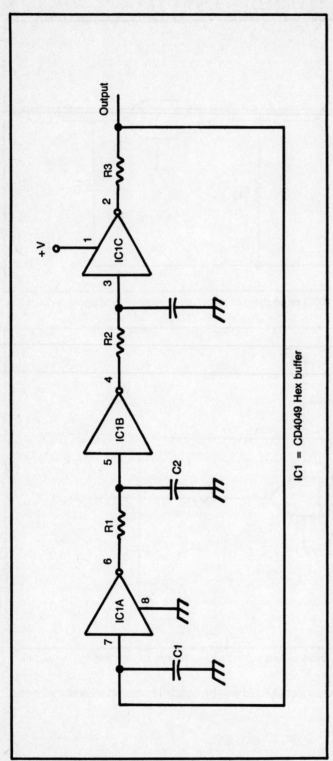

Fig. 8-28. A phase shift oscillator circuit using digital inverters. PROJECT #87

IC1 = CD4049 Hex buffer

For example, if R = 470 k, and C = 0.01 μF, the output frequency would be;

$$
\begin{aligned}
F &= 1/(3.3 \times 470{,}000 \times 0.0000001) \\
&= 1/0.01551 \\
&\cong 65 \text{ Hz}
\end{aligned}
$$

Digital devices are most suited to square waves, of course, but they can be "fooled" into creating other waveshapes. Figure 8-29 shows a digital function generator with two outputs. Output A is an ordinary square wave, but output B provides a modified triangle waveform. Both output signals have the same frequency. The frequency equation for this circuit is;

$$
F = 1/(1.4R_1C_1)
$$

R2 should be about a quarter of R1.
As a typical example, use the following component values;

$$
\begin{aligned}
R_1 &= 47 \text{ k} \\
R_2 &= 12 \text{ k} \\
C_1 &= 0.047 \ \mu F \\
C_2 &= 0.047 \ \mu F
\end{aligned}
$$

In this case, the output frequency works out to approximately;

$$
\begin{aligned}
F &= 1/(1.4 \times 47{,}000 \times 0.00000047) \\
&= 1/0.0030926 \\
&\cong 325 \text{ Hz}
\end{aligned}
$$

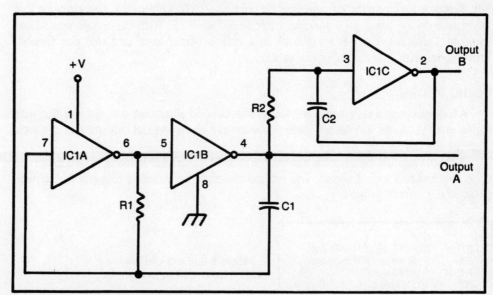

Fig. 8-29. This waveform generator circuit produces two waveforms. PROJECT #88

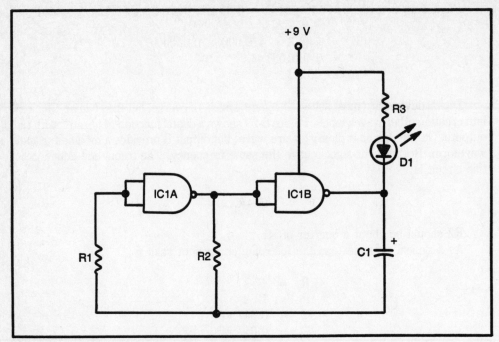

Fig. 8-30. A simple LED blinker circuit. PROJECT #89

LED FLASHER

A low-speed oscillator can be used to blink an LED on and off at a regular rate. If the frequency is too high, the LED will appear to be lit continuously.

A simple LED blinker circuit is shown in Fig. 8-30. The parts list is given in Table 8-6. Resistor R3 limits the current flow through the LED. Otherwise, this circuit is just a variation on the basic clock generator circuit of Fig. 8-25. With the component values listed in Table 8-8, the LED will blink at a rate of about once or twice per second. Experiment with other component values.

LOGIC PROBE

A logic probe is a very handy device to have around whenever you are working with digital circuits. At its simplest, a logic probe simply gives a visual indication of the logic state at the test point.

A simple logic probe circuit is shown in Fig. 8-31. The LED lights up when the probe tip is touched to a logic 1 signal. The ground clip must be attached to a suitable ground point in the circuit under test.

IC1	CD4011 quad NAND gate
C1	5 µF electrolytic capacitor
R1	1 MΩ resistor
R2	100 kΩ resistor
R3	470 Ω resistor

**Table 8-6. Parts List for the
LED Blinker Circuit in Fig. 8-30.**

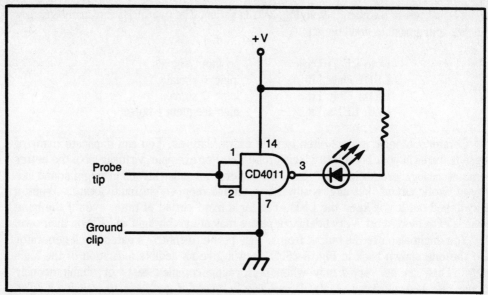

Fig. 8-31. A simple logic probe circuit. PROJECT #90

This circuit could also "steal" its power from the circuit being tested. Just put an alligator clip on the end of the V+ line and attach it to the supply voltage of the circuit under test.

While functional, the circuit of Fig. 8-31 may give ambiguous results under certain circumstances. An improved logic probe circuit is shown in Fig. 8-32. Essentially this

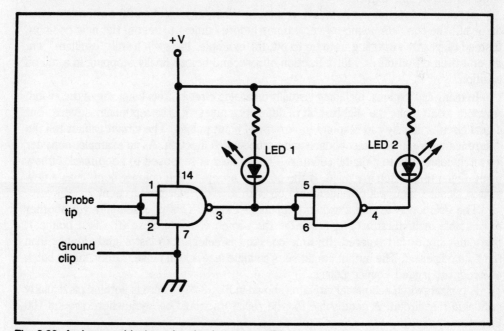

Fig. 8-32. An improved logic probe circuit. PROJECT #91

circuit is just two of the circuits from Fig. 8-31 in series. The two LEDs can unambiguously indicate four possible conditions;

Both LEDs Dark	no input signal
LED1 Only Lit	logic 1 signal
LED2 Only Lit	logic 0 signal
Both LEDs Lit	high frequency pulse

Commercial logic probes often include extra features. You can duplicate many of these features in your breadboard logic probe too. For example, virtually all of the better commercial logic probes include "pulse stretchers". A pulse stretcher might sound like a very exotic circuit, but all it really is is a simple monostable multivibrator. When it is switched on, it will keep the LED(s) lit for a fixed period of time, even if the input pulse is extremely short. Very brief input pulses may not visibly light an LED on their own.

You might also use the output from a logic probe to control a gated clock generator like the one shown back in Fig. 8-26. This will give an audible indication of the logic state. This can be very handy when performing complex tests or simultaneously monitoring several circuit points. It can also be useful if you have to wait for a pulse but aren't sure just when (or if) it will occur.

With a little bit of imagination, the simplest circuit can become the heart of a very sophisticated and versatile piece of equipment.

SWITCH DEBOUNCER

Mechanical switches seem simple enough, and for most applications they are. A switch is either on, or off. Right?

Actually it depends on how fast you look. When any mechanical switch is turned on or off, the contacts bounce several times before coming to rest in the new position. Instead of cleanly switching from on to off, for example, the switch will "oscillate" on-off-on-off-on-off-on-off . . . for a fraction of a second before finally stopping in a full off position.

In many applications, including virtually all analog circuits, this bouncing of the switch contacts won't make the slightest bit of difference unless it is exceptionally severe. But digital circuits usually can respond to very brief input pulses. The circuit cannot tell the difference between a contact bounce and a true switch function. As an example, consider a switch connected to a digital counter. The counter is supposed to keep track of how many times the switch is closed. If the counter accepts each contact bounce as a new switch closure, you will obviously end up with a wildly inaccurate count.

The solution is to use a switch debouncer circuit. This is essentially yet another monostable multivibrator. The first time the switch contacts close (the first bounce), the multivibrator is triggered. Its time constant is selected to last slightly longer than the bounce period. The output circuit sees a single nice, clean pulse, rather than a batch of irregular, jagged bounce pulses.

A typical switch debouncer circuit is shown in Fig. 8-33. There is nothing particularly critical in this circuit. A good value for the resistors would be somewhere around 100 k, or so.

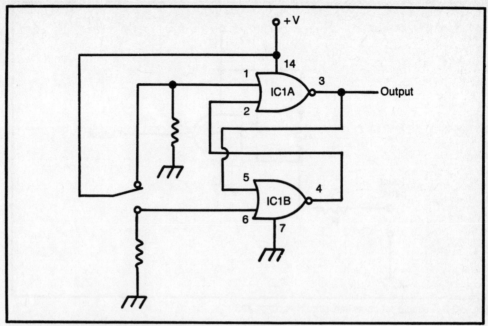

Fig. 8-33. Switch debouncing is needed in many digital applications. PROJECT #92

TOUCH SWITCH

A touch switch can be handy under certain circumstances. More frequently, however, such circuits are used just because they are fun and fascinating.

A simple digital touch switch circuit is shown in Fig. 8-34. The output goes HIGH when you short the two touch pads with your fingertips. A parts list for this project is given in Table 8-7.

IMPORTANT NOTE! Because the user will be touching a bare conductor, any touch switch circuit should be operated from batteries *only*. Do *not* use an ac power source, even through an ac-to-dc converter. If there is the right kind of short anywhere in the circuit, the result could be extremely painful, if not fatal. This bears repeating. USE BATTERY POWER ONLY FOR ANY TOUCH SWITCH CIRCUIT. It is not worth the risk.

A variation on the basic touch switch circuit is shown in Fig. 8-35. Basically, this circuit is something like a combination of the simple touch switch circuit of Fig. 8-34 and the switch debouncer circuit of Fig. 8-33. The result here is a timed touch switch. When you short the two touch plates the output will go HIGH for a specific period, and then go LOW again, even if the touch pads are being shorted continuously. For the component values listed in Table 8-8, the ON period will be approximately one second. Experiment with other component values.

Once again, please power this project only from batteries. Do not take foolish chances!

BINARY ADDER

A digital computer is made up of thousands and millions of digital gates. If you were

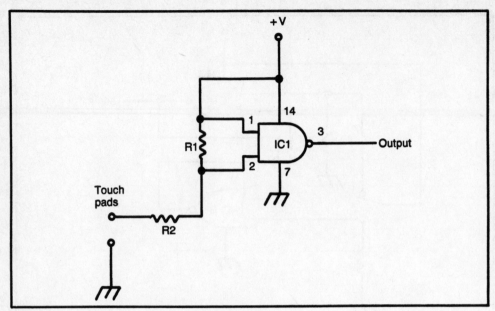

Fig. 8-34. A simple touch switch circuit. PROJECT #93

patient enough and had unlimited time, resources, and space, you theoretically could build a full computer from the digital gate ICs used in this chapter.

Obviously that would not be a very practical project. Dedicated LSI (Large Scale Integration) ICs will do the job more efficiently and cheaper and will take up considerably less room.

Even so, it is worthwhile to experiment a little on the gate level, so you will understand better how the more sophisticated digital devices work.

Figure 8-36 shows a circuit for adding two binary digits. The parts list is given in Table 8-9.

Since there are two possible binary digit values (0 and 1), there are four possible combinations of two single digit numbers;

$$0 + 0 = 0$$
$$0 + 1 = 1$$
$$1 + 0 = 1$$
$$1 + 1 = 10$$

Notice that in the last combination, the sum has two digits instead of just one. The carry output is used to accommodate this new column.

IC1	CD4011 quad NAND gate
R1	10 MΩ resistor
R2	220 kΩ resistor

IMPORTANT—USE BATTERY POWER *ONLY!*

Table 8-7. Parts List for the Simple
Touch Switch Circuit in Fig. 8-34.

202

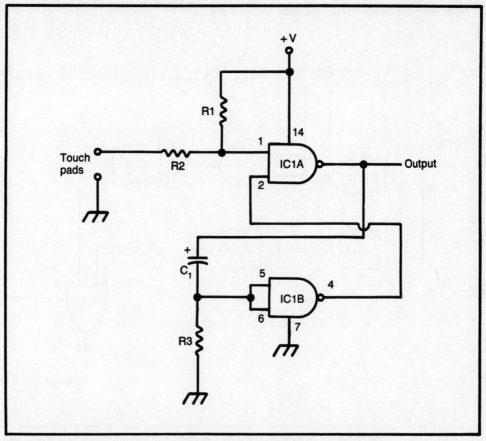

Fig. 8-35. This touch switch circuit features a built-in time delay. PROJECT #94

You can cascade several of these circuits in series. The carry input of each stage is then connected to the carry output of the preceding stage. Any number of digits may be accommodated in this manner.

If you are only working with single digit inputs, the carry input is not needed.

LINEAR AMPLIFIER

Figure 8-37 illustrates a circuit for one of the oddest digital applications of all. This circuit, which is made up of three digital inverters, actually functions as a linear amplifier.

Table 8-8. Parts List for the Timed Touch Switch Circuit in Fig. 8-35.

IC1	CD4011 quad NAND gate
C1	5 μF electrolytic capacitor
R1	10 MΩ resistor
R2, R3	120 kΩ resistor

IMPORTANT—USE BATTERY POWER *ONLY*!

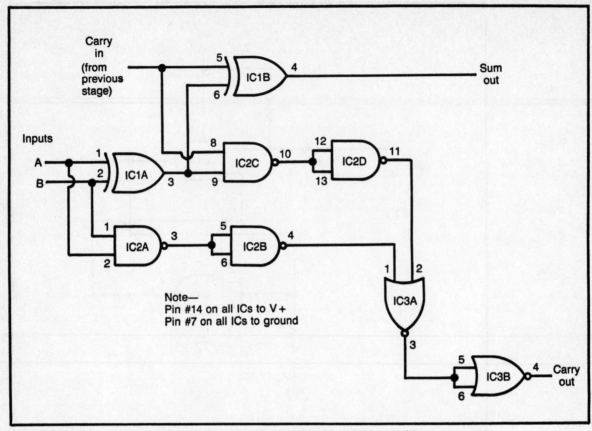

Fig. 8-36. Gates can be combined to perform complex functions, like this binary adder. PROJECT #95

The gain is determined by the ratio of the values of resistors R2 and R1;

$$G = R2/R1$$

For the component values listed in Table 8-10, the gain is 10.

The purpose of the capacitor is to block any dc component in the input signal.

IC1	CD4070 quad X-OR gate	
IC2	CD4011 quad NAND gate	
IC3	CD4001 quad NOR gate	

Table 8-9. Parts List for the Binary Adder Circuit in Fig. 8-36.

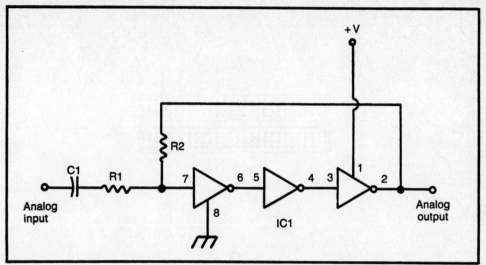

Fig. 8-37. This digital circuit functions as a linear amplifier. PROJECT #96

**Table 8-10. Parts List
for the Digital Linear
Amplifier Circuit in Fig. 8-37.**

IC1	CD4049 hex inverter
C1	0.01 μF capacitor
R1	100 kΩ resistor *
R2	1 MΩ resistor *

IMPORTANT—USE BATTERY POWER *ONLY*!

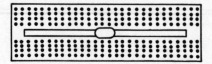

9

Flip-Flops

MOVING BEYOND SIMPLE GATES, ONE OF THE MOST IMPORTANT TYPES OF SUBCIRCUITS in digital electronics is the bistable multivibrator, or flip-flop. In a sense, this is a circuit with a memory. In fact, flip-flops are used in many simple memory circuits.

You should recall that back in Chapters 2 and 3 we were working with monostable multivibrators and astable multivibrators. The bistable multivibrator is obviously related to these devices.

A monostable multivibrator has one stable output state. The output will remain in this stable state until the circuit is triggered. The output will then go to the opposite (unstable) state for a predetermined period of time, before reverting to its stable state.

An astable multivibrator has no stable output states. The output continuously swings back and forth between states, at a rate determined by the circuit's component values.

As you have probably guessed, a bistable multivibrator has two stable output states. Its output can remain in either state indefinitely, as long as power is not interrupted. Each time a bistable multivibrator is triggered, the output reverses its state. Because the output flip-flops back and forth, the bistable multivibrator is widely known by the somewhat whimsical name, "flip-flop."

There are several different types of flip-flops. If you want to learn more about flip-flops and other digital devices, I recommend my earlier book, "Using Integrated Circuit Logic Devices" (TAB #1645). Besides memory circuits, flip-flops are widely used in such applications as frequency dividers, counters, shift registers, and sequencers.

FLIP-FLOP DIVIDERS

Each time it receives an input pulse, a flip-flop reverses its output state. If we feed

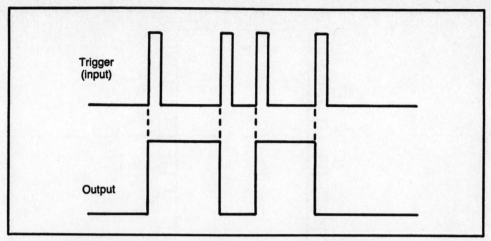

Fig. 9-1. A bistable multivibrator reverses its output state each time an input pulse is received.

a train of pulses into a flip-flop, there will be half as many pulses at the output, as illustrated in Fig. 9-1.

We will use two flip-flop devices in the projects of this chapter. The CD4013 dual D-type flip-flop IC is shown in Fig. 9-2, while Fig. 9-3 illustrates the CD4027 dual JK-type flip-flop IC.

It is easy enough to set up a flip-flop as a divide-by-two counter. A typical circuit is shown in Fig. 9-4. By cascading additional flip-flop stages, output to input, we can divide by any power of two. But suppose we need to divide by some value that is not

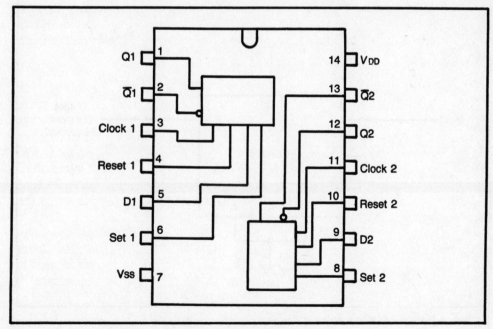

Fig. 9-2. Pin-out diagram of the CD4013 dual D-type flip-flop IC.

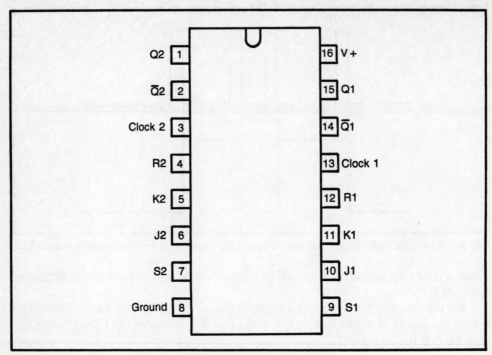

Fig. 9-3. Pin-out diagram of the CD4027 dual JK-type flip-flop IC.

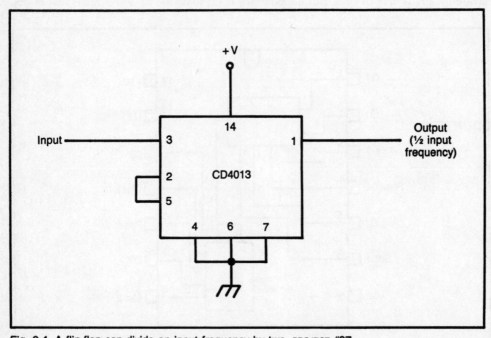

Fig. 9-4. A flip-flop can divide an input frequency by two. PROJECT #97

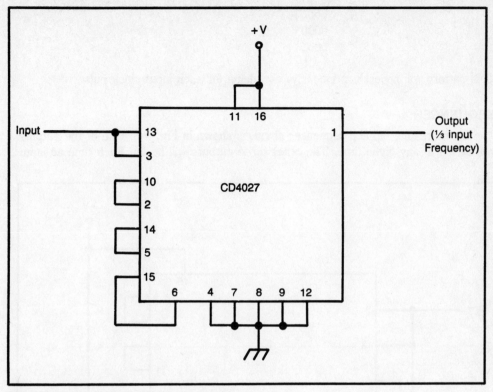

Fig. 9-5. A divide-by-three circuit. PROJECT #98

power of two? Just use a JK-type flip-flop and force reset it at any desired point. As an example, a divide-by-three circuit is shown in Fig. 9-5. A divide-by-five counter appears in Fig. 9-6. Note that the circuit in Fig. 9-4 used the CD4013 D-type flip-flop, but the circuits of Figs. 9-5 and 9-6 use the CD4027 JK-type flip-flop.

COUNTERS

A flip-flop-based counter circuit is really very similar to a divider circuit. We just tap all the intermediate binary outputs. Figure 9-7 shows a counter using D-type flip-flops (CD4013) that counts to eight then resets. The LEDs will light up in binary sequence;

DCBA	
0000	0
0001	1
0010	2
0011	3
0100	4
0101	5
0110	6
0111	7

1000	8
0000	0
0001	1

This pattern will repeat continuously, advancing for each input clock pulse.

SEQUENCER

An interesting flip-flop sequencer circuit is shown in Fig. 9-8. One of the outputs will be a 1 at any given time. The other three outputs will be 0s. Each time an input

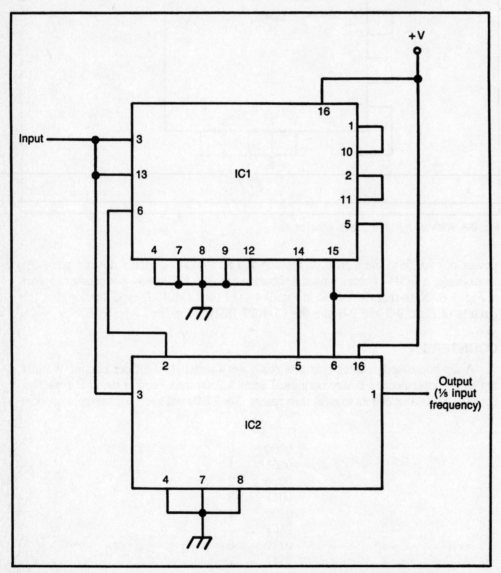

Fig. 9-6. This circuit provides one output pulse for every five input pulses. PROJECT #99

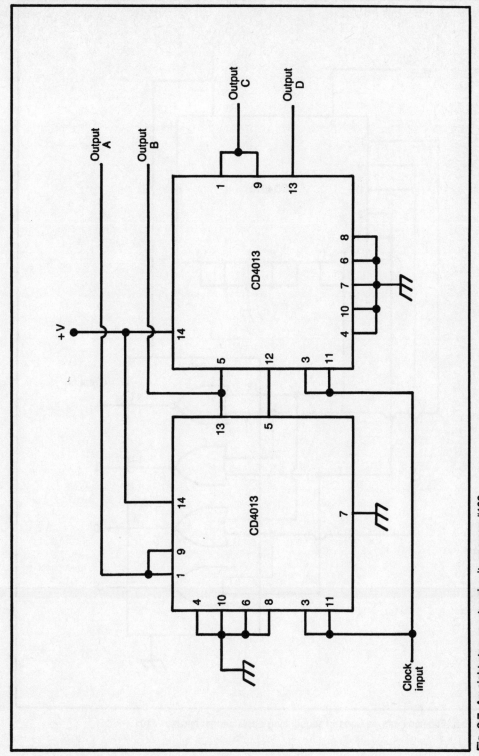

Fig. 9-7. An eight-step counter circuit. PROJECT #100

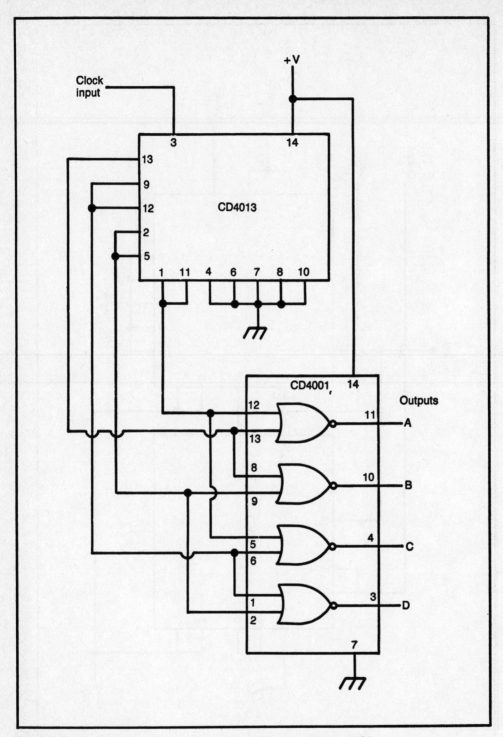

Fig. 9-8. Flip-flops can be used in sequencing applications. PROJECT #101

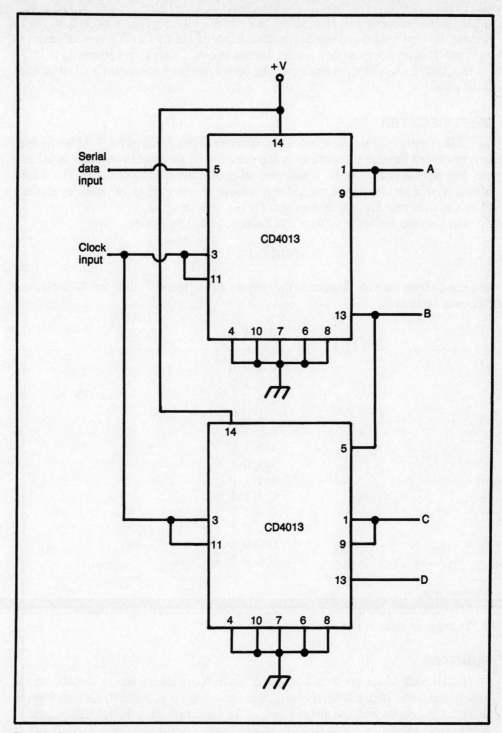

Fig. 9-9. A shift register is similar to a counter. BONUS PROJECT

(clock) pulse is received by this circuit, the current output will be switched off (go to 0), and the next output in sequence will be activated (go to 1). This type of circuit is very useful in applications that require certain events to occur in sequence.

A CD4013 is used for the flip-flops. The output gates are sections of a CD4001 quad NOR gate.

SHIFT REGISTER

Shift registers are similar in concept to counters. They are used for short term memory, or to step through a sequence. In this circuit, a bit pattern (1s and 0s) are fed into the data input serially. One bit is accepted on each controlling clock pulse. The output is displayed in parallel fashion on LEDs A through D. On each clock pulse, everything is moved over one place to make room for the new input bit.

Suppose the following pattern was being fed into the circuit:

1-0-0-1-1-0-1-1-1-0-0-0-

and just 0s from then on. Assuming the outputs all started at 0, they would display the following sequence;

```
0 0 0 0
1 0 0 0
0 1 0 0
0 0 1 0
1 0 0 1
1 1 0 0
0 1 1 0
1 0 1 1
1 1 0 1
1 1 1 0
0 1 1 1
0 0 1 1
0 0 0 1
0 0 0 0
0 0 0 0
```

and so forth.

The data may also be taken off serially at point D, delayed by the number of stages in the register (four in our example).

SUMMARY

In this book I have presented over one hundred circuits for you to breadboard and experiment with. With a little ingenuity, you can come up with countless variations on these basic circuits and use them singly or in combinations in literally thousands of electronics projects.

Index

324 op amp, pin designation for, 67

555 timer, 6-44
  astable circuits using, 18
  basic internal structure of, 9
  basic modes of, 6
  basic monostable circuits using, 9
  complex sound generator, 35
  features of, 8
  frequency divider circuit using, 40
  inverted input monostable
   multivibrator, 15
  light-off/light-on alarm using, 43, 44
  linear ramp astable using, 35
  linear ramp monostable timer
   using, 33
  low-frequency astable multivibrator
   using, 21
  missing pulse detector, 39
  monostable multivibrator
   demonstrator using, 11-14
  pin designations of, 8
  power supply specifications for, 9
  sequential timer using, 33
  sound pocket generator using, 26
  switch debouncer using, 15-17
  timer controlled relay using, 17
  triangle wave generator using, 25
  use of 556 dual timer with, 26
  use of 558 quad timer with, 30

voltage-controlled monostable
  multivibrator using, 14
556 dual timer, 26
  pin designation for, 28
  tone burst generator using, 27
558 quad timer, 30
  cascaded timer using, 30
  long duration timer using, 31
  pin designation for, 30

741 op amp, 60-125
  absolute value circuit using, 103
  antilogarithm amplifier using, 93
  comparator using, 81
  difference amplifier using, 77
  division circuit using, 99
  exponential circuits using, 100
  improved comparator using, 83
  inverting amplifier circuit using, 67
  inverting summing amplifier using,
   83
  logarithmic amplifier using, 88
  low-pass filter using, 106
  mathematical functions with, 88
  multiplier using, 95
  negative input inverting amplifier,
   72
  non-inverting amplifier using, 75
  pin designation of, 64, 65
  sawtooth wave generator, 123

  sine amplifier using, 101
  sine wave generator, 117
  specifications for, 66
  square wave generator using, 120
  triangle wave generator, 123
  variable frequency square wave
   generator using, 122
  variable gain inverting amplifier, 73
  variable width pulse generator
   using, 122
747 op amp, pin designation for, 66
7555 timer, 44

A
absolute value circuit, 103-105
alternate complex tone generator,
  57-59
AND gate demonstrator
  circuit diagram for, 179
  input expansion in, 180
  parts list for, 179
antilogarithm amplifier, 741 op amp,
  93-95
astable circuits, 555 timer, 18
astable mode (see timers, basic
  modes of)
astable multivibrator
  555 timer, 18
  audio-frequency circuit diagram
   for, 24

circuit diagram of, 18
LM339 quad comparator, 133-134
low-frequency circuit diagram of, 22
astable multivibrator demonstrator (audio frequency), 24
astable multivibrator demonstrator (low-frequency), 21
audio amplifier, 138-155, 138
  HA-2400, 148
  LM380, 144
  LM386, 148
audio-frequency astable multivibrator, XR2240, 55-56
audio-frequency astable multivibrator, 555 timer, 24

B

band-pass filter, 112-113
band-reject filter, 116-117
bandwidth, op amp, 63
bargraph, LM339 quad comparator, 134-136
base frequency, 20
basic amplifier circuit, LM380 audio amplifier, 142
battery power supply, 3
binary adder, 201
  circuit diagram for, 204
  parts list for, 204
bistable multivibrator
bistable multivibrator (see also timers, basic modes of)
  output reversal in, 207
breadboarding system, 1-5
  customized, 4
  Heathkit, 4
  output devices in, 4
  potentiometers and switches in, 4
  power supplies for, 3
  precautions when using, 4
  use of ICs in, 5
  variable signal source in, 4
bridged amplifier, LM380 audio amplifier, 146-148
buffer, 177

C

capacitance meter, LM339 quad comparator, 135-137
cascaded timer, 555 timer, 30-31
CD4001 quad two-input NOR gate, 186
  pin designation of, 187
CD4011 quad two-input NAND gate, 186
  pin designation for, 188
CD4013 dual D-type flip-flop, pin designation for, 207
CD4027 dual JK-type flip-flop, pin designation for, 208
ceramic cartridge phono amplifier,

LM380 audio amplifier, 144-146
chatter, LM339 quad comparator and, 129
circuit building
  experimental, 2, 4
  temporary vs. permanent, 1
clock generator
  circuit diagram of, 194
  inverter as, 193
CMOS timer (see 7555 timer), 44
combination gates, 186
common-mode rejection ratio (see op amps)
comparator demonstration circuit
  diagram for, 128
  parts list for, 128
comparators, 741 op amp, 81-84
complex gate circuit #1
  diagram of, 187
complex gate circuit #2
  diagram of, 193
complex sound generator, 555 timer, 35-40
complex tone generator, XR2240 programmable timer, 56-58
counters, 209
customized breadboarding systems, 4

D

difference amplifier
  741 op amp, 77-81
  op amp as, 61
digital gate driver, LM339 quad comparator, 129-130
digital gates, 176-205
  binary adder using, 201
  clock generator using, 193
  combinations of, 186
  complex gate circuits using, 187-193
  digital linear amplifier using, 203
  dual waveform function generator using, 197
  gated clock generator using, 194
  LED blinker using, 198
  logic probes using, 198
  phase-shift oscillator using, 194
  signal generators using, 192
  simple touch switches with, 201
  switch debouncer using, 200
  timed touch switch using, 201
  XOR clock generator using, 194
divide-by-five circuit, 209
  diagram of, 210
divide-by-three circuit, 209
  diagram of, 209
divide-by-two circuit, 207
  diagram of, 208
dividers, flip-flop, 206
division circuit, 741 op amp, 99-100
division circuits, 95

dual timer, 28
dual waveform function generator, 197
duty cycle, 20

E

eight-bit binary counter, XR2240 programmable timer, 47
eight-step counter, 209-211
equalization, 145
explosion/gunshot sound effect, SN76477 IC, 168, 171-172
exponential circuit, 741 op amp, 100-103
exponents, op amps for, 100

F

filters
  band-pass, 111
  band-reject, 116
  high-pass, 110
  low-pass, 106
  notch, 116
  op amp, 105
flip-flops, 206-214
  counter circuits using, 209
  D-type, 207
  divide-by-five circuit using, 209
  divide-by-three circuit using, 209
  divide-by-two circuits using, 207
  dividers, 206
  eight-step counter using, 209
  JK-type, 208
  sequencer using, 210
  shift register using, 214
frequency divider circuit, 555 timer, 40-42
fundamental (base frequency)

G

gain, op amp, 62
gated clock generator, 194
  circuit diagram of, 195
gates, digital, 176

H

HA-2400 programmable amplifier, 148
  operations summary of, 152
  programmable inverting amplifier using, 153
  programmable multifunction circuit, 155
  programmable sine wave oscillator using, 155
  selectable input stages for, 152
harmonics, 20
Heathkit breadboard, 4
heatsinking, 140
high-gain circuit, LM386 audio amplifier, 150
high-pass filter

circuit diagram of, 111
frequency response of, 110
house current power supply, 3
hysteresis, LM339 quad comparator
  and, 128

I

impedance, op amp, 62
improved logic probe, circuit diagram
  for, 199
integrated circuits
  LM339 quad comparator, 126
  pin #1 location in, 4
  removal of, 5
  timer, 6
  use of, 5
integrators, 105
interconnection pattern, 2
inverted input monostable
  multivibrator, 555 timer, 15
inverter, 177
  clock generator use of, 193
inverting amplifier circuits
  741 op amp, 67-71
  programmable, 153

L

LED blinker
  circuit diagram for, 198
  parts list for, 198
LEDs, 4
light detector, LM339 quad
  comparator, 133-135
light-off alarm, 555 timer, 43-44
light-on alarm, 555 timer, 44
limit comparator, LM339 quad
  comparator, 129, 132
linear amplifier, digital gate, 203-205
linear ramp astable, 555 timer, 35, 37
linear ramp monostable, 555 timer,
  33-35
LM339 quad comparator, 126-137
  astable multivibrator using, 133
  bargraph using, 134
  capacitance meter using, 135
  chatter and, 129
  comparator demonstration circuit
    using, 128
  design and use of, 126
  digital gate driver using, 129
  hysteresis and, 128
  light detector using, 133
  limit comparator using, 129
  loading effects with, 129
  monostable multivibrator using,
    132
  pin designations for, 127
  schematic for, 127
LM380 audio amplifier, 138-155
  audio amplifier circuit using, 144
  basic amplifier circuit using, 142
  bridged amplifier using, 146

ceramic cartridge phono amplifier
  using, 144
design and use of, 139
internal circuitry of, 141
pin designation for, 139, 140
RIAA phono amplifier, 145
LM386 audio amplifier, 148
  circuit diagram for, 149
  high-gain circuit using, 150
  low-gain circuit using, 149
loading effects, LM339 quad
  comparator, 129
logarithmic amplifier, 741 op amp,
  88-93
logic probe, 198
  circuit diagram for, 199
long duration timer, 558 quad timer,
  31-32
low-frequency astable multivibrator
  555 timer, 21-22
  XR2240 programmable timer,
    52-54
low-gain circuit, LM386 audio
  amplifier, 149
low-pass filter, 741 op amp, 106-107

M

mathematical functions, using op
  amps for, 88
missing pulse detector, 555 timer,
  39-41
monostable mode (see timers, basic
  modes of), 6
  555 timer experiment in, 9
monostable multivibrator
  555 timer, 11
  circuit diagram of, 10
  digital gates in, 200
  inverted input, 15
  LM339 quad comparator, 132-133
  voltage-controlled, 14
  XR2240 programmable timer,
    49-51
multifunction circuit, programmable,
  155
multiple LED flasher, XR2240
  programmable timer in, 54-55
multiplication circuits, 95
  schematic of, 96
multiplier, 741 op amp, 95
  741 op amp, block diagram of,
    98-98
multivibrator circuits, 6
  astable, 18
  bistable, 207

N

NAND gate, 178
  schematic of, 180
  truth table for, 181
NAND gate demonstrator, 181
negative input inverting amplifier, 741

op amp, 72
non-inverting amplifier circuits, 71
  741 op amp, 74-76
NOR gate, 179
  schematic diagram for, 183
  truth table for, 184
NOR gate demonstrator, 184-185
notch filter, 116

O

offset, op amp, 63
one-shot circuit, 7
op amps, 60-125
  bandwidth of, 63
  common-mode rejection ratio in,
    62
  difference amplifier use of, 61
  exponents with, 100
  filters using, 105
  gain in, 62
  ideal performance of, 60
  input and output impedance in, 62
  mathematical functions with, 88
  multiplication and division circuits
    using, 95
  offset of, 63
  schematic symbol for, 61
  signal sources using, 117
  sine amplifiers using, 101
OR gate, 179
  inputs for, 182
  schematic diagram for, 182
OR gate demonstrator, 183
oscillation suppression component,
  143
oscillators, astable multivibrator as,
  19
output devices, 4

P

phase shift oscillator, 194
  circuit diagram of, 196
phono amplifier, 144
pin designations
  324 op amp, 67
  555 timer, 8
  556 dual timer, 28
  558 quad timer, 30
  741 op amp, 64, 65
  747 op amp, 66
  CD4001 quad two-input NOR gate,
    187
  CD4011 quad NAND gate, 188
  CD4013 dual D-type flip-flop, 207
  CD4027 dual JK-type flip-flop, 208
  HA-2400 programmable amplifier,
    151
  integrated circuit, 4, 5
  LM339 quad comparator, 127
  LM380 audio amplifier, 139
  LM386 audio amplifier, 148
  SN76477 complex sound

generator IC, 157
SN94281 complex sound
generator IC, 174
XR2240 programmable timer, 46
potentiometers, 4
power supplies
555 timer, 9
battery, 3
house current, 3
variable, 3
programmable inverting amplifier,
HA-2400, 153-154
programmable sine wave oscillator,
HA-2400, 155
pulse stretcher circuit, 7

Q

quad timer, 30

R

ramp circuits, linear astable, 35
ramp timer, linear, 33
rectangle wave, 20
RIAA phono amplifier, 145
parts list for, 146

S

sawtooth wave generator, 741,
123-124
Schmitt trigger, 129
sequencer, 210
circuit diagram of, 212
sequential timer
555 timer, 33-34
XR2240 programmable timer,
50-52
seven-segment readouts, 4
shift register, 214
circuit diagram of, 213
signal amplitude, 4
signal generator
astable multivibrator as, 19
digital gate, 192
signal sources
op amps for, 117
variable, 4
sine amplifiers, 741 op amp, 101-104
sine wave, 118
sine wave generator
741 op amp, 117-118
programmable, 155
SN76477 complex sound generator
IC, 156
circuit diagram of, 158-159

dynamic control of noise clock in,
173
explosion/gunshot sound effect
using, 168
limiting values for, 166
pin designations for, 157-166, 157
space phaser sound effect using,
168
speeding car and crash sound
effect, 169
steam engine sound effect using,
168
triangle wave output by, 174
SN94281 complex sound generator,
170
pin designation for, 174
steam engine sound effect using,
173
solderless socket, 2
interconnection pattern for, 2
sound effects generators, 156-175
SN76477 complex sound
generator IC, 156
SN94281, 170
sound pocket generator, 555 timer,
26-27
space phaser sound effect, SN76477
IC, 168-169
speakers, 4
speeding car and crash sound effect,
SN76477 IC, 169, 172-173
square wave, 20
square wave generator, 741 op amp,
120
steam engine sound effect
SN76477 complex sound
generator IC, 168-171
SN94281 complex sound
generator IC, 173-175
step-down transformer, 3
summing amplifiers, inverting, 741 op
amp, 83-85
switch debouncer
555 timer, 15
digital gate, 200-201
switches, 4

T

timed touch switch, 201
timer controlled relay, 555 timer,
17-18
timers
555, 6-44
556 dual, 26
558 quad, 30

7555, 44
astable mode of, 7
basic modes of, 6, 45
bistable multivibrator, 7
integrated circuit, 6
monostable mode of, 6
multivibrator circuit, 6
tone burst generator, 556 dual timer, 27-29
touch switch, 201
simple, 202
timed, 201-203
triangle wave, 123
triangle wave generator
555 timer, 25-26
741 op amp, 123-124
truth tables, 177

V

variable frequency oscillators, 4
variable frequency square wave
generator
circuit diagram for, 122
variable gain inverting amplifier, 741
op amp, 73
variable power supply, 3
variable width pulse generator, 122
voltage-controlled monostable
multivibrator, 555 timer, 14

W

wave generation, 555 timer for, 35
waveshapes, 4, 20

X

XOR clock generator, 194
circuit diagram of, 195
XOR gate, 180
schematic diagram of, 185
XOR gate demonstrator, 185-186
XR2240 programmable timer, 45-59
alternate complex tone generator,
57
audio frequency astable
multivibrator using, 55
basic time period of, 45
complex tone generator, 56
internal structure of, 47
low-frequency astable circuit using,
52
monostable multivibrator using, 49
multiple LED flasher, 54
pin designation of, 46
sequential timer using, 50

Other Bestsellers From TAB

☐ **500 ELECTRONIC IC CIRCUITS WITH PRACTICAL APPLICATIONS—Whitson**

This comprehensive "nuts and bolts" reference is the kind of project book you've always looked for and never could find. More than just an electronics book that provides circuit schematics or step-by-step projects, this complete source book provides both a wealth of practical electronics circuits AND the additional information you need about specific components. You will be able to use this up-to-date guide to learn basic project-building skills and become familiar with some of the more popular integrated circuits.

Paper $18.95   Hard $28.95
Book No. 2920

☐ **ELECTRONIC CONVERSIONS, SYMBOLS AND FORMULAS—2nd Edition—Rufus P. Turner and Stan Gibilisco**

This revised and updated edition supplies all the formulas, symbols, tables, and conversion factors commonly used in electronics. Exceptionally easy to use, the material is organized by subject matter. Its format is ideal and you can save time by directly accessing specific information. Topics cover only the most needed facts about the most often used conversions, symbols, formulas, and tables. Basic mathematics are presented first, and follow-on formulas build from that base. 280 pp., 94 illus.

Paper $14.95   Hard $21.95
Book No. 2865

☐ **MICROPROCESSOR THEORY AND OPERATION—A SELF-STUDY GUIDE WITH EXPERIMENTS—J.A. Sam Wilson and Ron Walls**

This guide will take you into the central nervous system of computerized electronic equipment and explain bit-by-bit how microprocessors work with their associated circuitry. To give you hands-on experience, 15 easy-to-build, inexpensive experiments are featured: from construction of a bounceless switch, a clock circuit, a logic probe, and a counter, to more advanced ROM, RAM, and interfacing experiments. 224 pp., 127 illus.

Paper $14.95   Hard $21.95
Book No. 2791

☐ **ELEMENTARY ELECTRICITY AND ELECTRONICS—COMPONENT BY COMPONENT—Mannie Horowitz**

Here's a comprehensive overview of fundamental electronics principles using specific components to illustrate and explain each concept. You'll be led, step-by-step, through electronic components and their circuit applications, Horowitz has also included an introduction to digital electronics, complete with a description of number systems—decimal, binary, octal, hexadecimal. 350 pp., 231 illus.

Paper $16.95   Book No. 2753

☐ **HOW TO READ ELECTRONIC CIRCUIT DIAGRAMS—2nd Edition—Robert M. Brown, Paul Lawrence, and James A. Whitson**

In this updated edition of a classic handbook, the authors take an unhurried approach to the task. Basic electronic components and their schematic symbols are introduced early. More specialized components, such as transducers and indicating devices, follow—enabling you to learn how to use block diagrams and mechanical construction diagrams. Before you know it, you'll be able to identify schematics for: amplifiers, oscillators, power supplies, radios, and televisions. 224 pp., 213 illus.

Paper $12.95   Hard $20.95
Book No. 2880

☐ **POWER CONTROL WITH SOLID-STATE DEVICES—Irving M. Gottlieb**

Whether you're an engineer, technician, advanced experimenter, radio amateur, electronics hobbyist, or involved in any way in today's electronics practice, you'll find yourself turning to this book again and again as a quick reference *and* as a ready source of circuit ideas. Author Irving Gottlieb, a professional engineer involved in power engineering and electronic circuit design, examines both basic and state-of-the-art power control devices. 384 pp., 236 illus., 6″ × 9″

Hard $29.95   Book No. 2795

☐ **TROUBLESHOOTING TECHNIQUES FOR MICROPROCESSOR-CONTROLLED VIDEO EQUIPMENT—Bob Goodman**

With this excellent introduction to servicing these "electronic brains" used in everything from color TVs and remote control systems to video cassette recorders and disc players, almost anyone can learn how to get to the heart of most any problem and solve it skillfully and confidently. Includes dozens of handy hints and tips on the types of problems that most often occur in microprocessors and the easiest way to deal with them. 352 pp., 232 illus.

Paper $16.95   Hard $24.95
Book No. 2758

☐ **RADIO ELECTRONICS' STATE OF SOLID STATE—by the Editors of *Radio Electronics***

Have you ever wished that you'd clipped some of those solid state projects and explanations of solid state theory from *Radio Electronics* regular monthly column, "State of Solid State?" Or do you simply need some hands-on guidance in the he use of today's digital ICs? If you can answer "yes" to either of these questions, you won't want to miss this collection of articles from *Radio Electronics* Magazine's monthly feature: "State of Solid State!" 168 pp., 111 illus.

Paper $9.95   Hard $14.95
Book No. 2733

Other Bestsellers From TAB